THE PALINDROME ADVENTURE

CHRIS WALLACE

ISBN: 978-0-6459687-2-9

Published by Round Lake Publishing
Book cover design by Rainsford
Book design by Jana Lulovska
Back cover photo by Brett Tucker

*For **A** muse meant*

FORWARD

I was never sure where I belonged. I came to Australia to live in the 1990s because of a woman. We lasted less than two years. When my ex and I broke up, I had no friends of my own here. But during the first year, something happened. Unbeknownst to me, a musical I'd written in Hollywood was given to someone at the Victorian Arts Centre. They decided to produce it.

I had been an actor in New York and Hollywood. Before long a couple of guys asked me to be in an American play they were putting on. Then I did a another play. And another. I got an agent and had a completely unexpected acting career in Oz.

But I've always had the wanderlust. I now had a couple of bucks in my pocket and that longing to be someplace else beckoned. But where to go? I remembered the words of the ancient Greek philosopher, Heracleitas: **You cannot step twice into the same river, for other waters are ever flowing onto you.** *I thought about that for a while, then decided to test that premise. I hadn't been away from Oz for five years. I had always had a special thing for Africa and had friends in Nairobi. I had friends in Europe. I had family and friends in America. I decided to visit all of them and find out about those other waters.*

On the 8th of September, in the palindrome year of Two Thousand Two, I boarded a Qantas flight for a journey that would eventually take me around the world. What follows is the story of that trip. It's a different kind of travel experience, where past and present collided with the unimaginable. Hope you enjoy the ride.

CHAPTER ONE

The alarm went off at 3:30. I snapped awake instantly. Everything was packed. I had been ready for this trip for weeks. All I had to do now was get to the airport, board the Qantas plane and buckle into seat 23D. The first leg was a nonstop flight to Johannesburg over the South Pole. Once I settled into the flight, my mind began wandering back to the first extraordinary visit I'd made to Africa.

At that time I was working in New York at the flagship station of one of the three major television networks, producing on-air promotion. I was doing a series of promos for the news department and on this particular day went to Brooklyn with a news correspondent and her film crew to cover the arrival of a boatload of animals from Africa. The press release referred to it as "a modern day Noah's Ark." I tagged along because I would get a chance to shoot some footage of the news correspondent for my promo once her story was shot.

The guy who captured this menagerie, by the merest coincidence, had some years before hosted a kids tv show called Jungle Bob. He had been a pet store owner in a small town in the Midwest and parlayed that into a syndicated tv series. The program had been produced several years before and was about to begin airing on the station where I worked. I asked Jungle Bob, when I met him on the Brooklyn docks, if he'd like to come by and do some voice-over promos for his show. He agreed.

Anyone who grew up when I did, where I did, would have had a Hollywood-induced fascination with Africa. Tarzan movies and National Geographic were our guides to the Dark Continent. Never mind that the movie elephants were Indian and the animals didn't live in jungles but on the plains. Our interest was in concepts, not nuts and bolts.

Therefore, when Jungle Bob came by to do his voice-overs, I had a lot of questions to ask. The most important thing he said to me was that if I was really interested in seeing the animals, I'd better do it now because they wouldn't last forever in the vast numbers they currently were. The next most important thing he said was, "If you want to come over, you can bunk in with me." This was in the mid 1960s.

My wife worked for a major airline. Because of my wife's position, I had my choice of flying on a pass, that is to say, at no cost, assuming I could wait for a flight. Or I could purchase a ticket at a 90% discount and ensure a seat. The airline business was a wonderful fraternity then. Even on competitive airlines, you were treated like family and often upgraded when identified as an insider. Both my wife and I agreed that this was an opportunity of a lifetime and I must go.

CHAPTER TWO

I boarded a BOAC flight to London. I had been in London only once before and if not for the fact that I was expected in Nairobi on a particular day, may have considered staying longer. As it was, I boarded a plane that had a stop in Rome and another in Khartoum on its way to Nairobi. I was seriously tempted to get off the plane in Rome because there was a restaurant that I'd fallen in love with on another occasion and couldn't stop thinking about their cannelloni.

Perhaps I should explain that at that time in airline history, one could decide on virtually a moment's notice to stay longer in a place, then re-board another plane and continue the journey. It was only important that one had a ticket from A to C. If B was a stop on the way, it was not unusual to deplane for a stopover, then reschedule the continuation whenever it suited at no additional cost. I never had to worry about catching the next plane.

We arrived in Khartoum and passengers were deplaned for the refueling stopover. When my feet touched the ground in Khartoum, I felt as if they'd taken root, as if a part of me belonged on African soil. It was mystical. It could be that everyone who sets foot on African soil has the same sensation. All I know is that it was a powerful awareness for me. I belonged to this earth, this continent. It was palpable. I felt the DNA connection with Lucy as vividly as if I were only a generation removed, not centuries. In case you don't know, Lucy is the name given to the oldest set of fossilized bones ever discovered up to that time. She was found in Ethiopia in 1974 and was judged to be 3.2 million years old. We're all related to her.

This concept continued to swim in my head as we re-boarded the plane for its ultimate destination, Nairobi. The very sound of it filled me with excitement. Nairobi. Nairobi. It sounded so African, so exotic. The Sudan was unquestionably on the continent but to me Kenya was Africa. I was filled with an excitement that was beyond calculation.

Jungle Bob was there to meet me. I had been virtually sleepless for a couple of days. None of this seemed to matter. Every part of me was wide-awake.

First, we dropped my bags off at Jungle Bob's little house in the outskirts of Nairobi. Then we went to a tailor to have me outfitted in some safari gear, heavy twill khaki shorts and shirts with lots of deep pockets. The friendly Indian (or as they were referred to, Asian) tailor measured me painstakingly around the chest, meticulously around the waist, expertly around the hips, made copious notes and then sewed two sets of shirts and shorts that would have fitted Godzilla — with room to spare.

After leaving the tailor, Jungle Bob and I went to the Thorntree in front of the New Stanley Hotel for a cup of tea and a bite of lunch. Imagine the romance of arriving in Nairobi, then having lunch at this place of legend. It was *the* hotel, one of those colonial watering holes like Mena House in Cairo that overloaded the imagination. Hemingway, Ruark, Blixen, anyone who ever visited Nairobi would have sat here casually shooting the breeze before and after shooting the game. We sat in a shaded area that bordered the footpath. The brilliant equatorial sun made even the most subtle hues explode into breathtakingly vivid colors.

Today, Nairobi feels like a city. Back then it felt like a small town. And not just a small town but a small, mainly white town. The people who served us at the Thorntree were Africans, to be sure, but the clientele were not. The passersby, going about their daily chores, were, in my recollection at least, mainly white. You had to have business to be in this neighborhood. And only white people had business. The country had gained its independence in December of 1963 and became a republic one year after independence. Africans were not yet running things entirely and the whites who were there still thought of Kenya as theirs.

Many of them had been there through the Mau Mau uprisings or the fight for independence, depending on your point of view, when atrocities were committed by both Europeans and Africans. Both of these groups claimed ownership. I had read Robert Ruark's *Something of Value* before leaving New York and had some idea of the history from the white perspective, none from the African. But I knew enough about the British Empire to know there was definitely another side to the story.

No sooner had we sat down than someone walking past would spot Jungle Bob and come over to say hello. No matter what chores one had to accomplish, or even how important they might be, there was always time to stop for a cup of tea or a glass of beer and a chat. At least five times during our sojourn at the Thorntree, Jungle Bob said we needed to go to this office or that office for something or other, but somehow we never got up. There was always another old-timer passing by.

One chap had been in Kenya for forty-six years. He had been among the first operatives with the East Africa Company. The East Africa Company resulted when the European powers in the late 19th and early 20th centuries decided to carve up Africa among themselves, robbing it of its resources and dignity. The British, the Dutch, the Germans, the Italians, the Belgians, the Portuguese all claimed their share. While he sat with us, this gentleman spent a good deal of time bemoaning the fact that things weren't the same anymore like they were in the good old East Africa Company days.

"The bloody nig-nogs knew their place back then. Not so bloody uppity," he said as he sipped his Pimm's Cup, the gin based cocktail of choice, it seemed. When I had no response, he continued. "You'll see. They'll bloody muck this up before long. Mark my words. African government, my arse."

Jungle Bob rescued us and told the old timer that we had to move on, that we were leaving for the NFD (Northern Frontier District) the next morning and had to get our gear together.

"Going up to see Don Summers, are you?" the old timer inquired.

"Yep. For a few days. I want to show my friend here the bush before it disappears," Jungle Bob replied.

After another cup of tea and another half-hour of talk, we finally left the Thorntree and rushed from one office to another, barely completing our chores before they all closed for the day.

Back at his little house, Jungle Bob and I sat on canvas chairs and drank a beer while Magda, his Dutch girlfriend, prepared some food. This was the first chance we had to really talk. Since we met, I had developed an idea for a television program which I was calling, "Capture." The idea was to follow Jungle Bob around with a camera or two and document the process of capturing animals for the various clients he had developed. Some were zoos. Some were research facilities. Unfortunately, the idea was too far ahead of its time. My version never got done. There have since been plenty of others.

As we sat there in the diminishing twilight, Jungle Bob told me about his wife and children back in the US. He spoke of them with real affection, even showing me photographs of his children.

"My life's here in Africa now. I don't have anything in common with them anymore, even though I still love them all very much."

"What about Magda?" I asked innocently. "Do you plan to formalize your relationship?"

"I'm Catholic," he said. "I'm married for life to my wife back home." He got a look in his eye that I came to recognize later. It meant, *This conversation is terminated.*

A short time later, Shegi, Jungle Bob's whatever you might call him: servant, assistant, handyman, served us dinner, after which I slept as if I'd been drugged.

CHAPTER THREE

The vehicle of choice at that time in Kenya was the Land Rover. It was the status vehicle, the only one used in the bush. That's why I was surprised to find that Jungle Bob drove the Toyota equivalent. It was virtually unknown at that time. Japanese vehicles of that kind were only just beginning to penetrate the market. They were less expensive both to run and to buy. Being the shrewd businessman that he was, Jungle Bob saw before most others that Land Rovers and Toyotas both accomplished the same task. Only one was a hell of a lot cheaper.

We planned an early start. The drive to Isiolo in the NFD was a long one over dirt tracks which passed for roads. Shegi woke me with a cheerful, "Good morning, Bwana," and I awakened wondering where I was. When it dawned on me that I was in Africa, I was enraptured all over again. I drew in a deep breath and was conscious of what I was later to identify as the aroma of Africa. I had noticed it at the airport upon arrival. Now it claimed my attention again. It wasn't an unpleasant smell, nor was it especially pleasant. It was just African, a combination of earth, age, nature, vegetation, whatever – Africa.

The Toyota had a flat tire. We drove Magda's car into town to do last minute chores: pick up my clothing, buy food, fill the petrol cans and other odds and ends while Shegi changed the tire. When we returned, he was just releasing the jack.

The long ride to Isiolo was bumpy and dusty. There was bush on either side of us but no game that I could see. Not because it wasn't there but because my eyes hadn't yet adjusted to the proper frequency. I didn't know yet how to look. Later I learned how but at this time, I could only see vegetation and shadows.

We stopped about halfway there and Magda pulled sandwiches out of a hamper and poured hot tea from a large thermos. I glanced nervously around while the warm liquid washed down ham and cheese, still marveling at the notion that I was actually in Africa. Not only in Africa but in the African bush. *We weren't in Kansas anymore, Toto.*

Jungle Bob took out a portable short-wave radio and tuned it to the BBC overseas news service. Nowadays we could have pulled out a cell phone and talked to a pal in Keokuk or Kakadu. But at the time, I was awed by the idea that we could be out there in the middle of nowhere, not connected to anything electrical and listening to some guy reading the news from a little sound booth in London. It was equatorial Africa, for god's sake! It gave one enormous respect for Burton and Speke and Grant and Livingston and all the other 19th Century explorers who marched through that unknown landscape struggling with the variety of deadly and exotic flora and fauna with which it was populated. I had already relived those adventures in Alan Moorehead's two books, *The White Nile* and *The Blue Nile*. Now I was standing on the same earth listening to a man read the world weather forecast from over 4,000 miles away.

After a few hours, we turned off the main dirt track onto a narrower dirt track where we soon approached a triangular, red-outlined traffic sign that announced "Game Warden." A charming, single-story, rambling homestead was nestled under a couple of modest trees. A verandah stretched across the entire front of the house. A young African woman sat there with two children on a quilted comforter. There was a garage nearby and several African men, askaris, dressed in khaki uniforms like mine – except that theirs fitted -- standing around in the distance.

Don and Rachel Summers came out the front door as soon as they heard the Toyota's tires crunching up the track. Huge smiles split their handsome faces as they greeted Jungle Bob and Magda.

"Hello, Bwana," Don said, as he stretched out his welcoming hand toward me. "Welcome to our most humble, yet rustically appointed and comfortable abode. It's no New York City, Bwana, but we do our best."

"Oh, Donald, do shut up," Rachel teased. "Don't pay him any mind. He does tend to go on." She took my arm and led me into the house. "How was your flight?"

Don Summers could have just as easily been a product of perfect casting. He had striking good looks, brownish hair into which the strong, equatorial sun had bleached blond, almost white streaks. His perfect teeth were revealed whenever his engagingly crooked smile allowed them. He was about average height but large around the chest. His eyes were a piercing blue.

Rachel was his opposite. She was dark complexioned with deep brown eyes. Her figure didn't give away the fact that she'd had two children. It was supple and rounded, but just this side of *zoftik*.

They had met in Kenya. Don had originally come to Africa, as he told it, to keep from murdering the man who had stolen his girlfriend while he was off killing communists in Korea. Since he had been in the British military, he didn't hesitate when the call came from East Africa to join the police force, which was essentially a paramilitary organization whose mission was to halt the unrest among the natives. This unrest eventually mushroomed into the Mau Mau movement for independence.

Jomo Kenyatta, the Mau Mau leader, was no Gandhi when it came to overthrowing British rule. His followers did it with pangas (machetes) and whatever guns they could get their hands on. White settlers were slaughtered in their homes, sometimes in their sleep by Africans who may have been their cooks at one time, who may have looked after their children, who may have worked alongside them on their coffee plantations or tending their maize.

The war for independence was savage – which is probably redundant. Don told blood-curdling stories of the brutality on both sides. But when it was all over and Kenya was independent from

British rule, and the republic was proclaimed with Jomo Kenyatta as its first president, Don decided to stay on. He took Kenyan citizenship and became a game warden, as did many of his colleagues on the police force. Africa had permeated their bloodstream. It was a natural transition. They were adept at handling guns and leading a cadre of troops.

Rachel's family left Stuttgart early in the Nazi years. They were among the few Jews who were able to escape. Because Germany had an interest in East Africa -- Tanganyika had been a German territory before it became Tanzania -- her father made contact with people there and fled the Third Reich.

Rachel knew no other home than Africa. Her childhood was spent in the bush alongside an abusive and uncommunicative father and docile mother. She had lost all Jewish identity and eventually converted to Church of England, more in rebellion than out of any conviction or devotion. Her family had kept no Jewish customs, religious or otherwise, making her transition easier. But her ethnicity accounted for her dark, exotic, features.

Their courtship, if it can be called that, was initially one-sided. Rachel pursued Don, sometimes walking miles to be with him. When he finally realized that he wanted to be with her too, it was only a matter of a short time before they committed to one another. Now, two children later, they were also both committed to a life in Africa. His position in the Game Department was a civil servant position that eventually would be turned over to an African. But in the meantime, it was Don's show.

CHAPTER FOUR

We had a lovely dinner, prepared by Rachel and served by her staff. There was nothing affected about this arrangement. Everyone who could afford to had servants. And if you were white, you could afford it. It was a way of employing indigenous people. Now that the "troubles" had ended, it was perfectly respectable for Africans to work as domestic labor. It was regarded as a good job and from the white settlers' point of view, indispensable as a way of life. It's how things were in Kenya.

The chatter and laughter never stopped as we sat around the table together. For a guy who had spent the best part of his thirty-some years in a military-like situation, Don Summers was amazingly well read and had a keen knowledge of both Broadway and West End musicals, and could also quote a bit of Gilbert and Sullivan, if asked. Or even if not. Between us, we must have known every song ever written and regaled each other and the others with a kind of tag team performance. We went from Gershwin to Cole Porter to Frank Loesser to Irving Berlin to Rodgers and Hammerstein to Lerner and Lowe to Meredith Willson, one after another until around 11.

The next morning was going to get started at dawn so we all retired to our respective sleeping accommodations. There was one bedroom still unoccupied in the house. Obviously, Jungle Bob and Magda headed toward it in a familiar fashion.

"We'll put you out the back, Bwana," Don said, leading me through the kitchen. "There's quite a comfortable cot in that little room next to the arsenal." He led the way. "Don't leave your light on too long, Bwana. We'll be running off the batteries once I turn off the generator and we don't want to run them too long."

I went into the bathroom and brushed my teeth. It was under the same roof as my sleeping quarters but had to be accessed by an outside door. As I was standing there with the bathroom light burning, something flew in one window and out the other so quickly that I didn't have time to register what it was before it was gone again. It spooked me and I quickly rinsed, spit and got the hell out of there.

When I was comfortably in my cot, I snapped off the bedside lamp and lay there staring into the darkest blackness I'd ever experienced. I raised my hand and waved it around in front of my face. Nothing. I would like to have been tired enough to drop off to sleep but that wasn't going to happen either. Being in the African bush was far more interesting and entertaining when I wasn't on my own. This was scary.

After some minutes of lying there stiff and listening to night sounds that were completely unfamiliar, I heard one that was: footsteps. As quietly as possible, someone was walking on the gravel toward my screened window. During dinner, Don and Jungle Bob had spoken about a group of renegades who were still terrorizing white settlers. They were called the Shiftas and were known for creeping in at night and stealing weapons. I was next to the arsenal where there were a whole lot of big, high-powered rifles and lots of ammunition. I was shitting myself.

The footsteps got closer. It was obvious that the person was doing his best to be quiet but the gravel still crunched under his feet. I had nothing with which to defend myself, not even a belt buckle. I suppose I could have thrown a desert boot at him if he tried to come in but the crepe soles would probably not have done much damage.

The footsteps were right outside now. I froze. They went past the window. I waited to hear someone break into the arsenal. The footsteps continued and faded. Then there was silence.

Just as I began to relax, there was another sound that ripped through the night air. It was indescribable. It started as a kind of low moan or whoop, then became higher in pitch and faster until it became a shriek – a blood-curdling shriek. It scared the shit out of me all over again. Then silence. Then it started again and continued way longer than I thought I could stand. Then the crunching of the gravel came and the shriek stopped until the crunching faded and the shrieking began again. How long this went on I couldn't say. Eventually, out of sheer exhaustion, I must have dropped off to sleep.

It seemed that I had only just shut my eyes when Shegi tapped on my door and entered with a tray on which was a teapot covered by a cozy, a cup, warm milk and two pieces of toast. "*Jambo*, Bwana," he said, when he saw the panic melt from my face.

"*Jambo*, Shegi," I replied, happy to see that light was just starting to make its presence known in the eastern sky.

"How did you sleep, Bwana," Don asked brightly, when I went into the house to join the others.

"What the hell was that sound that sounds like someone's being murdered?"

"Must have been a tree hyrax. They're tiny little animals but they do sound a bit ferocious if you don't know them. Did one keep you awake?"

"No, what kept me awake was someone walking around outside my window. The tree hyrax just scared the shit out of me."

"I suppose I should have said something about the sentry. There are a lot of guns in the arsenal, you know, and we have to protect them against the bloody Shiftas."

"Right," I said. "Well, at least, tonight I'll know."

CHAPTER FIVE

After grabbing a banana and a couple of plums, I hopped into Don's Land Rover. Jungle Bob sat in the back with me while little Donny, the Summers' eight-year-old son, sat in front with his father. The askaris followed in another vehicle, driven by Don's sergeant.

The track we took was virtually non-existent. We were on our way to a farmer's property where some cape buffalo had ruined part of his maize crop. Game was so abundant and ubiquitous in those days that much of it was considered vermin – anything that came in conflict with a farmer's livelihood, in fact. But the government required that somebody official deal with the problem and not the farmer himself, unless, of course, there was an immediate threat. Hunting was a source of revenue for the Kenya government and licenses had to be obtained to kill virtually any animals. The buffalo were an annoyance and, therefore, reported to the local game warden so that he could take official action.

As we passed through the bush, little Donny would spot various animals alongside our track. To me, it was like being on a snipe hunt (*for those not familiar with this phenomenon, a college prank was to take an unsuspecting neophyte into the country and give him a burlap sack. He's told to hold it while the others go and scare the snipes into the burlap sack. Instead, they leave him in the middle of nowhere waiting for the snipes to rush into his burlap sack until he realizes he's been duped and is left holding the bag. Snipes are actually birds*). I nodded and said, "Oh, yeah," when something was pointed out but never once saw what everyone else was seeing. Again, all I saw was vegetation and shadows. If I had been able to see them, I'd have seen an abundance of Thompson's gazelle, impala, zebra, ostrich and giraffe. I felt particularly stupid when I couldn't see a 15-foot giraffe. But I couldn't.

We arrived at our destination and began tracking. The terrain was hilly and thorny. We each had a weapon, even though no one knew if I could shoot or not. I was told to keep the chamber empty until and unless told otherwise. I complied. We had a pack of dogs with us to aid in the hunting, as well as an old Turkana tracker.

The tracker looked around on the ground for a little while, then pointed unenthusiastically in a direction. The dogs were released, sniffed and led the way. At first it seemed they were merely excited about being free in the bush and seemed rather undisciplined. They were an interesting collection of canines, maybe seven or eight in all. There was one that was a combination St. Bernard and Great Dane, one of the unlikeliest looking animals I've ever encountered. It was huge and stayed at Don's heels the entire time and wouldn't give way to any competition, including human. Others looked to be mongrels of various stripe. And there was one small mongrel that looked completely out of place in this environment. It was fuzzy and cute and should have been in some dowager's lap, not trekking through the African bush in search of buffalo.

The dogs began to settle into the task at hand. Before long they were off and barking. They had picked up the scent and rushed ahead.

We quickly followed and, coming to an open area, saw the dogs nipping at a young male giraffe that was lying on the ground, its back legs entwined in a fence. He must not have seen the fence, and perhaps wondered what such a contraption was doing obstructing his path. I wondered myself. There is always something satisfying about seeing animals in their natural environment, whether it's kangaroo in Australia, bison in America or giraffe in Africa. As we humans continue to expand our needs for land, there can be only one consequence, birds and animals lose. At that time, in Kenya, Man's needs were still modest and animals roamed everywhere freely. Except for this fence, of course.

Don and the askaris called the dogs off and we could see the giraffe was injured on the inner part of one of his legs, no doubt from the fence post that had been pulled out by his thrashing. It was a chore keeping the dogs away and trying to get close enough to the giraffe to untangle the wire from his legs, at the same time staying clear of any thrashing he would do. There was also a danger that he would fracture his own skull. And despite the fact that it is a relatively docile animal by African standards, a giraffe can still cause injury to the unprepared. Its kick can kill a predator.

This one appeared to be about ten feet tall. Carefully, the animal's legs were released from the wire and it quickly jumped to its feet and went off, relatively uninjured except for the small amount of exposed flesh on its leg. It was followed by the barking dogs until they got tired of chasing.

Until the dogs returned, there was little to do but wait. The Turkana tracker and the askaris sat around on the ground while Jungle Bob, Don, Donny and I poured a cup of tea from a thermos that Rachel had packed for us.

One by one, the dogs returned. They were winded but still excited. The old tracker was talking to one of the askaris when a dog came to his blind side, sniffed and peed all over his heavy wool Army coat. When the other askaris noticed it, they fell down with laughter. The old tracker turned, gently shooed the dog away, wiped the piss from his coat and laughed along with the rest of us.

Eventually all the dogs returned and we finally reached a maize field where the buffalo tracks had led us. Now it got really exciting. First the buffalo tracks are found. You follow them. The tracks appear to be fresher. Then you determine that there are several animals, one of which is huge. The dogs begin to get more excited. Without anyone saying anything, the pace quickens. You're traveling through thick thorn bush that scratches your arms and legs but you don't notice the sting. The tracks are very fresh now and everyone proceeds silently.

You hear shells click into place in the chambers of the rifles. In the excitement, you nervously force a cartridge into the chamber of your rifle but it jams and you keep pace while trying unsuccessfully to get the shell to move one way or another. The others begin making hand signals indicating the direction of the herd. Now there is fresh scat and little drops of uncoagulated blood appear on thorns. The party divides. The separated members whistle to keep the others informed of their location. You try to stay as close behind Don as possible but that fucking monster dog takes up the space and won't let you in. Suddenly you break into a trot and crash through the bush as if you were the animal being pursued. Adrenalin pours through your system. By the time you catch up to the buffalo, the only thing on your mind is to shoot it for dragging you through this uninviting terrain. You hear shots fired ahead of you.

You watch as the buffalo romp across an open area into a forest. Whoever fired either didn't shoot to kill or missed. None of the animals appears to be injured and there is no blood on the ground. Unnoticed by the others, you manage to extricate the cartridge that was jammed in the rifle and return it to your pocket, grateful that it wasn't needed.

When I had time to digest my first bush experience in Africa, a few years later, a number of things occurred to me. With the exception of a few times with my older brother and his friends when we went rabbit or pheasant hunting – in my mind, more a rite of passage than an activity I enjoyed – I was relatively indifferent to the sport and not particularly competent. I owned a shotgun and a .22 caliber rifle, another rite of passage, but rarely used them. In the army I had been required to qualify with a weapon and look after it but I had virtually no interest in actually wanting to shoot anything, particularly after I had murdered a chipmunk as an adolescent and can still see it in my mind's eye dropping slowly from the bark of a tree, dead as a doornail. I had no objection in principle to hunting and could even make the argument that it was sometimes necessary. I just didn't care to do it myself.

With that disposition as a background, I was, nevertheless, willing to shoot and kill in Kenya. Was there something in the air, as it were, that drove this passion? Was it a Hemingway or a Teddy Roosevelt thing? Did my testosterone demand it? I couldn't figure it out. But there was no question that I was a different person in Kenya than I had been anywhere else. Maybe it was genetic. Perhaps it was fundamental and natural to be a member of the dominant species in this our birthplace where instincts replaced reason. I've never figured it out.

CHAPTER SIX

That evening, following the buffalo adventure, some friends popped in, as is the custom in those rather desolate regions, and we all had another rousing time of conversation and singing.

Among those who decided to stay on in Kenya after independence, there was an understandable bond. They had been the masters in a British colony, whether farmers or administrators or businessmen or policemen. Anyone who knows anything about the history of the British Empire knows that this was mainly an advantage for the colonials and not for the indigenous people.

It's always a hard thing to balance: the subjugation and exploitation of millions of people of color against the fact that the world now has a principal language. Was it worth the cost? It depends. Maybe yes because virtually anywhere anyone goes, if they can speak English, they can communicate. No because of the human suffering that goes with colonialism, whether in India, Australia, Canada, the U.S. or any of the countries Britain invaded. It would have been a lot more humane if there had been another way to spread the language around the globe. But history teaches us that the more humane way of doing anything rarely, if ever, wins out.

The next day began in leisurely enough fashion. There were no emergencies that Don had to deal with until afternoon when he received a call from another farmer, a real old timer named Percy Kyneton-Smythe. He was an 84-year-old bachelor who had come to Kenya when he was in his fifties, an extreme example of a mid-life crisis. Percy reported that there was a very large, very dead giraffe on his property and he couldn't tell what it died of. He wouldn't move it until the Game Department signed off on the fact that the animal didn't die of a disease that might be passed on to his cattle.

We arrived at Percy's place with a full family entourage, Don, Rachel, Donny and his sister, Rebecca, and Jungle Bob and me. Magda stayed behind to read. The giraffe was a seventeen-foot bull. It was definitely dead. From this vantage point, you could see how massive the animal was. Normally one could never get close enough to it. While the kids frolicked around the dead animal, Don examined it more closely.

One of the things I learned quickly was that succinctness is not necessarily a conversational virtue with Don. The same information and observation must be repeated endlessly, each time, as if it had never been uttered before, and it must always be done with sincerity and conviction.

Don began his monologue. "There are no holes in the skin, Bwana, that's certain. If there were any penetration by a bullet or spear, there would be blood. Since there's no blood, I think we can assume that nothing penetrated the skin. No weapon. No, that's fairly certain. This animal was not shot or speared. If it had been, there would be some evidence of it. A hole or some kind of skin penetration – and blood. From the size of this *ndume* (male animal), there would certainly be blood somewhere. No, I think we can rule out any kind of injury from a bullet or spear. That leaves us with another possibility. It must have died of another cause. Without any sign of a bullet or spear, something else must have killed this *twiga* (giraffe). It could have died of a disease. It certainly wasn't shot. He appears to have been healthy. No reason to think otherwise. Look at the size of him. A disease would have caused him to waste away, not die in such a healthy condition. Well, I think we can safely rule out several options. He wasn't shot or speared and he doesn't appear to have died of a disease. But something killed him…"

While all this conjecturing was going on, an expanding number of local Turkanas, about twenty, congregated at a safe distance away from the animal. They were waiting for the verdict from the white

Bwana. When he made his official proclamation, depending on whether or not the animal had to be quarantined, they would be able to get at the meat and have a feed.

Don was still weighing alternatives when he noticed something. "See here how his neck is swollen. This could mean that something happened to him. Right under his chin here, it looks like he's a bit swollen. Giraffe don't normally have this kind of swelling around this area. No, something could well have caused that. There are no bullet holes or spear holes so we can rule that out. But something could have caused this swelling just under the jaw here…"

This monologue went on for some time until Don glanced to one side and noticed a small tree that had been uprooted from somewhere else. "This tree obviously wasn't around here anywhere. There is no evidence that suggests this tree comes from anywhere around here. It must have been dragged here somehow. If this tree…"

The light went on. Don concluded, after another ten minutes of to-ing and fro-ing, that the giraffe had somehow gotten its neck lodged in the fork of this tree, tried to get itself free, was strangling in the process – thus the swelling -- and in its death throes, flung the tree away from itself, perhaps bashing its own head against the ground to add insult to injury.

Sherlock Holmes may have come to the conclusion quicker but no more reasonably. "I think we can let these people have a bit of *nyama*, Bwana," Don said to me.

"*Nyama?*"

"Meat. I think we could do with a bit ourselves. Let's see what kind of shot you are, Bwana."

Jungle Bob, Don and I got into the Land Rover. Before the engine turned over, the locals had already begun butchering the giraffe. One long incision was made down the side with a huge panga. Chattering and laughing, they hacked away for dear life. This was going to be a celebration. Fresh meat. Despite the abundance of game, these poor natives were not permitted to legally kill animals. First the Europeans, now their own government decided that what these people had lived in harmony with for eons was now too valuable for tourism.

We drove to a remote area away from the others when Don pulled to a stop. In front of us was a herd of at least fifty zebra. At our approach, they started off. We tried to keep up with them, and eventually positioned ourselves so that they would have to cross our path. When they thundered past, it was a spectacle. These magnificent, stunning animals stormed in front of us at a gallop, free and stark in the brilliant sunshine.

After they passed, Don said, "Have a look over there, Bwana. See? There are some tommys and some impala. See that male tommy?"

The animal was about one hundred yards away among other Thompson's gazelles but it was clear which one Don meant. "Yeah, I see it," I answered.

"Take a shot. We need some *nyama* for the dogs." He handed me the loaded rifle. I took aim and squeezed off a round. The gazelle flopped. "Looks like you got him, Bwana." But then the animal jumped to its feet and high tailed it out of there. The velocity of the bullet must have knocked him down but he was uninjured.

"That must have been close," Jungle Bob said.

Looking in another direction, Don spotted a small herd of impala. "Let's see if we can get a little closer to those impala."

We began stalking them once it was established that we were down wind of them. When we got within a hundred yards, Don suggested I take another shot. "Aim just at the top of his forelegs. That's the perfect shot. If you hit him, he's killed instantly. You break both his legs and burst his heart in one shot."

I got down on one knee and braced my elbow against it, took careful aim and squeezed the trigger. In an instant, the young buck was down and dead. I couldn't have been prouder of my shooting if it had won me an Olympic gold medal. Making that shot was the only thing in the world. It established my manhood. It validated me in the eyes of these real men. I look back on it now with embarrassment. But at that moment, I was erupting and overflowing with testosterone.

As we started back, Don spotted another tommy. "Have a shot at that one, Bwana."

Again, I went down to one knee, aimed and fired, bringing this young buck down as well. *All right! Don't fuck with Bwana Chris, you ferocious, man-eating gazelles!*

"I think we've got a bloody marksman on our hands, Bob," Don said. The words filled me with masculine pride. It takes very little to inflate an ass's ego.

We couldn't have been gone more than twenty minutes but when we returned, the Turkanas had chopped the entire animal into chunks that were distributed around the ground. For the next fifteen minutes, Don regaled old Percy with tales of my shooting prowess.

"You should have seen it, Percy. He gave that first tommy a shave and a haircut, then dispatched the impala and another tommy. Christ, what a shot. I told him to aim for the heart, told him just where to aim and *whap*. The bullet hit and brought him down like a stone. Brilliant shooting. Couldn't have done it better myself. Got down on one knee, took his aim and squeezed it off. Aimed right for the top of the legs. A perfect shot, Bwana. A real marksman, this Yank. Make no mistake about that. The lad took his time, down on one knee and down went the antelope. No, you won't find better shooting than that, I'll guarantee you…" And on and on while I tried, unsuccessfully, to maintain a façade of modesty.

By the time he finished, the Turkanas had vanished and the only evidence of the monstrous, seventeen-foot giraffe was the huge stomach, which was filled with grasses and would have been inedible, along with some blood that had seeped into the ground. Everything else was gone. Not a bone or piece of skin remained. Not a horn or a hoof. Hyenas may have left some of the carcass behind. Not the Turkanas. Everything was usable.

We drove back to Percy's homestead for sundowners, usually gin but in this case, tea. His place was rough and rustic, as eccentric in appearance as he was. A leopard skin was draped over one upholstered chair that had long ago seen its best days. Lumps of stuffing peeked through under the leopard's legs. Three huge snake skins hung from one wall, reaching from ceiling to floor, a distance of maybe fifteen feet.

There was a print over the fireplace of Wilson's Last Stand. Wilson was the equivalent of an African Custer. The picture depicted a white man, Wilson, surrounded by Africans closing in. He looked sufficiently valiant and they properly menacing. It was explained to me that after Wilson was defeated, the Africans rewarded his bravery by carrying his body aloft and burying him with some dignity.

A lantern hung in the middle of the room, presumably old Percy's light source after sundown since nothing electrical was visible. The rest of the furniture was also over-stuffed and virtually worn out. Old Christmas cards were stacked on the mantle and a brownish photo of a nephew and his Belgian wife leaned against them.

For the most part, Percy talked about the Great War. It was his reference point in life. He had been wounded, he said, four times by the bloody Huns. Then his conversation jumped, perhaps for my benefit, to Iowa.

"They bloody well don't know how to manage their soil. That's for sure. It's the richest soil in the bloody world. Beautiful soil. Grows anything. But they don't know the first thing about managing it. They bloody well take things out, but don't put a bloody thing back into it. You'll see how long it lasts if they keep that up. Bloody idiots."

"Have you been to Iowa? I asked.

"Never," Percy answered with a defiant look that said not to ask anything further.

Rachel had made tea and toast. "You must try some of Percy's biltong," she insisted.

"What's biltong?"

"It's dried eland meat. You add salt, pepper and some spices, then shred it and sprinkle it on hot buttered toast," she explained.

I took a bite and that same smell I had associated with Africa permeated the biltong, the same gaminess, the same atmosphere, the same Africanness.

CHAPTER SEVEN

My reverie was interrupted when the captain of the Qantas flight came on the intercom.

"G'day, folks. We're above Antarctica now and you've got a real treat. Normally, there's so much cloud cover that you can't see anything. But if you want to take a look down, you'll see a rare sight."

I waited my turn at one of the portholes near the galley and had a look down. The view was extraordinary. It was also foreboding. The landscape was more barren than anything I'd ever imagined, let alone seen. It was gray. The water was gray. The snow was gray. It looked cold, even in the sunlight. I was glad to have seen it but wasn't curious enough to want a closer look. Before long the clouds reformed and nothing was any longer visible.

As the meal was served, I found myself remembering more incidents of that first visit to Africa.

The day after our giraffe adventure at Percy's, Jungle Bob got a call from one of his clients and had to return to Nairobi to discuss business. Originally, he was meant to stay for a few more days in the NFD. For my part, I was not eager to leave the beauty and fascination of the African bush. But I was too timid to invite myself to stay. That's why I was ecstatic when Don and Rachel Summers suggested that I stay on for a while longer.

"You can always meet up later on," Don suggested.

"If you don't mind," I said.

"You'll be a more than welcome," Rachel added.

Jungle Bob left at around midday with Magda and Shegi. I became – in my own mind – assistant game warden for the Northern Frontier District of Kenya.

My first assignment in this position was the following day. It was suspected that a lion, which had been killing some cattle, was hanging around some leopard baits that had been set out in a nearby forest. Don, Donny, a few askaris and I went to check it out.

A zebra had been shot and wired in place as the bait. It was virtually intact except for a portion of its head that had been chewed on. Apparently the diner was a connoisseur since normally it was the guts that were consumed as an appetizer. This one went for the head and left the guts alone.

As we approached the spot where the zebra was, I noticed a sound I hadn't noticed before. It was a kind of drone that I couldn't place. It was constant, unrelenting, a double-bass continuum that the other forest sounds sang over the top of. When we got within sight of the animal, a black cloud whooshed up from the carcass and the drone became a screaming zing as the insects soared away. It was like a fly convention with all nations and species represented. You wouldn't think there were that many flies on the planet, let alone in that one forest on that one zebra.

Another bait was hanging from the branch of a nearby tree. Don checked it and found that something, probably a lion, had tried unsuccessfully to climb the tree for the meat. Why a lion would attempt that rather than partake of the feast on the ground was an unsolved mystery.

"Looks like a *simba* (lion) tried to climb this tree to get at that *nyama*, Bwana. Not too successful, it seems. See these claw marks here? I would say these are definitely made by a lion. Much too wide apart for a *chui* (leopard). Looks like he may have even made it up to the limb but it might have been too precarious for him and he climbed back down. See how the bark is ripped up here. If it had been a leopard, it would have climbed straight up, don't you worry. The *chui* is a climber. They can climb a tree with a whole impala in their teeth. Pound for pound the strongest cat there is. No, these were definitely made by a lion. Poor bugger couldn't stay up there long enough for a feed. There are places in Africa where lions will climb a tree almost as handily as a leopard but not often around here. No, lions in these parts hunt and eat on the plains. Looks like he tried to climb this tree to get at that *nyama* up there…"

The sergeant noticed some long, light colored hairs. Soon some tracks were found that could have been made by a lion. Don concluded that a lion had been around but certainly wouldn't be now. We started back toward the Land Rover. I spotted a ball of what appeared to be the same kind of light colored hair. I couldn't have been prouder and more excited if I'd discovered King Solomon's mine or the headwaters of the White Nile.

Just as Don began congratulating me, we heard something crashing through the bush. The sound came closer and as it did we were able to locate its direction. It was not on the ground but somewhere above us. In a moment, a Colobus monkey was swinging through the trees, making a hell of a racket. These are large monkeys and have a distinctive ring of long, light colored hair around their throats. Mystery solved. The hairs weren't from a lion. They were from a monkey.

Because the game was so abundant at that time in the NFD, there were often reports of lions where people would prefer they not be. By the time we arrived back at the homestead, there had been another report of a lion. This time it was in Isiolo itself, the principal village in the NFD. There was always a fear that lions in such close proximity to people would eventually become man-eaters. To the lion, *nyama* is *nyama*. The easier to kill the better. Human beings – except for the Masaai -- were not equipped to fend off a lion without bullet propelling weapons. A Masaai warrior proved his mettle by killing a lion *mano a mano*, with only a spear and a shield as his standard issue. The report from Isiolo said that two native girls had been killed and eaten by what was referred to as a rogue male. Everyone was depressed at the news.

Next day, we went out looking for that lion. Don shot a zebra to use for bait. The zebra was skinned and the bloody carcass lay there on the ground. No sooner had that flesh been exposed than shadows began swooping across the ground at our feet. Looking up revealed a flock of vultures that had to number at least five hundred, circling at varying heights above our heads. More were in the trees nearby – watching, waiting. As soon as we left that place, the vultures descended to the blood soaked ground where the corpse had been, looking for any leftovers.

We drove to the area where the bait would be placed. We dragged it to the chosen spot and wired it to the ground, leaving a scent for the lion to follow. An advance vulture scout was already in a tree, watching intently as we piled thorn bushes over the carcass to protect the meat against anything but a large predator. Vultures would be discouraged by the thorns, as would jackals and hyenas. We took branches and swept the dirt in a wide circular area around the bait so that anything that approached would leave tracks in the smoothed dirt. We would come out again tomorrow and learn more about this killer.

After a quick wash, we all went to the Samburu Lodge, traveling through country so packed with game that even I could see it. Waterbuck, impala, baboon, giraffe, zebra, wild dog. The place was teeming with game, running free, in the wild, as it had done since forever.

Around the Samburu Lodge I saw for the first time a different part of the human component that is also the story of Africa. People without modern medical care can develop some pitiful physical characteristics. The amount of deformity was shocking. There were Africans with withered limbs, crooked limbs, abbreviated limbs. One man crawled along on his hands and knees. His knees were so calloused that they looked like stumps that extended three or four inches beyond his kneecaps. It looked like he had brown cans on his knees with useless legs trailing behind him, dangling as he pulled his way along the ground. The people I saw represented a fraction of the misery that was their normal, everyday lives. It was sobering to think that all this existed in the same world that I and my friends, family and acquaintances shared.

Next day when we returned to the lion bait, the tracks told a story, but not the one Don had wanted to see. The thorn bush was scattered on the ground a short distance from the pristine, cleanly polished zebra bones that glowed in the African sunshine. The tracks coming in and going away from the bones appeared to be made by tire treads about a foot long and spaced a stride apart. The local Turkana men often made thong-like footwear from old tires.

"No lion tracks, these, Bwana. No. We've got ourselves a different kind of predator. My guess is that this gent came in with his *panga* and whacked as much *nyama* as he could carry, then left the rest for the vultures. They did a fine job of cleaning up this zebra, didn't they? I'd hate to live off what they left around. It's good they're here though. Them and the jackals and hyenas -- and the maribou stork. They keep the bush tidy. This way there's enough for everybody. No. Not much more we can do around here, I'm afraid."

CHAPTER EIGHT

Julian Brown, a former member of the police force and game warden fraternity, had taken the next likely step and become a professional hunter. By law, he was required to make sure the local game warden knew his whereabouts. Julian had contacted Don to tell him that he and his Texan client would be hunting in the NFD, somewhere near Isiolo.

Rather than return to the homestead, Don suggested we see if we could find Julian's tracks and visit him in camp. I was all for it. I had now been in the bush long enough that I was not only comfortable but eager for the next escapade. It was like living in a dream.

While his sergeant drove, Don invited me to sit on the roof of the Land Rover with him, our legs dangling into the cab, while he followed the nearly illegible tire tracks that led to Julian's camp. How he saw what he saw was another of those talents developed after years in the bush. The terrain was the roughest I'd seen to date.

As we made our way through this raw, unadulterated bush, we saw herds of buffalo numbering from twenty to seventy animals. There were rhino, wild dog, ostrich, plains animals by the scores and even a lone leopard.

After much winding around and about three-quarters of an hour, we approached an area that had a few trees visible straight ahead of us. "*Sawa-sawa*, Sergeant," Don said, indicating straight ahead with his hand.

Julian saw us bouncing our way toward his camp and walked towards us. There were "*Jambos*" all around and introductions made.

"This is my client, Harv Driscoll. He's from Dallas."

Going on a hunting safari was definitely a rich man's game. To begin with licenses had to be bought and licenses for large animals were exorbitant. Then there was the cost of trucks, tents, food, the professional hunter, skinners and trackers, not to mention airfare. After that, having the trophies taxidermied and shipped back home piled on even more expense. Today's packaged tours, with buses full of people with cameras hanging around their necks, didn't exist. National parks, while they did exist, didn't have a corner on the game market. It was everywhere.

"Hey, boys, come and look at this," Harv beamed. "He's a good 'un. Got damned if he ain't."

He led us to a lion that he had only killed a short time before. It hadn't been skinned yet. It was as close as I'd ever been to a *simba* – even including my visits to the zoo. I could get right up in his face.

It was a large male. His head was massive. His mane was a dark brown and thick and coarse. His face looked angry, with a "don't fuck with me" sneer on his lips even in death. One of his forepaws had a hole in it, indicating that he'd had his share of battles. This old boy had survived everything but a bullet. His weight was estimated at around four hundred pounds. This was one of the most impressive sights I had ever and have ever seen.

"Brought him down like a stone, didn't I, Julie?" Harv said. Julian visibly winced at hearing this diminutive of his name. He rolled his eyes upward for Don to see, as if to say, "This is the price one pays for escorting these wankers around the bush," proving that in any context, a gig's a gig.

As if longing for another human being's company, Julian invited us to stay for dinner.

"Hell yeah," Harv added. "You can help us celebrate this dead ol' *simba*. Got damn, that boy's gonna make one hell of a trophy." The only thing Harv didn't do was YeeHaaaaa!

Canvas chairs were set up around a fire in the middle of the circle of tents. Glasses of whiskey were distributed with a choice of mixers. Individual bowls of salted nuts were given to each of us. Harv was still excited about his kill and tried to insert his prowess into the conversation at every opportunity. But Julian and Don skillfully directed the conversation to other, local issues that managed to leave Harv smiling and pumping up on his own. In the midst of Harv's coarseness and bravado, I had already conveniently forgotten what an ass I had been after shooting a helpless gazelle. I saw in him what I had been unable to see in myself. Africa tended to bring that out in us foreigners.

After a while, I wandered back to the lion. By now the skinners had done their work and I was able to see the muscle structure of this beautiful cat. It was an anatomy lesson. As you would expect, there was no fat visible anywhere. His shoulders were hugely muscled and sinewy. What I would identify as his biceps and forearms housed bulging veins that indicated enormous strength. I imagined him being able to run alongside a gazelle or zebra and bring it down with one swipe of this mighty foreleg. This animal was as beautiful and impressive without skin as it had been with it. I was absolutely in awe.

Dinner was a much more elaborate affair than I would have guessed. Fresh vegetables and freshly baked bread, wine and butter, tasty beef and fancy dessert, cheese and brandy and coffee. It could just as easily been Le Grenouille in New York.

Harv was still crowing as we left Julian's camp. It was dark by now and the almost invisible track that we'd come in on was a virtual figment of Don's imagination on the way out. In an area where the only sounds at night were the occasional "Woof" of a lion on a kill or the cackling of hyenas, and the only light was provided by the moon, this Land Rover was making its presence abundantly clear. Because this was Shifta country, Don and I were both armed to the teeth. We each had a 12-guage shotgun. I had a .300 magnum rifle; he a .375. I had a .38 caliber pistol, he had a 9 mm. All were loaded and ready.

Somehow, Don was able to lead us back to the main track and we arrived without incident at the homestead, where Rachel greeted us with a cup of tea.

CHAPTER NINE

There was little to do the next morning. A tremendous rainstorm pounded down for a few hours. In this equatorial region, there was no climactic or meteorological subtlety. When it rained, it bucketed down. When it was hot, it was stinking, steamy hot. When the sun was up, colors were magically vibrant and intense. When the sun went down, the only outdoor light came from the sky. What we have come to recognize as the light of civilization, the light that illuminates cities, the light that makes most humans both diurnal and nocturnal animals, has no place in this fundamental, organically basic world. Nature is the clock.

Just after lunch, Jungle Bob called and suggested I make my way down to Nanyuki to the Mt. Kenya Safari Club. As it happened, Rachel would be able to drop me off on her way to Nairobi. I said a reluctant goodbye to Don and off we went. The time had been so concentrated, as it is when we are away from our everyday environment, that it felt as though it could have been days or months or years that I spent in the Northern Frontier District. Each moment had been so supersaturated and intense that it seemed as if nothing outside it existed. Visiting any new place can be that way. But being in Africa seemed to intensify it a thousand-fold for me.

Jungle Bob and Magda were sitting under an umbrella by the pool at the Mt. Kenya Safari Club when we arrived. The Mt. Kenya Safari Club was founded in 1959 by the movie actor William Holden, oil billionaire Ray Ryan and Swiss financier Carl Hirschmann. Its membership was by invitation only and exclusive. Members included Winston Churchill, Bing Crosby, Charlie Chaplin, David Lean and other assorted influential people. You could only get in if you were a member or the guest of a member. Jungle Bob was, of course, a member and sponsored my one-night, temporary membership, which allowed me to stay there. It was the closest to five-star accommodation that I'd seen so far – in a rustic, African sort of way.

A large table of us met for dinner. I wore a jacket and tie for the first time in so long that it felt odd. And I didn't much like it. But proper dress was required in the dining room. Very pucka. My dinner companions included a man from South Africa named de Beers, Bill Holden (who was between pictures),, a pilot for East African Airlines, a New York attorney, a writer and his female assistant, a wildlife photographer and several other movers and shakers who had a *thing* for Africa.

Because I was there and a friend of Jungle Bob's, it was naturally assumed that I belonged. I put on a respectable front and with my recent bush experience, was able to make a unique contribution. My African *thing* was every bit as real as theirs. However, I soon discovered that African *thing* or not, people could be just as ill informed, opinionated and boring at the Mt. Kenya Safari Club as anywhere else in the world. One person thought Chiang Kai Shek was head of Communist China. Another calmly announced that slavery had been a benefit to the African people. The conversation ranged between sophomoric psychological tests and absurd supernatural tales, and made me long to hear a million flies buzzing over a dead zebra's carcass. Bill Holden must have seen the writing on the wall because he excused himself early and went to his room.

Next day, Jungle Bob, Magda and I drove back to Nairobi. Jungle Bob had business with a zoo director and Magda was expecting a guest. I checked into the New Stanley Hotel and wrote cards while I figured out what to do next.

We all had drinks together that evening and it was suggested that I might like to hop over to Uganda and have a look at Murchison Falls. Jungle Bob was going to be in Tanzania for a few days and Magda had business in Somalia.

Next morning, after a leisurely breakfast in my room, I went to East African Airlines and, thanks to my membership in the airline family, bought a ticket to Entebbe at a 75% discount. Once that was all sorted out, I returned to the New Stanley, sat at the Thorntree and waited for the world to pass by.

Before long, the pilot from the Mt. Kenya Safari Club strolled by and stopped for a beer. Not long after that, the New York attorney showed up. In a little while, Rachel popped in for a cup of tea before returning to the NFD. People each of them knew joined us over the next few hours. It was like old home week. In the short time I'd been there, I had become accepted as one of them. Certainly, some of it had to do with the fact that I had met several of these people, socialized with them and not pissed anyone off. But part of it had to do with something unspoken: we were all white. This bonded us as nothing else could. There was definitely an "us and them" mentality among the residents and others gathered at the Thorntree, which led to certain social assumptions on most of their parts. It made me uncomfortable. I had never thought of myself as that kind of white.

CHAPTER TEN

I arrived in Uganda and took a bus from the airport in Entebbe to the Lake Victoria Hotel. I was expecting to spend a night or two, then push on to Murchison Falls with a tour of some kind. When I arrived at the Lake Victoria Hotel, I learned that the tour I was looking for left from the Grand Hotel in Kampala. So it was back on the bus and back to the airport to try to catch a different bus to Kampala. Somehow, we intercepted the right bus on the way and I made the transfer.

This bus was more of a van. I was seated in one of the middle seats. A very large African gentleman was sitting in front next to the driver. I had noticed him on the plane from Nairobi. He kept looking back over his shoulder and staring at me so often that I began to get nervous. Then he leaned toward the driver and said something I could not hear and even if I had, wouldn't have understood. The drive had seemed endless already when the driver nodded to the large man and pulled off the main road into some back streets.

These were back streets like none I had ever seen. Kampala was hardly a metropolis to begin with. Off the beaten track was actually *on* the beaten track. The roadway was compacted dirt. The dwellings that lined the streets were humble, bordering on slums. Certainly not a place that the Kampala Chamber of Commerce would have put on their brochure.

I had bought a beautiful bone-handled steel hunting knife at Abercrombie and Fitch in New York and carried it in a special compartment in my luggage. As the driver wove his way through these side streets, my anxiety built to a Wagnerian crescendo. Any minute I expected to have to fight for my life. I had the knife securely in my grasp and was holding it down between my knees. The van eased to a halt. Then the interior light flicked on. Both the driver and the large man opened their doors and stepped out of the van. I brought the hunting knife up onto the seat beside me, at the same time trying to keep both of them in my sight.

The driver walked around to the back of the van from his side while the other man did the same from his side. Only swiveling lizard eyes could have kept them both in view. I heard a sound behind me. I snapped around. The driver opened the tail door of the van and took out the man's bags. They exchanged some pleasant words. The man gave the driver some money. The driver returned behind the wheel and we drove off. I had been petrified with fear and now realized what an innocent thing it had been and what a drama I'd made of it. Fortunately, there was no one there to observe my stupidity. The driver had made a couple of extra bucks by giving this guy a lift home.

Without further incident, real or imagined, we pulled up at the Grand Hotel. I hadn't made reservations. The hotel was full. I was in Kampala without a place to stay or anyone to call. I pleaded with the Indian desk clerk.

"Don't you have any rooms at all?"

"No, sir. All our rooms are booked. This is our busy season."

"Yeah, but there are always some rooms set aside."

"Not here, sir. We are booked out."

"There must be something, a bed somewhere…"

"We have no beds, sir."

"But I'm taking your tour to Murchison Falls day after tomorrow."

"I would suggest you try at the Speke Hotel on the other side of the street. They may have something."

"What if they don't?"

"I'm sure they'll have a room for the night. I'll have one of our bellman escort you."

"I don't need anyone to escort me." I was thinking I was being worked for a tip.

"You could go there on your own, sir, but I would not recommend it."

"Why's that?"

The look he gave me answered my question but he added, "I think you'll be safer, sir." He called a bellman. "Take this gentleman's bag to the Speke Hotel, please. We'll see you in two day's time, sir."

The Speke Hotel had a room on the second floor (or first floor by European standards) that overlooked the main street. The Grand Hotel was up the street to my right, toward the main part of Kampala. My room had a small balcony from which I could look into a very large park across the street. There was nothing fancy about the place but it had a bed and a tub and that was all I required.

I was going to have a day in Kampala before the tour so I unpacked what I needed and went to sleep.

The daylight brought with it a sense of security. I was awakened at 7 a.m. when a pot of tea and some toast were brought into my room. I took my breakfast out onto the balcony and watched the modest hustle and bustle of Kampala play out beneath me.

The weather was a bit closer in this more inland country. Kampala sits on the northern part of Lake Victoria, the second largest fresh water lake on the planet, about the size of Ireland. To the north of Uganda is Sudan. North of that, Egypt. To the southwest, Tanzania and Rwanda. To the west is the Congo and Kenya is to the east. The headwaters of the White Nile poured into Lake Victoria. I felt as though I had come to the real Africa, not a European version, but the real thing.

After I ate and dressed, I decided to have a walk around the town. Nothing was very far away and I soon made my way to a café where I had a cup of coffee and read whatever newspapers were available. Unlike the Thorntree's passersby, the people who drifted before me were far less cosmopolitan. African women, with the poise of Paris models, paraded by with huge, heavy baskets loaded with all sorts of things rocking easily on their heads. The pace was slower than

Nairobi's. More men in Arab-like dress were to be seen. There were fewer European looking people around, fewer people altogether.

A lone European woman came into the café and sat at a nearby table. We were the only people in the place. Before long, we struck up a conversation.

I laughed as I told her about my experience in the van on the way to the hotel the night before.

"You were very lucky," she said with a distinct French accent.

"Was I?"

"Very. It is *tres* dangerous here. They tell me never to go out alone at night."

"They wouldn't let me walk across the street from one hotel to another."

"Is very dangerous. They have men who block the roads and rob drivers. They roll a log on the road and make the car stop. Is very dangerous. They tell me this often."

We had a glass of whiskey together and then she disappeared as mysteriously as she had arrived. I didn't even learn her name.

I had an early dinner alone on my balcony. Just at dusk, I noticed, way over to my left in the direction of Entebbe, what appeared to be the beginning of a dotted black line. The line then widened until it now appeared to be a black, silk cloth that waved and fluttered across the sky. As it came into the middle of my field of vision, it got wider still and was accompanied by a shrill, high frequency sound that was so piercing as to be nearly deafening. The sky was now a band of dense black before me and the enormous traveling cloud vibrated with what must have been millions of bats. They crossed through the frame of my balcony lens until they vanished, taking their eerie noise with them.

CHAPTER ELEVEN

It was raining hard next morning. I could barely make out the park across the street through the downpour. The humidity had been rising noticeably for the past few days, an indication that the wet season was approaching.

In front of the Grand Hotel were the two Volkswagen minibuses which would take my traveling companions and me to Murchison Falls. Already seated in the vehicle I entered were an American dowager-looking woman, an American secretary from Saudi Arabia, and a European gentleman of unknown origin. I greeted them and climbed aboard.

Murchison Falls is in the northwest corner of Uganda. In the mid-to-late 1800's there was an insatiable desire to discover the source of the Nile. The speculation had begun with Diogenes in 350 BC and continued through to the Victorian Age. Some of the greatest names in England's arsenal of Victorian explorers went on this quest: Richard Burton, John Hanning Speke, Stanley and Florence Baker (she being the only woman involved in the various expeditions), James Augustus Grant and Henry Morton Stanley (who found the lost) Dr. David Livingston.

Illness, animal and human attacks, treachery, starvation, blindness and various other depravations complicated even the successful expeditions. The prize was to be the first. As Mark Twain wrote in *The Innocents Abroad*, "To do something, say something, see something, before *anybody* else – these are the things that confer a pleasure compared with which other pleasures are tame and commonplace…"

It was the Bakers who first made their way to our destination, Lake Albert. In his diary, Stanley Baker wrote: "It was with extreme emotion that I enjoyed this glorious scene…No European foot had ever trod upon its sand, nor had the eyes of a white man ever scanned its vast expanse of water. We were the first and this was a key to the great secret that even Julius Caesar yearned to unravel, but in vain. Here was the great basin of the Nile."

Our journey to Murchison Falls would take most of the day with a stop at Misindi for lunch. As we left Kampala farther and farther behind, the sun burned through the clouds and revealed a bright, hot, sunny day.

The dowager lady – let's call her Mrs. Jones – felt it necessary to maintain a running commentary as we progressed toward Misindi. She said nothing of interest or consequence. It was more as though she couldn't stand silence.

At one point our path was blocked by a herd of ordinary cattle, there being but one thoroughfare between Kampala and Misindi. As we very slowly eased our way past these bovines, Mrs. Jones would "ooo" and "aah" over each "calf," which she pronounced with a Boston accent, leaving one with the impression that she'd never seen one before. "Isn't that one cute?" she'd say repeatedly. The secretary, the unknown gentleman and I looked out the window at nothing in particular.

We arrived at the Misindi Hotel bored with Mrs. Jones but otherwise intact. The grounds around the hotel were alive with brilliant color. As one traveled deeper into the continent, the foliage became more intense and vibrant, denser and more spectacular. Bright reds and yellows and greens and oranges shimmer in the sunlight. Exotic birds flutter among the trees and plants. In every direction you see a natural rainbow of beauty.

After I had a bite of lunch, I took a walk around the grounds. I wandered down the entrance path to the main road. Across the way were two older African people, a man and a woman. Their hair was gray and they were dressed in what appeared to be woolen coats despite the temperature. They were seated under a large tree, looking in my direction. I approached them and saw that their limbs were rounded off where fingers and toes should be. These smoothed nubs were discolored pink and nearly white in contrast to their natural, chocolate complexion. The expression on their faces was forlorn and pathetic as they looked up into my eyes. I will never forget it.

I couldn't speak to them. But even if I had been able to, I wouldn't have known what to say. "Are you lepers?" was what I wanted to ask, even though the evidence made it obvious that they were. "What can I do to help you?" may have followed. Instead, I reached into my pocket and took out some money. I offered it to them haltingly. I didn't want to offend them if they were there for some other reason. Their eyes acknowledged the money and the man took it from my hand with a discolored stump that had once been a thumb and his palm. I returned to the hotel sobered.

The second minibus had made this journey from Kampala behind us. There were two British women in it who asked if I'd mind switching vehicles with them so that there would be five in each and allow more room for everyone. As much as I hated the idea of missing Mrs. Jones' commentary, chivalry got the better of me and I acquiesced.

The second bus had its own special character – or perhaps I should say, characters. There were two British women on this one and two Germans who insisted they were "making cinema." Judging by the way they pushed and shoved and called for silence and generally ordered everyone around, including the driver, it must have been very important cinema indeed – at least to them.

I sat quietly and tolerated their abuse as long as I could. Then I went Yank on them. "Hey, guys," I said, "This is not your vehicle and it is not your tour. We all paid the same money for the same experience. Please, stop ordering everyone around. Stop telling the driver what to do and kindly shut the hell up."

The two Germans had a sufficient grasp of English to understand the gist of my outburst. For that matter, if I'd expressed myself in

Mongolian, they'd have caught the gist. The English women understood perfectly and nodded their heads. When I started to apologize to them for my language, one quickly said, "No need. Good show."

As we approached Murchison Falls National Park, the two women displayed their knowledge of African flora and fauna in a way that brought a quiet smile to my face. One saw a warthog resting in the shade under a tree. "Look!" she said, "There's a rhino!" Mrs. Jones would probably have nodded in agreement or maybe said, "Isn't he cute?"

When we entered the area where our camp was set up, there were traffic signs indicating that elephants always had the right of way. It seemed quaint and amusing until we saw the vast herds of elephant that populated this pristine habitat. They were everywhere. Hundreds, thousands dotted every horizon. All sizes, all ages. In groups numbering up to fifty or sixty animals. Their ubiquitous presence filled us all with joy.

At one point we were close enough to an adult female to get her attention. The two German "cinema makers" stuck their heads out of the top of the minibus and began shouting, "Yumbo, Yumbo. Hier. Yumbo," in an effort to get the animal to turn toward their camera. The elephant glanced around at them indifferently, dropped about three-and-a- half tons of elephant shit and slowly walked away.

When a small herd of antelope bounded across the road in front of us, the second English lady said, "If my Quarters could run like that, I'd win the Downs."

We continued to bounce our way slowly toward our campsite. The would-be Fritz Langs needed to amuse themselves. The two British ladies had fallen asleep. The two Germans carefully lifted the women's hats from their heads and put them on themselves. They giggled and snorted and minced, then turned to me so that I could also enjoy this hilarious joke. In spite of myself, I couldn't keep from smiling at their idiocy.

We arrived at our destination with only a modicum of lingering hostility and each of us went to their assigned tent. Each tent had two cots in it, but owing to my lack of a traveling companion, I was given a tent to myself.

After dinner in a common mess tent, we were told that it would be an early start in the morning and it would be wise to get some rest. This suited me and I retired to my canvas home just as the sun was going down.

I had a momentary flashback to my first night in the African bush when an unfamiliar sound grabbed my attention. It was too close to ignore. Once I was able to identify it as a lizard scurrying across the canvas roof of my tent, I paid it no more heed and soon fell off into a peaceful slumber.

Sometime during the wee hours a massive storm blew up. Deafening thunder claps and dazzling lightning bolts competed fiercely for attention; the wind blew savagely and the rain poured down in torrents. I became just conscious enough to wonder if the tent would blow away; decided that I'd pull the blanket over my head if it did, and slid back into unconsciousness. It was one of the soundest, most refreshing sleeps I'd had so far in Africa.

CHAPTER TWELVE

In the morning, after the night of the storm, tea was brought to my tent at 7 a.m. I shaved in front of the tent, Army style, and went to the mess tent for breakfast. Three *"guten morgens"* and six "good mornings" greeted me. It turned out that the unknown man from the first bus was also German. I joined the group. Our vans took us to the shore of Lake Albert.

We walked out onto a humble, but practical pier from which we boarded the craft that would take us out onto Lake Albert. It was a unique sailing vessel: a rickety, chugging, motor-powered, rectangular-shaped device with a wide, flat deck. It looked like a houseboat without the house. It was sea-worthy, but just barely. As we putt-putted along, we saw a lake filled with hippo and crocodile in such abundance that they soon became commonplace.

The boatman maneuvered us near an embankment and we were told to look for some tiny creatures swimming near the shore. Newly born, three or four inch baby crocs could be seen wriggling through the water. Just above them, on the bank, were the torn-open, leathery looking eggshells from which they had emerged. Nearby, from time to time, the attentive mother croc would surface just long enough to see that we were causing no harm to her brood, just like any other mother.

We approached the place where three hundred cubic meters of water per second squeezes through a gap in the rift valley escarpment that's only twenty-four feet wide. It then cascades one hundred twenty feet to the bottom. This is Murchison Falls, one of the most dramatic and powerful waterfalls on the African continent. Samuel and Florence Baker were the first explorers to see it. It was they who named it in honor of Sir Roderick Murchison who was president of the Royal Geographic Society in London. During Idi Amin's reign, it was renamed Kabalega Falls. But when he went, so did the name he gave it.

Later we were loaded into our vans and taken close to where the cascading water completed its dramatic fall. The spray gave us a refreshing spritz. But Murchinson Falls was equally impressive from either vantage point. I thought of Stanley and Florence Baker and Speke and Burton and all the others. What must they have thought? How would they be able to rationalize the ease with which we observed what they spent years and suffered so much in seeking?

Since my visit to that game rich resource, Uganda has lived through the murderous regime of Idi Amin and a decimation of the seemingly endless elephant herds. Wildlife experts warned years before that if the elephant population was not managed, the animals would eat themselves into starvation by consuming everything edible in the huge park. Their warnings were not heeded. When an attempt was finally made to cull the remaining animals, they had already completely destroyed the vegetation. A little reason and management could have protected the glorious sight I was able to behold. Jungle Bob had been accurate in insisting that I see the animals while there were still such enormous numbers of them roaming free.

We returned to Kampala by way of Misindi, again stopping there for tea and a modest rest. Back in Kampala, I went to my old haunt, The Speke Hotel, checked flights back to Nairobi and read for a while before dropping off to sleep.

Next morning, after a quick breakfast, I caught a bus for Entebbe, flew back to Nairobi, checked into the New Stanley and then went to a local cinema. Whatever film I saw was totally forgettable.

CHAPTER THIRTEEN

I was surprised awake when the phone rang. I certainly wasn't expecting a call and wondered who even knew I was there. It turned out to be Gerald Hastings, the pilot I'd met at the Mt. Kenya Safari Club.

"Morning. I took a chance that you might be in town. Just got in from London. Meet me at the Thorntree in half-an-hour."

After a quick bath and shave, I went downstairs and out to the Thorntree. In a few minutes Gerald showed up.

"I just got in last night myself," I said. "I was in Uganda, Murchison Falls."

"Have you seen Jungle Bob?"

"No. I think he's still away on business. But he left a message for me to take Shegi and the Toyota if I wanted to go on safari anywhere around here."

"Perfect," he said. "I've got a few days off. Let's go down to Amboseli and have a look at Kilimanjaro."

After breakfast we went to Jungle Bob's little house where Shegi was wiping down the Toyota. He greeted us with his customary, broad smile, revealing about two-thirds the standard issue of teeth. He nodded and handed us the keys when I told him we were going to take the vehicle.

Since Gerald knew the way, he elected to drive. Amboseli National Park is located in the southwestern part of Kenya, near the border with Tanzania. Mt. Kilimanjaro is actually in Tanzania but clearly visible from Amboseli.

We got on *the* road, unpaved, of course, and made our way south. It's inaccurate, not to mention insulting to proper roads, to refer to this track as a road. It was a cleared path wide enough for two vehicles to pass one another. Essentially we were driving through the bush.

By now I had developed my "game" eyes to some extent and saw an abundance of animals and birds of all sorts as we rolled along. There were lots of both Grant and Grevy zebra, impala, tommys, Grant's gazelle, ostrich and in an especially climbable tree, a monkey. I asked Gerald to stop.

"What are you doing?" he asked.

"I want to climb up that tree and see how close I can get to that monkey." I don't know what possessed me. Gerald made a sort of "hmmm" sound and pulled to the side of the road.

The lowest limb was easily within reach. I grabbed it and swung myself up onto it. Adrenalin pumped through my body as I got to my feet on the limb and reached for the next higher branch. As I climbed higher, the monkey did too. It chattered at me in a language that any animal, human or otherwise, could easily understand. He was saying, "Fuck off!" The adrenalin must have also fogged my other senses. As I continued climbing higher and higher I was suddenly aware of a peculiar odor. I paid it no attention at first. But it reached a point where it could no longer be ignored.

"Something really stinks," I yelled back to Gerald, who was sitting patiently in the Toyota.

"It's probably you," he said calmly.

It was then that the light flashed on. Monkeys had been living in this tree since the dawn of time. It was their home. It was where they ate and climbed and chattered and fucked and, logically, where they shit. I had been essentially climbing through this monkey's toilet.

I was soon back on the ground and in the Toyota. "If you don't mind," Gerald said, again calmly, "stay as far away as you can. You reek of monkey poo!"

We had our eyes peeled for rhino, but in vain. We came across a herd of elephant but no rhino. We came upon a zebra that was lying beside the road. It was alive but didn't move as we approached. We slowed and could see that one of its hind legs seemed to be broken.

"That poor bastard's going to be someone's lunch," I said. "Look at his leg."

Gerald stopped alongside the zebra and we were closer than we had a right to expect when the animal struggled to its feet and hobbled off in the direction of a small herd.

"He'll still be someone's lunch," Gerald observed. "A *simba* will spot that game leg in no time."

Closer to the entrance to the park, we were greeted by a dust storm that obliterated everything beyond the windshield from view. It lasted about two minutes but seemed like an hour. With all the windows and vents closed tight, we still ended up spitting dirt after the storm had passed. It was another example of the lack of subtlety in this part of the world. It is all in your face: the good, the bad, the exotic, the treacherous, the serene. All *in extremis*.

The accommodations in the park were rustic and comfortable. From my little verandah I could have seen Mt. Kilimanjaro, assuming the clouds which mostly surround it had allowed. As it was, I spent most of my time smashing about forty thousand mosquitoes which had joined in a combined effort to suck the life out of me.

In the early morning, before the clouds had a chance to assemble, I was able to take in the full majesty of Mt. Kilimanjaro. I looked at it as long as I could, until the clouds began to enshroud its flat summit, then met Gerald for breakfast.

We continued in quest of rhino to no avail. There were baboon and wildebeest and hartebeest and everything else overflowing the park. At one point, we stopped on a small hill and scanned the landscape. We could see from horizon to horizon. As we looked across the vast plain, Gerald pointed out a giraffe in the distance. It took me a moment to focus my game eyes on it. Once I did, I realized that I had been looking at countless numbers of giraffe. They had somehow blended into the landscape so perfectly that they were unnoticeable before. Now I could see hundreds at various distances, in groups, standing individually, peacefully going about their business.

We came upon a group of deserted Masaai manyattas made of mud and cow dung grouped in a ring called a *boma*. The Masaai would live here for a while, then abandon this location in favor of their next nomadic home. I was too curious to pass it by.

"I wouldn't go in there if I were you," Gerald cautioned. "Remember the monkey tree."

"I have to," I responded and ducked my head inside one of the huts. It stank like nothing I'd ever smelled before – including me after the monkey tree episode. I stepped completely inside. Flies whirled around this humble domicile in a fever of ecstasy. I would have been tempted to stay longer if there was anything more to see. As it was, I left the flies to their orgy of delight and ducked out again. I don't know what I expected. Family photos? Snake skins like at Percy's? A portrait of Jomo Kenyatta? Who knows? All I saw was bare, brownish walls and a dirt floor.

As we continued our quest for rhino, we saw a lone, enormous male elephant with a colossal pair of tusks.

"How is it he's still alive with ivory like that?" I wondered out loud.

"That's Craig," Gerald said. "He lives here and is one of the park's attractions. They are very careful that he is protected from poachers – for obvious reasons. He's kind of like the grand old patriarch of Amboseli."

It was thrilling to see this handsome animal, knowing that his life wouldn't be cut short for the sake of a greedy merchant or collector or a hunter.

At our next turn we came upon a group of Masaai who were watering their cattle. Cattle represent wealth to these red-clad, red-skinned, red-haired nomads. The red on their skin and in their hair comes from ochre that they use for dye. Most had extensive beadwork, for which this tribe is famous, hanging from or encircling their various body parts. The men all wore toga-like apparel, also dyed red. Or in some cases, actual blankets or cloth which were purchased – but always red. Some wore the homemade footwear I'd seen in the NFD, a piece of tire held on by straps.

When I raised my binoculars to have a closer look, they became agitated, thinking that I was taking photographs. They made it clear with their stern expressions and wagging fingers that photos were definitely not allowed. I put the binoculars away and we moved on.

We decided to give up on the rhino, call it a day and return to Nairobi. It was about 11:30 in the morning when we started out of the park. Gerald's sense of direction matched my own and it was nearly three hours before we found the exit that pointed us toward Nairobi. It should have taken about twenty minutes.

But during the time we were lost, at last we found two rhino. One was relatively calm and placid. The other was less pleased to have us on his turf. To see one this close was to see how massive the animal is. This was a black rhino and weighed all of a ton, maybe more. As stupid as I had been in climbing the monkey tree, Gerald was equally stupid in taunting this inhospitable rhino. We were too close. It decided to stop playing around and looked in our direction, head bowed, horns aiming straight ahead. These animals are known to charge vehicles and topple them.

"I think we should leave him. He doesn't look very happy," I said.

"Oh, let's have a bit of fun," the otherwise conservative Gerald said.

He ripped around in the dust, playing tag with the rhino until it decided enough was enough and made a serious charge. Gerald mashed down on the accelerator and we left the rhino pawing at the dust.

"Now we're even," Gerald smiled.

"Even?"

"Monkey poo."

"Oh. Right."

We finally found the exit and made it back to Nairobi by around 6 o'clock.

I had a cold bath – the hot water wasn't working – ate and then called Rachel Summers, hoping that I'd get an invitation to return to the NFD before bringing my African adventure to an end. She didn't disappoint.

CHAPTER FOURTEEN

Shegi and I left Jungle Bob's reasonably early the next morning on our way to the NFD. As I hadn't driven a four-wheel drive vehicle before, nor on the left side of the road, getting out of Nairobi was challenging. In the city, I didn't notice the sluggishness of the Toyota. When we were on the road, something was definitely not right. I couldn't accelerate beyond a very unacceptably slow speed without the engine sounding as though it was going to have a hernia.

I was certain that I'd ruined the transmission or something worse, but had no one to ask what to do. Shegi was of little help beyond telling me that something was wrong. As long as I stayed below a certain speed, the Toyota seemed to function properly. Therefore, we limped along toward the NFD, stopping far too frequently as a precaution against overheating.

It seemed to take forever but somehow *Ngai*, the god who lives on top of Mt. Kenya, must have been smiling on us. We arrived at the familiar homestead without the engine burning up. Shegi unloaded the provisions that I'd brought with me while Don Summers had a look at the Toyota.

One glance and Don saw the problem. I had not known how to take the Toyota out of four-wheel drive. I had driven the entire distance from Nairobi to the Northern Frontier District at the speed that you'd use to get out of mud. Once Don adjusted the four-wheel drive gizmo, the vehicle purred like a kitten. How it got into four-wheel drive to begin with was a mystery, but I strongly suspected that I must have somehow done it before we left. No one had driven the Toyota since Gerald and I had returned from Amboseli.

The plan was to spend a day with the Summers and then return to Nairobi, catch a flight to London, then New York and try to adjust to not being in Africa anymore. We had a light dinner, then retired.

This time I got to stay in the main house with the adults.

After breakfast, Rachel and a neighbor drove down to Nairobi on business. In my role as self-appointed assistant game warden, I was keen to have a final adventure in the bush. It wasn't long before Don's phone rang and he was told that some buffalo were menacing a nearby farmer's maize crop.

Don hailed his trusted sergeant and a couple of other askaris, loaded the dogs and off we went. We soon arrived at the farm and once they'd settled, the dogs found the trail. It was still fresh enough for them to take off with some vigor. But it wasn't long before they got sidetracked.

Whichever dog was the leader, assuming there was one, got to sniffing out a rhino instead. With this and the young giraffe incident as evidence, I concluded that the dogs were less discriminating than one would like in tracking game. To them, it seemed, all wild animals smelled the same. This change of heart pointed them in a new direction and soon we could see them running toward a forest on the heels of a very large, fast-moving rhinoceros. We watched as they followed the rhino into the forest, then, realizing that nothing could be done without the dogs, sat down to await their return.

Eventually they all returned. The little fluffy one that I thought should have been a lapdog was limping badly. Closer examination revealed that the rhino had gored the poor little thing. Fortunately for the dog, the hole made by the rhino horn entered its chest away from the heart and exited behind the shoulder. The rhino must have flipped the dog over its back. It was obvious that the dog had to be treated immediately so the buffalo hunt was called off and we returned to the homestead.

Don looked after the little guy with tender care, applying some kind of disinfecting salve to the wound and stitching it up securely. He was certain that the dog would survive to chase after another wild animal fifty or a hundred times its size.

For all practical purposes, the workday was ended. I retired to a long, hot bath after a cup of tea. And with Rachel gone, Don and I were invited to a neighbor's for dinner. I went to bed that night with the knowledge that it would be my last in Africa. My heart was heavy.

It lightened immediately when, at breakfast the next morning, Don suggested that we have another go at the buffalo. I rationalized that I could always send a telegram to the television station in New York saying that I was lost somewhere in the African bush and couldn't get out. What choice would they have but to buy it? It never occurred to me that they'd wonder how I sent a telegram.

On our return to the farmer's field, we were stopped by the manager of a cattle farm. He had called the homestead and spoken to Angela, the African woman left in charge of the house and children. Therefore, he knew where to find us.

"Hello, Bwana," Don said in greeting. "This is a friend of ours from New York."

The man shook my hand in a perfunctory way and got down to business. "I think we've got a predator problem."

He led us to where a calf lay dead, its innards exposed as if the stomach had been ripped open by some very sharp teeth. "This is just the way we found this poor beast."

Don's analysis began. "Something appears to have ripped out its guts. It could be a lion or a leopard. A leopard would have tried to haul it up a tree after it had a feed to keep it for another meal or two. If it was a lion, it must have been a single male. The females hunt in groups and there wouldn't be anything left of this poor bugger. Hyenas could have done it. They hunt on their own sometimes. Not often. Normally they go after someone else's kill. But they will hunt if necessary. But they must have been scared off if they did make this kill. There's too much meat here. No, it's a mystery, Bwana. It's certain that something killed this poor beast and not very mercifully, at that. But what? That's the question. A leopard would have dragged it away, up a tree to keep some for another time. A leopard wouldn't be able to eat all this meat at one time like a lion might. A lone male lion could have done this if he was on his own, run off from the pride by a stronger male. The females would have consumed all this meat in a flash, don't you worry about that. Jackals only live off other's leftovers. Could have been hyenas. A hyena will hunt if forced. No, it's not likely it was a leopard. Could have been a male lion if he was on his own…"

After about the fourth or fifth time through, Don decided that the only way to find out would be to sit up and wait for whatever it was to come back. He was certain that the killer would return after dark. There was too much meat left.

"How would you like to spend a night in a tent out here, Bwana?" he asked me.

"Sure!"

We returned to the homestead and gathered the equipment we'd need for an overnighter in the bush.

Don picked a spot for our tent that would be close enough to the calf for a good shot but far enough away not to scare anything off. We drove a long peg into the ground next to the dead calf and wired the carcass to the peg so it couldn't be hauled away. Whatever came to feed on it would have to do it within shooting range.

We packed some sandwiches and a large thermos of strong coffee, thinking it would do a better job of keeping us awake than tea. We set up the tent and Don lashed a sturdy limb that he'd hacked off a nearby tree onto the tent pole where the canvas opened in front. It made a Y so the rifle barrel could rest comfortably and securely in it, making it an easier and more stable shot.

We laid our comfortable sleeping bags out on the floor of the two-man tent and had our sandwiches before the sun went completely down. A whole new soundscape began as the darkness spread. The hum of insects, which had been so ubiquitous that it was like white noise, faded and was replaced by a different insect choir. In the distance, the baritone "woof" of a lion echoed. Soon the careful sound of approaching carrion-eaters could be heard. Even the faintest sound anywhere within miles, it seemed, was audible.

"We'll take turns sleeping and watching, Bwana. If something comes up, we'll only have one shot at it. So remain quiet once it's dark. We don't want to scare it off. I'll take the first watch."

I nodded. In fact that's what I did during most of my watch too. I kept nodding. When Don was on watch, I slept. When I was on watch, I also slept – only this time sitting up instead of prone. How I could be so relaxed in the midst of this unique excitement is beyond me. But I was. I don't know how many times during the night I heard his voice whispering my name, but it was many. Sometimes I would be sitting up when he woke me. Other times I would find myself flat on my back.

The rifle was tied in place so that it only needed to be raised into firing position. Sometime during the night, Don whispered that I should get the torch ready. My job would be to aim the bright light in the direction of the calf and his was to get off a shot. It had to be timed perfectly.

He brought the rifle up to his shoulder. Something was out there. We could hear teeth gnawing on bone. When he whispered, "Now," I was to shine the torch.

"Ready?" he breathed.

"Yeah."

"Now."

I turned on the torch and in doing so was slightly off target. By the time I got the light shining in the right direction, all we could see was something racing off away from the calf. It was impossible to tell what it was. It wasn't a rhino or a giraffe, that was certain. But what it was Don wasn't able to see. I thought it may have been a hyena but not too much attention was paid to my opinion.

"Might as well get some sleep, Bwana," he said. "Whatever it was won't be coming back tonight."

I felt like an idiot.

CHAPTER FIFTEEN

Don and I got back to the homestead after a decent night's sleep in the tent. Rachel had returned and we had breakfast together. Again I counted my last moments in the bush before returning to Nairobi and catching a plane for London, then New York.

I started to pack my bag when the phone rang. Don "uh-huhed" a few times then hung up and asked if I wanted to have another go at the buffalo.

What the hell, I thought, *What's another day?*

Don called to the sergeant and told him to assemble some askaris. In a short time we were off again to another cornfield.

The chase was as exciting and thorny and exhilarating as the others. It all had to do with being in the open and tracking game. There was something so primal and honest about it even though the hunt was not strictly to gather meat for the clan. The instinct of it was strong and satisfying.

By the time this hunt was finished, at last we had found animals in the field creating havoc with the crop. Five of them were killed, the rest escaped. A group of Kikuyu people had heard the shots and when the firing ended, they had already gathered with pangas in hand to help themselves to fresh *nyama*.

It was still early enough for me to drive back to Nairobi. And I would have except Rachel had taken the Toyota to do some chores and I couldn't. I had to credit this new delay to Kismet. It was obviously not to be that I leave – yet. If it were up to me, I would have stayed forever.

But, without any further excuses, I left with Shegi for Nairobi the next morning at around 10 o'clock. Right before we left, there was a report from Isiolo that another native girl had been found dead, perhaps killed by the same rogue lion. Because of this, there was an additional sadness permeating the atmosphere as I said my final goodbyes.

I had grown so close to these people during the time of their generous hospitality that leaving was actually harder than I had thought it would be. It was clear that we had touched each other and the assurances to keep in contact had a genuine ring to them.

The drive back was uneventful. I spent the entire time re-living my experience with Don and Rachel and their two youngsters. When you think your heart is filled to capacity, it's always a surprise to find that there's just that much more room for something new. I had come to Africa with not the slightest hint or hope of making such good friends. Yet that is precisely what happened.

All the while that I was sitting in the passenger lounge at the airport in Nairobi, I tried to think of a scheme that would bring me back to Africa as soon as possible. Again, long before there was such a thing as "reality" programming, I conceived a program which I intended to call, "The African Summers," that would chronicle the lives of these extraordinary people. But life took me on another path and my return to Africa would be delayed.

In the meantime, since I left Don and Rachel, we managed to remain much closer than I would have expected. Don and I began corresponding regularly and kept up with each other's lives. He kept me up-to-date on the lives of the other people I'd met as well.

Gerald Hastings married a lovely Indian woman, breaking all taboos. They met in London when he was there on a flight. She had just finished her studies in economics. It was love at first sight and they returned to Nanyuki and were married at the Mount Kenya Safari Club.

In a later letter, Don told me that Gerald and his wife had come up to the NFD for a visit. The Summers family had adopted two lion cubs that were found abandoned, probably the result of their mother having been killed. The cubs barely had their eyes open when they were taken in by Don and Rachael, but mostly by Donny and Rebecca. The children looked after the cubs and bonded with them. It was not unusual to see them romping together anywhere around the homestead. As the cubs grew, they remained tame and wandered freely in and out of the house – until they became too fond of the furniture. Then they were easily shooed outside where they were harmless. They even played with the dogs.

When Gerald and his wife came to visit, it was to show off their newborn daughter. They had been told about the lion cubs, to be careful not to leave their daughter unattended. But one afternoon, when Don and Gerald were in the bush and Rachel had gone into Isiolo for provisions, Gerald's wife had left her baby unattended on the verandah.

The lion cubs saw the kicking bundle and became curious. As they were approaching the child, Gerald's wife returned and screamed, frightening the cubs away. She grabbed up her baby and ran into the house.

She was still hysterical by the time Gerald and Don returned. In the meantime, Angela had taken the cubs into the garage for safety. Without asking or hesitating, Gerard went to his car, took out a .45 caliber automatic and went to the garage. He shot both cubs dead without apology or explanation.

I was especially touched by this letter because Rachel had sent me photos of the kids with the cubs. I felt I knew them. It seemed so brutal and unjust. But then I remembered how brutal and unjust life can be there. Life can only be judged by African standards: if it can cause you harm, kill it.

Don had succumbed to the pressure and did what everyone who knew him thought he should do: become a professional hunter. His charm and wit would go a long way in keeping clients amused and happy. After he had made this transition, he had occasion to come to New York. There were always prospective clients to romance and former clients to catch up with. His client list included names that would be known by everyone: film people, politicians, the superrich and the super-powerful, a gluttony of name-dropping .

Whenever he was in town, we always spent a lot of time together. On some occasions he stayed in my apartment with me and whomever I happened to be living with at the time, either a wife or a significant other.

It was during one of these visits that he told me that he had discovered Rachel had been unfaithful to him. Again, he claimed that he was prepared to kill the man, just as he had been upon returning from Korea. The community was so small in Kenya that it would have been impossible not to have eventually learned about it. Don appeared to be devastated by this betrayal.

His way of compensating was to take advantage of the many offers he had from the partners and wives of his clients who graciously offered themselves to him. In some cases, it was under the noses of their men, often wandering surreptitiously into Don's tent in the middle of the night. At other times, it was in places like New York or Paris or London or Beverly Hills, wherever he went in search of new clients.

Yet, he and Rachel never parted. During those intervening years, I had been married again and divorced and lived with another woman and separated. His letters were always full of praise for my courage or wisdom or whatever he perceived to be a positive trait I had for not staying in an unloving relationship. When I suggested that it was only a matter of making a decision and that he was also capable of doing the same thing, he was unable to. Still he continued to complain and do nothing.

I could only conclude that he and Rachel must have come to some kind of understanding. Or their need for each other was something beyond love. Or any number of other possibilities that I couldn't imagine.

Then one day, I got a letter from Rachel. Don had been out on a buffalo hunt with a client. They had picked out a big male with a beautiful spread of balanced, arching horns. It was facing them in a defensive position, ready to protect the herd. Don, always mindful of his client's ego, insisted that the client take the first shot. But he was equally prepared to take the second immediately after to ensure an instant kill. The cape buffalo started charging. "Now," Don shouted. "Shoot now!" The client hesitated. The bull was coming close, too close. "Shoot now, goddam it!" Don insisted. The client froze. The bull was on top of them. Don shot, hitting the animal, slowing it, but not killing it. It continued its charge. Don pushed the client aside and the buffalo hit him, knocking Don to the ground and then falling and pinning him with its weight. Since the animal was not dead, it began thrashing with Don pinned under it. The faithful sergeant, whom Don had taken to be a part of his safari team, was concerned for Don's safety, thinking that the animal might gore him. "Shoot," Don assured him. The sergeant raised his rifle and fired into the buffalo's heart. The high-powered bullet instantly killed the buffalo but passed through its body and shattered Don's foot.

Don had a series of operations that attempted to reconstruct his splintered foot. Eventually, with only a portion of his foot remaining, he was fitted with specially made shoes and could walk again unaided. His safari days would be over. But by now, young Donny was of an age where he could take over the business with Rachel's help and Don's supervision.

During his ordeal, Rachel wrote asking me if there was any way I could come to Africa, that he was in desperate need of a friend and classed me as one of his best. I was broke, barely making ends meet since I'd recently embarked on a total career change in the most precarious of professions – acting. I could barely afford to feed myself. But I kept sending as much moral support through the mail as I could.

It was my assumption that this injury had brought Don and Rachel back together. It wasn't long after I moved to Hollywood that they both came to Los Angeles for a visit. It was wonderful being with both of them again. I had no reason not to maintain my affection for Rachel. Also, Don had more than made up for her single indiscretion with multitudes of his own.

Not long after their visit, Donny came out to L.A. to romance some clients. He had grown into a handsome man, a male version of Rachel's dark, good looks. He invited me to the house of one of his clients, a hugely successful Hollywood producer. For me, it was a rarefied look at how the other – I would say half but that would be inaccurate; one-hundredth of one percent is more like it – lived. The home was luxuriously furnished and had art on the walls that even I recognized.

After I came to live in Australia, we maintained our closeness. But Don was not as punctual about writing back as he had been. And at times, seemed unnecessarily fussy about insignificant things, like commenting on my penmanship. Whenever he did write, his main subject matter was often another reference to how wise I had been in getting out of bad relationships and how he wished he'd have had the courage to do the same.

CHAPTER SIXTEEN

All that history created the frame in which adventure was now set. That was then. This was now. When the Qantas flight arrived in Johannesburg, it was still daylight. We had been traveling with the sun. I had made reservations at a hotel recommended by the travel agent. My flight to Nairobi left the following day.

Already I knew I was in a different Africa. At the airport, several young men competed aggressively with one another to take my bags from me and escort me to the hotel transportation. There were armed, uniformed men at the entrance and in the parking area of the hotel.

The hotel complex included some shops, eating places, all of which were connected and enclosed like a mall. It was not necessary to step outside the hotel for anything. And certainly not encouraged. Most of the people walking around inside this African Disneyland seemed to be transients.

In this environment, everyone was pleasant and helpful and seemed to be unselfconscious and natural. There was a sense of pride among the African staff that suggested that, at least, their political struggles were over. It was their country and these were their jobs. They were completely at ease. There was nothing obsequious in their manner. They were my hosts. I was visiting their country.

I returned to my room after stretching my legs a bit and ordered a sandwich and coffee from room service. It was my plan to watch the finals of the US Tennis Open. Pete Sampras had reached the finals once more and was being challenged by Andre Agassi. It was certain to be a terrific contest. And I was hoping Sampras would win just once more before his inevitable retirement. I was a big fan.

I had checked the time, made sure my television set worked and settled back. The match never came on. Try as I might, contact whom I might, I couldn't get the damn thing. I had been forcing myself to stay awake to watch this battle of the titans and couldn't get it. I was heartbroken. But it had been such a struggle to stay awake that I reasoned that I may well have fallen asleep in the middle of it anyway.

I went down to the hotel dining room next morning for breakfast. Rested, I was able to take in more. First of all, I was conscious of being back in Africa in a way I hadn't been the day before. People get squishy and romantic about lots of different things. For me, Africa does it. Everything I felt the first time my feet touched African soil returned.

There was something wonderful about watching people of all shades working side by side in the various jobs around the lobby with no color line of demarcation. The concierge was black as coal and a woman. The bellhops were brown, beige and tan. The woman polishing the front windows was white. In the dining room, the waiters were friendly with an air of confidence. The buffet was crammed to overflowing with exotic fruit: guava, passion fruit, oranges, mangos, grapefruit, papaya and melons of various and unknown variety. I knew I was romanticizing – there were millions of people outside these walls who were suffering the worst imaginable deprivations – but I was content and happy that this abundance had been my first re-introduction to the continent.

After breakfast I packed and headed for the airport. Outside the hotel, I now noticed the brilliant South African flag flapping all its colors in the sun. The armed guards were still visible but my perception of them had changed with rest too.

This flight would stop in Zimbabwe before continuing to Nairobi later that day. There is something about words that begin with or contain the letter Z that have a special resonance when associated with Africa. Zanzibar, the Zambezi River, Zulu, Zimbabwe. I love saying them. I love hearing them. I was looking forward to spending a little time in Harare just to take in some of the sense of Zimbabwe.

The contrast couldn't have been sharper. There was no Mandela in Zimbabwe, no conscience. During the several-hour layover, I saw no people aside from the airport staff and one other transit passenger. No planes took off or landed. No shoppers wandered among the duty free shops. There was no cheerfulness, no courtesy, no confidence. Everything looked parched and lonesome.

A conversation with a woman in one of the shops revealed that there are long queues for bread and other daily necessities. Only money talks. And it only talks on the black market.

In the transit lounge I struck up another conversation, this time learning that all of this woman's family had moved to South Africa. She had a white grandfather who lives in Australia but couldn't claim migrant status because her branch of the family is illegitimate. She told me that in one month's time the real value of her wage dropped by 50%. She was openly hostile toward Robert Mugabe's government but, like most other citizens, felt powerless. All they could do was wait.

There were local newspapers in the transit lounge. When I looked through the editorial section of one, I was surprised bordering on shocked to see criticism of the government clearly spelled out in black and white. In the intervening years, things have only gotten worse. If I remember correctly, dissent of any kind is no longer tolerated, a reminder that this is also Africa.

It was dark when the other transit passenger and I boarded our flight to Nairobi. Once we were airborne and away from Harare, the flight took on an eerie and unique quality I'd never experienced before. Looking out of the window was meaningless. There were no lights to be seen anywhere coming from the ground. Nothing but black nothingness all the way from Harare to Nairobi, the same intense blackness I had experienced in the room next to the armory at the Summers in the NFD years before.

CHAPTER SEVENTEEN

The airport in Nairobi was in the midst of renovation and apparently had been for some years. There were half-finished sections all along the way from where I de-planed to the customs area. Also all along the way were uniformed men in camo fatigues, toting automatic weapons with crescent shaped clips of ammunition stuck into them. I hadn't remembered this Kenya at all.

Once I passed through customs and emerged, I saw Don and Rachel. Now I felt as though I had really returned. It had been 30-some years. Their familiar faces had aged even since the last time I'd seen them in Los Angeles, Don's much more than Rachel's, but then, so had mine. My automatic impulse was to hug them both. Rachel greeted me warmly. Don seemed to be self-conscious about showing this kind of affection but tolerated my embrace.

Because it was nighttime, there was nothing I could have seen out the window on the drive to their home. It wouldn't have mattered anyway. We were too busy talking. It took quite some time before we reached the Nairobi suburb where they now lived. I had no idea what to expect. I knew that Don's safari business had made him quite comfortable by any standards.

Rachel drove off a paved road onto a dirt one that was marked with speed bumps at regular intervals. On this cul de sac, there was also a guard shack with a gate that needed to be raised in order to pass. At the gate, the uniformed man saluted a casual salute with his index finger to his brow and raised the gate. A little farther along we arrived at a barbed wire topped fence where a proper, locked gate had to be opened by a young woman who came running out of the little house barefoot at the sound of the car horn. A little beyond that was a second locked gate, again with a barbed wire atop the fence. It was opened by a man dressed in khaki.

Rachel stopped on an expanse of gravel where a new-ish sedan was parked. Two large German shepherds and one other large but unidentifiable dog bounded up to us as we stepped out of the car. All three greeted Don and Rachel with enthusiasm and came to me for an identifying sniff, which it was their job to remember. My mind immediately flashed back to the big dog that was always at Don's heels when we were on a buffalo hunt in Isiolo.

Because it was dark and the place was unfamiliar to me, I merely followed as Don and Rachel led the way down a path, past the back of the house and into the kitchen. It was large enough for a table that would seat perhaps six or eight people, some side cabinets and a small pantry. There were two doors to the outside and one leading into the main part of the house. A large refrigerator stood next to ample counter space with a sink and more counter space perpendicular to it. It felt homey and unpretentious.

"Let's show you where you'll be staying, Bwana," Don said, leading me out the other door. "Then we'll have a cup of *chai*. You can muster up some *chai* can't you, Rachel?"

"It'll be waiting for you."

I noticed Don's rocking gate as he led the way to my room. I also noticed how much weight he had gained. Since I'd seen him in Hollywood, where he had already expanded noticeably, he had broadened his girth even more. I wouldn't have been able to reach around his gut. In all his letters, in addition to complaining about his marriage, he had bemoaned his weight gain, often referring to himself as fat. It was clear that he had taken no more action on this front than on the domestic front.

"This is Rachel's garden. I'll show you all this tomorrow." We passed through a little gate that separated the garden from the rambling lawn, passed through another small gate and onto a lovely little verandah. Don dug a key out of his pocket and unlocked the door to what was to be my room, handing the key to me once the door was open.

"We've only just finished this wing. You're the second person to stay here." He flicked on the light, illuminating a large room with two double beds, night tables beside each, throw rugs scattered on the floor, African scenes on the walls, some hand-painted water colors, some prints, a desk and chair at one end and earth-toned curtains on the windows. There was a bathroom with a shower, a welcome and noticeable difference to the ubiquitous tub I'd been forced to use on my previous visit. In the little kitchen area were an electric kettle, cups and the makings for coffee or tea, plus a small refrigerator that contained unopened juice and cartons of milk. I knew that I would be more than comfortable here.

While I was looking at my new surroundings, Don asked, rather bluntly, "Do you dye your hair?" His once brown, blond bleached hair had turned silver. He still had it in ample supply, however. My hair had a slight fringe of gray at the temples but was otherwise its original color. I was also several years younger than Don.

"No," I answered, taken slightly aback. "Why would I do that?"

He nodded and said no more about hair. "Hope you'll be all right here, Bwana."

"Beats being next to the arsenal," I said jokingly.

"We do our best," he answered blandly.

As we returned to the kitchen for a cup of tea, I was conscious that this was indeed an utterly different person than the one I'd previously known in Africa or even in America. There was something different in Don's manner. Something guarded. That ancient Greek didn't even let me unpack before he started showing me other waters. I passed it off as unimportant and allowed my mind to return to its new African home.

CHAPTER EIGHTEEN

Next morning, Don was at my window, calling to me to join him on the long verandah that spanned the middle of the house. Now I had a chance to see the place properly. The entire house was a large rectangle all on the ground level, ranch-style, and sprawled over an expanse of ground. This long verandah looked out upon an enormous lawn. One large tree stood just to the right of center, with several much smaller ones dotted here and there around the grounds. In the distance, you could see the Ngong Hills. Tall shrubs enclosed the entire grounds, or appeared to until I learned that through the shrubs in one direction was another large house where the bachelor Donny now lived and in another direction a house where the divorced Rebecca lived with her young son.

The entire property consisted of 10 acres. There were quarters where the staff slept that I never saw. But after morning tea, Rachel took me on a tour of her well-looked-after garden. There were three massive avocado trees with fruit dangling from the branches, banana and apple trees dotted around and a large expanse of garden where fresh vegetables were grown both for their own consumption and for the up-scale safaris that Donny now conducted.

Rachel was basically her son's partner in the business. Don was officially retired but never hesitated to offer guidance or an opinion whether asked for or not. I saw in Rachel much of what I'd remembered. She was a bit stouter but not nearly as careless with her weight as Don. Her face still looked young and when she smiled, it was bright and genuine.

When we sat down to lunch, later in the day, I noticed that Don's eyes were constantly scanning the area, both immediately in front of us and in the distance toward the Ngong Hills. It was a quality I remembered. People who live in such close proximity to the natural world have senses that are always alert for the unusual. At one time or another during lunch, as a punctuation to the conversation, Don commented on some mysterious looking smoke in the Ngong Hills or a dozen or so vultures that were circling in the distance or a predatory bird that was coming too close to the nests of the Weaver birds. Each of these things I also saw once they were pointed out, but I hadn't especially noticed them in the first place. My senses were focused with my attention on my immediate surroundings.

In the afternoon, Don and I drove to his grandson's school to pick the boy up. "Do you know how to drive?" he asked.

"Of course. Why?"

"I hate driving. I've just bought this car and I don't know a thing about it. You wouldn't like to drive, would you?"

"I have no problem except I don't know where we are or where we're going."

"Right you are."

He parked in front of the exclusive, private school and we waited. The school was situated on a large, lovely campus and served grades one through six. The children coming out to the waiting cars were a miniature United Nations. Every color and hue, every religious and cultural background could be seen among the running and laughing and rough housing children. It was enough to fill one with hope for tomorrow's Africa, except for the fact that these children all came from privilege and may or may not have a social conscience.

After picking up the boy, we stopped for petrol and to buy the boy an ice cream. Being the attentive grandparent that he was, Don couldn't allow the boy to have an ice cream alone. So he had one as well.

"I have to stop eating so much," he said, licking the cone. "How do you stay so trim, Bwana?"

"I pretty much watch what I eat. I exercise. It's not rocket science."

He seemed to weigh my remark to see if it contained any sarcasm. "Right you are."

We returned to the car after the attendant had filled the tank. Don tried repeatedly, without success, to start the vehicle.

"That bastard's done something to my car. It won't bloody start." He tried again and again, each time with the same result and the same harangue about how the attendant had sabotaged his car.

"I gave the bloody bastard instructions to service my car. Nothing more. Nothing less. But he's bloody well sabotaged it. Can't get the bloody thing to start. That bastard's done something. That's certain. It was working just fine until he got his hands on it. You can testify to that, Bwana. But he's done something. He's monkeyed with something under the hood, no doubt. No. The bastard's done something to keep the car from starting…"

I looked down at the gearshift. "I think you have to put it in P to start it." I tried not to sound like too much of a smartass when I said it.

Don looked down, moved the lever from N to P and the engine kicked over. Neville, the grandson, laughed a little too heartily for his grandfather's liking.

"Don't you dare say anything about this, you little bugger, or no more ice cream for you."

On the way to and from the school, I noticed the endless number of African people walking alongside the road in both directions. Some looked toward the car as we passed. Most just ambled along. Clearly there were few people who could afford public, let alone private, transportation. They walked – as they had always walked. To my urban eyes, this was as strange a thing to observe as the smoke in the Ngong Hills was to Don.

Back at the compound, Neville ran off toward home while Don called into the kitchen for some tea to be brought out to us on the verandah.

"Any women in your life these days, Bwana?" he asked, looking out toward the Ngong Hills.

"No. No one special."

"Any poontang?

"Well, all the equipment works. It's not like it was when I was twenty but I do all right." All I could think was that any time I've had a conversation of any length with any man that I knew, it would eventually include women and, more specifically, sex. It never failed. It was secret men's business.

"I don't get it up so easily anymore. But you don't have to stick it in to enjoy the feel of a woman," Don said.

This intrigued me. "What woman are you feeling these days?" It was clear to me that Rachel was not a candidate.

He gave me his crooked smile. "Niamani. She's away on holiday just now. You'll meet her. But keep your bloody hands off her."

"Don't worry." I was still curious. "What do you do with her? What does Rachel think?"

He ignored my question about Rachel. "Niamani slips in in the afternoon from time to time. I fondle her, feel her. It's enough."

In spite of myself, my mind immediately flashed back to a cotton plantation in the ante bellum Deep South. The old Massa would have his way with the slave girls and there was no one to object.

While we were in the midst of this enlightened discussion, a young woman approached. She asked for work for a day or two in her native Swahili.

Don answered her in his fluent Swahili, telling her that there was no work. She persisted. He continued to explain to her that there was no work. Still she persisted. Finally, he reached into his pocket and pulled out a large roll of currency. He peeled a couple of notes off and handed them to her, telling her to go see one of the other women on staff.

"I've told her to go see Matilda. She'll give her a job raking leaves."

The dogs began barking again as another woman approached. She had a daughter and young grandson tagging along behind her.

Don shouted at the dogs to stop, then told the woman to go see Matilda.

"Rachel doesn't like it when I help these poor buggers out. But what's a person to do? I told this one to go see Matilda, get a feed for her and the youngsters and spend the night in the quarters."

The dogs were always at Don's side and, after they got accustomed to me, mine. They tried to cuddle up to or somehow touch whoever was nearby. The two shepherds were magnificent. They were very large with beautiful, healthy coats, had intelligent faces and sleek, strong bodies. The other one was called a "sport" because even though he was in a litter of German shepherds, he had been sired by a Rottweiler. He was equally massive but had the disposition of a puppy.

Our principal meal was always in the afternoon. Just as in the old days, Rachel still did most of the preparation and supervised the rest. Later that evening, as the sun was going down, Rachel joined us for tea and a snack before we retired to the lounge room and a DVD. We never picked up after ourselves, of course. There was always someone on staff to do all that.

Before we entered the house, I saw one of the eight guards that patrol the grounds during the night and thought back to the crunching gravel outside my window by the armory. The barbed wire and electrical fences and guards may have kept everyone out, but they also kept everyone in. I couldn't help wondering if we were protected or imprisoned?

CHAPTER NINETEEN

Storm clouds piled up to the left as we sat on the verandah next day. Rain was on everyone's mind – or I should say, the lack of rain. We watched as the dark, heavily laden clouds moved across our field of vision, dumping thick lines of precipitation onto the Ngong Hills but leaving our area tinderbox dry.

It was now clear to me that Don and Rachel had what could be described as a cordial relationship, maybe correct would be a better way to describe it. The words exchanged were always proper, polite and rarely strayed into uncharted waters. It was as if they dared not touch on anything not completely acceptable and neutral. Each was, relatively speaking, warm to me. But they were experienced hosts and were practiced in conducting themselves accordingly.

Donny had returned from safari the night before and came over for tea in the late morning. He had taken four couples from Texas out and they would be coming for a farewell lunch later. I had seen Donny as a younger man in Hollywood. Now he was mature and very much in his element. He had been born and raised in the African bush. He was also charming without pretense. His relationship with both parents was easy, but a special bond seemed to exist with Rachel.

While we sat there, yet another African woman approached. She was a former employee and came to pay her respects – which, translated, meant she wanted money. It was pitiful to see these people reduced to this kind of penury. But it was how things were.

Two other women were out sweeping the leaves around the huge tree that dominated the lawn. They worked slowly and steadily, sweeping everything into one large pile. Soon after they finished, the wind kicked up and scattered the leaves all over the lawn again. No one seemed to mind. It merely meant that they would sweep them up again, justifying the few shillings they were paid for this make-work.

Rachel was less tolerant than Don when it came to these people coming up for what she regarded to be handouts. "They don't do a bloody thing but have babies," she observed. "It's all they're good for. They've bloody well populated themselves into permanent poverty. It wouldn't do anyone any harm if a few million of them went ahead and died of AIDS."

"That's a little harsh," I said.

"You saw what it was like before," she insisted. "If you were to go up to Isiolo now you'd see another sight, I can assure you. The population has ballooned. No one has work and they come to us because they think they deserve what we've worked for."

"We had a bloke in the house a while back," Don added. "He was stealing whatever he could get his hands on. I threw a bloody spear at him."

"I wish you'd killed him," Rachel said.

"Bastard broke right into my house. I thought I was in a time warp with the bloody Mau Mau."

"You have no idea," Rachel said. And she was right, of course. I didn't have any idea what it was really like in Kenya in the 21st Century. The romanticized version I had known was long gone.

Now, under the rule of Jomo Kenyatta's successor, Daniel Moi, the stable and progressive society which was the showcase and ideal of Africa, had been squandered. Moi had been in power since Kenyatta's death in 1978. Corruption, nepotism and dissension characterized his twenty-four years as head of the government. Services were irregular at best. It wasn't unusual for the electricity to drop out at far too frequent intervals with no explanation or recourse. If these people, who enjoyed financial independence were inconvenienced, imagine what the people with nothing suffered.

Still, I thought, even though it isn't the same as it was, it is how it is. Longing for days past was an activity of the old timers I'd met on my previous visit. As daunting as the task ahead may be, it had to be faced and dealt with politically. Otherwise, Kenya could become another Zimbabwe, something no one in or out of the country desired.

The four Texas couples arrived and we went to a large table that had been set under the trees near Rachel's garden. There were more than enough people to serve the food which Rachel had prepared with the help of her kitchen staff. The variety and quality were brilliant.

Conversation centered around the fabulous experience these people had had on safari. They felt as though they had become friends with Donny and his staff. It had been the experience of a lifetime for all of them. I understood these sentiments very well.

After they left, each of us retired to our own activities. Rachel went to putter in her garden. Don went to his room for a kip. Donny went through the hedge back to his house. I got my book and sat on my little verandah to read.

Before I opened my book, I made some notes in my diary. It was then that I realized that it was September 11th, the first anniversary of the World Trade Center disaster. In this relative isolation, it had slipped by virtually unnoticed. I confess that it was an immense relief to me not to have to be bombarded by the myopic world media with that horror again.

Don, Rachel and I assembled again later on the verandah for tea. Rachel brought out a Scrabble game. Being a lover of board games, I was keen to get into it.

Before long, it was clear that Don was accustomed to winning. He made up words, became strident when challenged and gloated when he scored big. There was an undertone to this game that became uncomfortable.

At one point, I challenged a word Don insisted was correct and proper. When we attempted to find it in the dictionary, no such word was to be found. Don insisted nevertheless.

"It's not a word, Don," I said.

"It bloody well is a word. Add up my score."

"But it's not a word," I repeated.

"And I say it is a word," he said, raising his voice.

"Donald, it's clearly not a word. It isn't in the dictionary," Rachel joined in.

"There you go again!" he exploded venomously, in a way completely out of proportion. "You never take my side! No matter what anyone says, you always agree with them instead of me!" His face contorted. He was furious. This was obviously not about Scrabble.

"There has never been a time in our lives when you've agreed with me about anything!" he continued to rave.

By now, Rachel was displaying the pain that she must have carried with her all the time. "How can you talk to me this way?" She was near tears. The stoic façade was cracked and crumbling.

"I've had to put up with your indifference and hostility for thirty years and I'm bloody well sick of it!" he thundered.

"You're a horrible person," she shouted, wiping away her tears and walking into the house.

I excused myself and walked through the hedge to Donny's house. He was there with his lady friend, a beautiful Pakistani woman.

"Mind if I join you for a few minutes?" I asked when he came to the door.

"Are they at it again?" he asked, without having to guess why I was there.

"They sure are."

"Come in and have a drink."

CHAPTER TWENTY

I got in the habit of taking my morning tea alone on one of two small verandahs outside my room. One faced a little flower garden and had a soft couch to sit on. The other faced a rose garden in the foreground with avocado trees in the background, and had a small glass-topped table with four chairs in the shape of elephant ears around it. Since Rachel had asked me what I liked for breakfast, there was always a bowl of fresh fruit: melons or oranges or papayas or mangos or apples, always bananas and avocados.

Sitting on either of these verandahs was a daily joy. I would awaken at around 7 o'clock. The staff members would be scurrying past and always raise their hand and smile a *mzuri sana* to my *Jambo*. The sky was always overcast at this time of the morning. The shadows slowly gave way on a diagonal across the flowers and trees, little by little until by 8 o'clock the clouds had burnt off and everything was exposed to bright sunlight. Each time it was like going from Kansas to Oz. Colors exploded into glory.

As soon as the sun brought the two birdbaths out of the shadows, they filled with splashing and fluttering and chirping and cooing and whistling and colorful little birds that darted in and out of the water, back and forth to various tree limbs, in an orderly, but frantic business-like fashion, each in turn awaiting its opportunity. I identified one of the bird calls as coming from what I dubbed the "Danny Boy Bird," so named by me because it repeated over and over and over, in perfect pitch and tempo, the first four notes of that classic song.

I watched two golden colored weaverbirds build a nest one morning. They built this architectural marvel at the very tip of a fragile looking branch on some kind of evergreen tree. One at a time, the birds would weave a supple stick in and out of the slowly emerging hanging, basket-like nest. When each bird finished and the limb was free of the bird's weight, the partially completed nest would whip back up to its natural height and position intact, securely fastened. Then the other bird would return, the limb would bow again and this one would weave in its piece. It was utterly fascinating. At every departure, you expected to see the nest flung off the tree and into oblivion. But it never happened.

The flowers in this little garden ranged from little white blossoms to poinsettias to something bright, bright orange to something else a vivid yellow to a few others moving in the direction of purple, all brilliant enough to hurt your eyes. These verandahs became my little sanctuary. Whatever had transpired the day or night before was quickly disposed of by this gentle, morning ritual.

I had expressed some interest in buying a few small, portable gifts for the people I'd see on the rest of my trip and others back in Australia. (I had brought a hand-blown piece of glass art for the Summers). Don and Rachel took me to a market – Rachel always driving, of course – that was located near the embassies and United Nations headquarters. As one of the most stable governments in East Africa, if not the most stable, Kenya became a center for all sorts of international affairs. This market was where those embassy and aid people tended to congregate. They felt relatively well protected despite the terrorist bombings of the US embassies in Dar es Salaam and Nairobi four years earlier.

On the way to this market I got my first real glimpse of local commerce. Shops, if they can be called that, lined the main, and I might add, partly paved road -- where it was paved there were gouging potholes, where it was unpaved it was subject to whatever the elements had in store: mud during the wet season, dust the rest of the time and potholes all the time. These "shops" were patched together with bits of discarded corrugated iron and whatever odds and ends of wood that could be found, sometimes looking like a slat from a packing box, sometimes looking like a tree limb. All were makeshift and primitive, but functional.

Near any shopping area large groups of indigent men could be seen standing around, waiting for an opportunity to help someone with a package for the sake of a few shillings. Here was a man holding up a still boxed computer game for sale. There was another holding up a puppy. Elsewhere was a man crawling around on kneepads at an intersection picking up the coins that people threw toward him from their automobile windows, reminding me of the man with the dangling legs in front of Samburu Lodge.

And speaking of automobile windows, I was advised not to keep my window open wide enough for anyone to reach in. People had lost the wristwatches from their arms, necklaces from their necks and anything else that could be grabbed quickly from a stopped car.

Farm produce and small plants were also available on the roadside. Rachel often stopped at these makeshift stalls to purchase fruit, vegetables or plants. Further along there would be a spot where newly made wicker furniture gleamed in the sunlight.

And the most dominant sign of commerce of all was the ubiquitous red and white Coca Cola logo. The entire side of a building may be painted with that well-known logo. Shacks alongside the road were filled with case upon case of the stuff. On an enormous billboard at one of the principal intersections in Nairobi was a seductive photo of three very young African girls, their beautiful, smiling faces radiating happiness with a bottle of Coke in each of their hands. To me it appeared to be as close to corporate malfeasance as I'd care to see. In any other country, there would have been laws protecting children so young from this kind of advertising. Not here.

We arrived at the market and immediately entered a different world. The people were colorfully dressed, some in traditional clothing like saris and turbans, but most in modern, generic, global clothing. There were Indians, Arabs, Europeans of every variety,

Africans, all bustling around, chattering in their native tongues, going about their shopping and social business.

On the upper level, in the direct sunlight, was what was called the Masaai Market. Once a week, craftspeople were allowed to come to this market and sell their handmade wares. In some cases, they were actually working as shoppers passed by. (I still wear a beaded belt that a Masaai woman was just finishing when I approached her) And even though it was referred to as the Masaai Market, other tribes displayed their goods as well.

The Masaai are known for their intricate and imaginative beadwork. Others are known for their woodcarvings. Others for their pottery. Individuals sold their own art, whether batiks or prints made from banana leaves or paintings of every variety.

These vendors were not as aggressive as, say, someone trying to hustle you into a strip joint on Bourbon Street. But they were not entirely placid either. This was an opportunity to make a few bucks and even the least sophisticated of them recognized it and intended to capitalize on it.

On the other side of the ledger, this same merchandise would cost a fortune if one were to buy it anywhere else. Here there was no middleman. This was direct business, from the maker to the buyer. The authenticity was guaranteed. And the products were unique and beautiful and existed in great variety. I bought as many things as I thought I could comfortably haul around the world with me. Rachel bought a few things as well. Some of the artistry was stunning.

Don approached a young African artist on my behalf. He had some batiks and banana leaf pictures that I found interesting. All the way around the market, Don and Rachel surprised most of the Africans with their fluent Swahili. They didn't expect this white, overstuffed city dweller or this well-dressed Memsaab to be able to converse with them, bargain with them and joke with them in their own tongue. Because of this, both he and Rachel could always get a better price than I would have on my own.

In addition to the shops that were scattered around this large, international market, shops for electronic gadgets, appliances, clothing and other necessities, there were a number of eating establishments that catered to an equally eclectic clientele. Most had open-air seating so that whether you were eating German, Thai, Chinese, Italian or Indian food, you could see everyone else. Even in this human sanctuary, Nature was nearby. Hawks were visible above the buildings, circling, hunting.

A European friend, a businessman originally from Sweden, but a Kenya resident for many years by now, joined us for lunch. After the courtesy questions about how I was enjoying my stay, etc., the three of them began discussing what can only be thought of as local issues – local to their continent, that is. Sometimes it can slip your mind where you are. Then the talk turns to something that happened in Egypt or someone being transferred to an office in Malawi or a political situation in Uganda or an arrangement between Zimbabwe and Libya. You realize that people are talking about things in their own backyard; in this case the backyard is all of Africa.

The atmosphere was once again cordial but non-committal when we had tea on the large verandah that evening. The Scrabble game, however, stayed in its box.

CHAPTER TWENTY ONE

As generous as Don and Rachel were, I still felt I was getting a very distorted picture of 21st Century Kenya. Within the compound, I could have been anywhere, apart from the Africans who waited on me and washed my clothes and made my bed and looked after my every need. I wanted to get out amongst the people. Both Don and Rachel were content to stay where they were, going out when necessary to do errands or rent a DVD, almost exclusively from Indian merchants. But otherwise they were unadventurous, happy to stay within the security of their little Ft. Knox after nightfall.

In an attempt to accede to my wishes, Don telephoned an African who had at one time been in his employ. It was clear from this end of the conversation that Don was not talking to a friend, but someone he expected to do as he wished, the inference being that there would be some money in it for him.

"Listen, Ngatia, I've got a friend here from Australia who wants to go hear some African music. When can you come by and take him along somewhere? --- Isn't there a concert on Sunday afternoons at the Zanzi Bar? --- Come by on Sunday and pick him up. --- Just for the afternoon. --- I know you don't have much money. This won't cost you a penny, just a little of your time. --- You'll be here, won't you? I'm not going to have to call you again, am I? -- All right, Ngatia. Don't forget now. -- All right."

Don returned the phone to its cradle. "He's a shifty bastard, this Ngatia. You'll have to watch your money around him. Caught him stealing here once. That terminated his employment in a hurry, I can assure you."

"Why would you send me out with him?" I asked.

"He knows these spots. You want to hear African music. I don't know anyone else, Bwana."

There was a woman from Nairobi whom I met at an artists' retreat in Australia. I had been trying to locate her since I arrived. The number Lydia had given me was no longer working. I still hoped to find her and get a look at the Kenya of 2002.

When that Sunday came, Ngatia didn't show up. My contact with African people would have to remain within the compound. Everyone was gracious to me. I was able to establish a modest relationship with Robert, the only man among the household staff. He seemed interested in seeing that I was enjoying myself at what he also regarded to be his home.

One of the staff who tended to look after my needs was a 30-ish woman named Margaret. She was never without a broad, engaging smile on her face. She was one of the most genuinely cheerful people I'd ever seen. When she brought fruit to my window in the mornings, it was always with an enthusiastically cheerful "good morning".

When she spoke, her hands constantly fluttered independently, like two birds that were attached to her wrists. It was impossible for her not to wave her hands about whenever she spoke.

One afternoon, when she brought tea to Don and me on the verandah, Don went into a routine I had already seen several times and was destined to see several more.

"Margaret, tell me how was your holiday. And don't use your hands."

Margaret would start, a smile already creeping onto her face, to tell about visiting her family in her village away from Nairobi, her hands plastered uncomfortably at her sides. Before a sentence was completed, her hands were waving around in their manic, uncontrollable way.

"No. Don't use your hands, Margaret. I'm not a deaf mute. You needn't talk to me with your hands. Just your mouth. How is your mother? Now, don't use your hands."

Another vain attempt to speak without those agitated, animated hands flying all over the place. By now she was also smiling and giggling uncontrollably, enjoying the joke on herself as much as we were. But try as she might, she could not get through a sentence without her hands flailing directionless and disconnected from her words.

"Are you being disrespectful, Margaret?" Don asked teasingly. "I asked you specifically not to wave your hands around like a windmill and yet you stand there and they whirl away."

By now Margaret would be laughing out loud and trying to talk without her hands appearing to be excited by something her brain was thinking. It was impossible. She just stood there, laughing and smiling infectiously.

"All right then, Margaret, if you're not going to tell me about your holiday, you might as well go back to Mama Kali."

Margaret returned to the kitchen, laughing all the way.

"Mama Kali?" I asked.

"That's what the staff call Rachel. Kali means fierce or sharp or even savage. You've seen Rachel around here. She rules with the authority of a field general."

It was true. A regular morning sight from either out my bathroom window or from the little verandah was Rachel, her parrot, Genghis, perched on her shoulder, the three dogs at her heels, striding around the property giving orders to the staff regarding the things she wanted them to accomplish that day. The staff knew that while Don was far more bark than bite, Rachel was to be heeded.

It was also interesting to witness the organic nature of African life in the matter of mortality. Death seemed to be a constant awareness in Africa, an essential and inevitable part of life, even in this protected environment. It lingered in various forms just beneath the surface of daily activity. Things live. Things die. Perfectly natural. Life goes on.

We had passed a shantytown one day that had recently been the scene of a murderous rampage by one hundred or so men who stormed through it with pangas and chopped and slaughtered the starving and destitute inhabitants for what were justified as "political reasons." It was grisly murder.

On another occasion a similar band of marauders stormed into a church and butchered the people worshiping there. It always gives me pause when I realize that these are all human beings acting out some ridiculous thought process, as if killing fellow human beings would somehow bring them closer to their own distorted goals. Regrettably, this kind of behavior isn't confined to Africa.

There was a student protest one day that was loosely organized at best. The nature of the protest was modest. No one advocated the overthrow of the government or threatened Daniel Moi. They were just expressing their displeasure on a university matter. Police arrested a person they decided was a ringleader. Another student approached the police, wanting to inquire about the treatment his soon-to-be incarcerated friend could expect. The policeman he approached raised his weapon and shot the student in the middle of his forehead without any explanation or seeming cause. No disciplinary action was taken.

Any animal was slaughtered for food whenever found, wherever found. There was virtually no game anywhere near the city except in the reserved areas. And even then the animals were not entirely safe. As if to balance the ledger, two people were recently killed by a lion. Even in 2002, it was, after all, Africa.

This unrelenting consciousness of death had been part of the life that Rachel and Don knew and had known since their earliest days. They were at the same time realistic and compassionate. If something needed killing, it was killed. If something died that had been held a part of the family, it was mourned – then released. This included pets and friends, with the same fondness and recollection. It was all part of accepting what was the natural rhythm of Africa. Things live. Things die.

We sometimes watched documentaries on television that dealt with the animal life in Africa. There was a bizarre quality about watching these films of animals that were actually just a relatively short distance away. It was like our world *was* a National Geographic special. When watching a program about honey badgers, Rachel was nearly in tears when a young member of this animal clan was mauled by a predator. The tears turned to sighs of happiness when a new honey badger was born.

There was a nature show playing itself out in the large tree that dominated the lawn. A pair of gymnogenes, African Harrier hawks, had nested in the tree a while back. Gymnogenes are large predatory birds. Because they naturally feed on smaller birds, Don and Rachel were concerned for the safety of the multitudes of much smaller birds that lived on the property. After much too-ing and fro-ing, it was decided to have someone get as high up in the tree as possible, destroy the nest and hope the pair would go elsewhere to live. The nest was destroyed and the pair left. But there was an unexpected hitch.

A lone chick was found in the nest. Rachel and Don didn't have the heart to destroy it and, instead, decided to raise it. When it grew up to be a healthy adolescent, they let it go. It immediately went back to its original home in the big tree. True to its nature, the bird, now dubbed Clarence, took the easiest prey he could to survive: the small birds that decorated and thrived on this property.

Without fail, sometime during every day for the entire time I was there, there would be a discussion about what to do with Clarence. Should they have him shot since nothing seemed to scare him away? He couldn't be poisoned because other birds could also die. What to do. What to do. What to do. Something certainly had to be done. But what?

It was a reliving of the past to hear Don go on about Clarence. "We have to do something about that gymnogene. He's much too comfortable here with all these little birds around, the weavers, the finches, all of them. They're too easy prey for old Clarence. We should have wrung his neck when he was a chick. Then we wouldn't have this problem. But something has to be done, that's certain. We could ask Donny's friend, Ian, to take a shot at him. Ian would bring him down. Good shot, Ian. If we could get up in the tree, we might be able to poison him. But the other birds might get hold of that poison and that'd be the end of them too. No, we definitely have to do something to get rid of Clarence. Gymnogenes are predators, you know. They'll feed on these other small birds we've got around here. They're much too easy prey. We have to get rid of him somehow. I hate shooting him but it might be the only way. We could get Ian over here and he'd get it done in a flash. He wouldn't miss, not Ian. Poisoning is too dangerous to the other birds. I don't like the idea of killing old Clarence but it may be the only way. He's too much of a threat to these weavers and finches. No, we definitely have to do something".

I heard that monologue at least a thousand times. It never reached any conclusion or resolution. The Clarence saga went on. In time, Clarence was seen flying off into the distance and returning.

A variation on the theme then began. "I wonder if that bastard's trying to entice a female over here. Well, he won't be long for this world if he does, I can tell you. No, old Clarence will be a memory if he brings a female here. Too much of a threat to the little birds as it is without having another mouth to feed. I'm guessing that's where he goes when he flies off like that. Probably looking for a mate. He'll bring her back here if he finds one. No, that poor bugger is looking at his final days. We'll bring Ian over here. Ian won't have a problem clipping old Clarence's feathers. I hate killing him though. He's such a handsome and majestic bird, old Clarence. But we can't have him nesting with a mate up there. The little birds would disappear, you can be sure of that…"

The next variation began when Clarissa arrived. "That bloody bastard's brought a female here. They're building a damn nest up there. We have to put a stop to it, no doubt about it. No, we can't allow them to nest here. God knows it was bad enough for the weavers and finches and all when Clarence was here on his own. Now that he's got a wife, he'll soon have a little Clarence. They all need to eat and those little birds are easy prey for a gymnogene. We have to get rid of them. That's all there is to it. Poor Clarence is living on borrowed time. So's Clarissa, for that matter. They're going to have to go. I hate killing them but that's the only way we'll be able to protect the little birds. No question about it. Their days are numbered. We'll get Ian over here and dispatch both of them. It's the only thing we can do. They'll just have to go…"

The gymnogenes were still living in the big tree when I left. Unless Clarence destroyed his own nest and committed a murder/suicide, he and his family are likely still there and will be for generations to come. And Don will still be deciding what to do.

CHAPTER TWENTY TWO

Don and Rachel had planned an outing for me. We were going to Nakuru, a government protected game park northwest of Nairobi. In order to get to the main road, which was in fact the main highway – if it could be called that – between Nairobi and Kampala, we had to pass through a – I don't know what to call it. It wasn't a town exactly. Town sounds too dignified. Village? Maybe. Let's put it this way, Don and Rachel had nicknamed it Shit Creek and that wasn't an altogether inappropriate name.

The little village where Rachel went to do errands: pick up mail, do her banking, buy food, etc. was adequate. It had two banks, a post office, a petrol station and a few shops. Whenever she pulled in to park, from four to ten men of varying ages would *Jambo, Memsaab* and *Jambo, Bwana* from the time we got out of the car until we entered a shop. This was their job, their only opportunity to earn a few measly bob by carrying a package or opening a door. Rachel always gave these men money as we returned to the car with the instructions that they share it. She would grumble about them once we were moving, but she always gave them something.

Had these men lived in Shit Creek, they would have been the pillars of the community, the capitalists, the plutocrats, the devil-may-care *bon vivants* with all that loose change jingling in their pockets – assuming they had pockets.

If you think you know what abject poverty looks like, I will challenge you to go to Shit Creek and have a look around. The entire length of the mud puddle that passed for Downtown Shit Creek, perhaps a hundred yards long, was lined by hundreds and hundreds and hundreds of people who were standing around looking lost. Dismal little – how can I call them shops? – enclosures, wooden slats for walls, sometimes with barely recognizable fruit hanging in front, were spaced along the way. A few people appeared to be doing something, either carrying something or going somewhere. But mostly they just stood around amongst the squalor. There were also children among the multitudes, equally enervated. How would you ever begin to address a situation like this?

We crept along in the four-wheel-drive at a snail's pace, easing through mud-filled potholes, ever-so-slowly weaving back and forth from one side of the road to another, picking the potholes that appeared shallower to traverse. It felt sometimes as though the vehicle was on a 45-degree angle as we crept in and out of these tank traps.

I looked at the faces as we painstakingly rocked past the assembled citizens of Shit Creek. They were all vacant, hopeless. Not a smile. Not a wave. No attempt to make any kind of human contact. Not even the children. No frolicking. No hijinks. Nothing. Only blank faces. I couldn't help commenting as we passed a shabby building with crudely painted letters spelling G-R-A-N-D H-O-T-E-L. Perhaps someone had a sense of humor in Shit Creek. Or perhaps not. All these people were fundamentally like me, my species. Born the same way. Had interchangeable body parts. Capable of the same emotions. Yet look at the differences in our lives!

Naivasha is about halfway between Nairobi and Nakuru. We stopped at what had once been a grand old colonial icon, The Belle Inn. As we sat on the verandah with our tea, local artists would approach the railing and pass hand-painted cards up to us. Each was unique and it was clear that the artists were talented. Was there a Matisse or Dali among them who would never be able to leave Naivasha? Rachel bought several cards from different artists so that all would make a little money.

When we arrived at Nakuru, it was a familiar scene. At the front gate there was a congregation of degradation. Hopeless looking people of all ages stood on the roadside and looked at us as we passed. They had nothing to sell, nothing to offer, nothing to do – except wait for a handout. This was the scene on one side of the threshold to the park. On the other side of the threshold was an African wonderland, the one I remembered.

On the way to our cabin, we spotted a lone zebra. It seemed strange at first. All the time I'd been in Africa and this was the first time I'd seen any game, not counting Clarence and Clarissa. All my recollections of the first visit to the Dark Continent began to trickle back into my consciousness. But whereas before it had seemed natural, now, after what I'd been exposed to in and around Nairobi, this seemed artificial, like a Disney version of Africa.

The animals themselves would not have had this perception. They were living as they had always lived: breeding, migrating, trying to avoid predators or hunting if they were predators, completing their life cycle as they had throughout time. This protected park was just part of their vast neighborhood. This time the fences protected them.

Our cabin was rustic and picturesque. Heavy wooden beams, lashed together with thick sisal ropes spanned the low ceiling. There was a large stone fireplace and rough-hewn wooden furniture in the lounge room. Colorful rugs decorated the tiled floors. The dining room contained a massive wooden table with leather director chairs around it. Mosquito netting enclosed the beds in each of the two bedrooms.

The verandah looked out upon the vast plains. Buffalo, impala, zebra, Thompson's gazelle, all grazed within view. A commotion was caused when some kind of disagreement broke out among a troop of baboons as they made their way past our cabin onto the plain. It must not have been serious because it was over in an instant, perhaps a little family spat. Or perhaps a normal baboon conversation.

We had brought a game scout, Nzomo, with us. He was one of Donny's safari staff. He had been to Nakuru before and knew his way around. The park is 120 square kilometers in size, or about 47 square miles. Late in the afternoon, toward dusk, one of the two optimum times to view animals, we drove along some of the well-defined tracks. The ubiquitous antelope were there. We saw five rhino in a group, a fairly large herd of Cape buffalo and a single ostrich. As before, it took me a little while to adjust my eyes to spot game.

When we got back to the cabin, Rachel prepared a simple but tasty dinner; then in a most courageous move, brought out the Scrabble box. After the embarrassment of the previous Scrabble session, everyone was on good behavior and there were no incidents. During our game run earlier, I noticed that relations were especially cordial between Rachel and Don. The conversation was restricted to the animals, something they both shared a passion for and history with. No controversial subjects or opinions.

We rose just after dawn the next day, had tea and some fruit and went on an early morning game run, the other optimum time to view animals. The plains were once again filled with Grant's and Thompson's gazelle, impala, zebra, buffalo, rhino, waterbuck, warthog, jackal. By now my eyes had adjusted and I spotted the game only a fraction later than the old hands in the front seat did.

Even to them, these animals remained an endless fascination and wonder. They cooed at the sight of newborns of every species, as if sighting these young animals somehow ensures the survival of their Africa for a little longer, at least one more generation.

One of the things that was pointedly obvious was the lack of elephant in this park. Without them destroying vegetation, a healthy balance was struck between these vast numbers of plains animals and their few predators.

We wandered toward Lake Nakuru. As it came into sight in the distance, you could see what appeared to be a dense, pink fringe encircling the entire lake. Closer examination revealed an uncountable number of flamingo, clacking and honking and fussing, creating such a din that in another environment it could be thought of as noise pollution. Other birds shared this sanctuary: pelican,

Maribou stork, Egyptian geese, royal ibis, all flying and landing and flapping and drinking and feeding naturally at one enormous, common banquet table.

When we'd had our fill of birds and animals for the moment, we stopped in a shady glen for tea, prepared on a portable gas burner, accompanied by, of all things, Neiman-Marcus chocolate chip cookies.

As he frequently did, Don commented on the quality of the grub by saying, "Damn fine cookies, Memsaab. Damn fine." In another instance it would be "Damn fine roast beef, Memsaab. Damn fine." Or "Um, damn fine pudding, Memsaab. Damn fine." Whatever the victuals were, his enthusiasm was consistent. When Don sprawled out on a blanket Rachel had brought along, I was able to see what a massive gut he now carried. Even lying prone, his girth was immense. It was a struggle for him to get back on his feet from the ground. All his complaints about being fat came flooding back to mind.

Back at the cabin, while Don had a nap and Rachel busied herself with some task, I sat out on the verandah and read, looking up from time to time at the parade of animals that crossed my field of vision. There was a water hole about fifty yards from where I sat which attracted them. Once, when I looked up, I saw a troop of at least fifty baboons. Another time approximately the same number of impala. Their presence was calming.

We had another game run in the afternoon, seeing more of the same. But there was a difference. There had been a shower during the day which settled the dust and brought out a wonderful, earthy aroma, the same smell of Africa that I had identified those many years ago. My nose remembered it and welcomed it like an old friend.

That night, when Rachel and Don were asleep, I sat up and watched the roaring fire become glowing embers. A candle supplied the only other light in the room. When I finally got sleepy and started toward my bedroom, I passed the window that looked out on the verandah. Spaced out wooden slats made up the overhanging roof of the verandah. An almost full moon illuminated the plain and shone through the slats, creating an unforgettable pattern of diagonal stripes. A cinematographer would have salivated over it.

We did a kind of farewell tour just after dawn next morning. It was a brilliant morning. Now, eland and dik dik were added to the antelope list. We took another swing past Lake Nakuru and the flamingo now mirrored themselves on the lake's still surface, their thin legs holding the ones above the waterline up while the perfect images below the waterline seemed to dangle from the same legs directly beneath.

We returned to the cabin for breakfast and a quick Scrabble game. All had now been forgotten, or at least forgiven for the time being. Nzomo had packed the car so that after the last tile was played, we were on our way out of the park.

Rachel decided to go out in a different direction. As we bounced along, we spotted a large giraffe off to our right. He would take a few strides then look back in the direction from which he had come. Take a few more strides. Stop and look back. As we looked to our left to where the giraffe was looking, we saw a large male lion. He stopped in the shade of a small tree and stretched out, looking like one of the lions in front of the New York Public Library, his eyes never leaving the giraffe.

"Could that lion bring down a giraffe that big?" I asked.

"If he's hungry enough," Don said. "And assuming he's fit."

It looked like a formidable task. Then I remembered the muscle structure of Harv the Texan's skinned lion and changed my mind.

The exit track we were on went through a rather densely forested area. Nzomo, who was sitting next to me, always had his eyes peeled. Suddenly he said, in Swahili, "Stop, Mama. Back up."

Rachel stopped immediately and put the vehicle into reverse. Through the brush, no more than ten feet away, was a very large male leopard. He was walking in the same direction we were going. We stopped. He walked toward the front of the vehicle, unconcerned. As he reached the left front of the vehicle, he glanced disdainfully toward us, sneering just enough to show his sharp teeth, ears back. He seemed to dare us as he slowly passed by the front of the vehicle and disappeared into the tall grass to our right, tail flicking menacingly.

"I could have reached down and slapped him on the back," I said.

"Just as well you didn't," Rachel said with a smile.

"I believe that's the most fantastic leopard sighting I've ever experienced," Don said. "You must bring good luck, Bwana."

"That was good, Nzomo," Rachel added.

"*Asante sana*, Mama."

We stopped at the house of a couple, old friends of the Summers, who still lived modestly off the land. There were a few domestic animals in pens which included four donkeys they had saved. According to them, the Africans were not very kind to their animals and these four donkeys were close to death when they were rescued. They also had a small herd of goats.

The house was comfortable and rustic with a large garden that supplied most of their fresh produce. A small creek ran along the property not far from the house. It was a water source not only for the homesteaders but any animals that might be passing by. One night a leopard had stopped by for a drink, must have seen the light in the house and nearly made it through the window before George got to it and beat it away with a rifle butt.

We lunched on freshly shot guinea fowl and fresh vegetables. After lunch, we took our coffee in the lounge room, the dominant feature of which was a massive lion skin which filled one wall and ended at the floor where the head rested on a short stool, looking at us.

The rest of the drive was quiet as we were lost in our own thoughts.

CHAPTER TWENTY THREE

On a lovely Saturday afternoon, two weeks into my stay, Rachel invited a few people over for luncheon. The guests at any of their gatherings were likely to be interesting. This occasion was no exception.

There was a couple originally from Kenya who had lived in South Africa for some time and were now returning to Kenya. They, like Don and Rachel were old Africa hands and shared experiences and yarns that were often based around their mutual frustration with the Africa of today. Donny without his Pakistani girlfriend, Rebecca with her son, Neville, and an American named Phil rounded out the party.

It didn't take long for Don to do his favorite party trick. I had already seen it once and was destined to see it another time or two before I left. The trick was to tell a story, always to an unsuspecting woman, about a tailor who was making a suit of clothes for a gentleman.

"He marked the jacket for pockets at the breast. Then he marked the jacket for pockets at the sides. Then he marked the shoulders. The gentleman asked if the pockets at the breast were necessary. 'Not at all, sir,' the tailor replied.'" And at this point in the story, Don would wipe the imaginary chalk marks from the breasts of the jacket.

Except the breasts he wiped were always the woman's to whom he was telling the story. This provided him with a cheap feel and her with a shock, followed by a forced laugh from everyone witnessing the performance.

Phil and I, both being Americans, naturally gravitated to one another.

"And what do you do? I asked.

"I'm in security," he answered, as if I should know what that meant. He noticed the blank expression on my face.

"We provide body guards for important people, government officials, multinationals, that sort of thing. We also provide guards when they have to move gold from the mines to the places where it's made into bars, like in South Africa."

"Sounds interesting," I mused.

"Well, it's actually more than that," he continued. "Mercenaries, per se, are no longer referred to as such. Nowadays they've been legitimized. They are hired by governments to do the work that they cannot legally do or endorse or condone. Like, they will prop up regimes that are friendly to a major country. Some companies have their own armies."

He didn't name the United States but it immediately came to mind. Now he began to warm to the task.

"Some of these soldiers of fortune are former French Legionnaires but many of them are South Africans left over from apartheid. There are a lot of Germans too. The South Africans are considered the best because they have no hesitation about being brutal."

Phil said all this so mater-of-factly that I couldn't help but be shocked by it. At the time of this conversation, the United States had not yet invaded Iraq. There was no Abu Graeve, no Guantanimo, no out-sourced interrogation, no defense contractors, none of the things that have subsequently come to light. Phil continued.

"It's possible to not only mobilize an army overnight," he said. "You can mobilize an air force overnight too, complete with aircraft and ordinance. A lot of our clients are African countries and Middle Eastern countries. They have an easier understanding of the value. They tend to rule with an iron fist and don't necessarily have the local manpower to keep everyone in line. That's where we come in."

I could only think how distant these concepts would have been from the average person's consciousness and how completely unreal and improbable they would seem. He was very businesslike in explaining his work, as if it was nothing out of the ordinary, nothing that wasn't already known and accepted as good business practice.

Like a dominatrix I had once spoken to in Los Angeles, Phil was convinced that he was performing a necessary service.

* * *

Donny had some clients from New Jersey who would be arriving in a few days. He had an arrangement with the Masaai to camp in a particular part of the Masaai Mara Game Reserve, an area of 600 square miles or, roughly, 1,500 square kilometers.

Since the tents were going to be set up anyway, he offered the camp to Don and Rachel to let me have a look at a 21st Century safari first hand for a few days before the clients arrived. Whereas in Don's day, these expensive safaris were for hunters, nowadays, with hunting banned in Kenya, the safaris tended to be luxury holidays for couples or groups of good friends.

The Masaai Mara Game Reserve is situated southwest of Nairobi. We proceeded out of Nairobi toward the border with Tanzania in one of Donny's vehicles, driven by an older Masaai tracker named Lambat.

On our way to Narok, another of those old colonial towns of days gone by, we drove along the escarpment of the Rift Valley. Looking down onto the valley floor, you got another view of Africa. Game was visible. Many people could be seen walking down there, some tending goats, others tending cattle, all carrying staffs or sticks of some kind, their version of a walk up the avenue.

We passed through Narok. Whatever importance it had enjoyed during colonial times had vanished leaving a squalid outpost of interest only to the people who lived there – and maybe not even them. The twisty main road, unpaved of course, went past shops of various stripe, selling services like tire changing and auto repair. It was hard to believe anyone could make a living at that in these parts.

If you look on a map of Kenya, the roads look like any other roads on any other map. This is deceptive. The roads we traveled on were primitive. There were places where there was evidence of an attempt in some long gone day to lay rocks on the track. There was even evidence, though scarce, that an attempt had been made to actually pave the road. The present day result is as quaint as the Apian Way, but perhaps not as well cared for. You could never build up any speed for fear of hitting a pothole that would rupture the suspension system and perhaps fling the vehicle into orbit. Either that or one of the rocks might fly up and do unpredictable damage of its own.

In all our travels away from Nairobi, there was only one very brief stretch of what passes for highway in our modern world. It was actually paved. When you arrive on this totally out of place stretch, after plodding along so carefully over dirt tracks littered with rocks of all sizes, it's like time travel to some future society. You suddenly remember what it feels like to ride along smoothly at a reasonable speed.

The only such stretch was on the road between Nairobi and Kampala, a major African artery. It lasted about ten miles. The reason for this aberration was that the surface had been laid by Israeli workers and paid for by the Israeli government. Whereas other governments would give money to the Kenya government to repair its roads -- which money would then disappear into the pockets of corrupt politicians and their cronies – the Israelis said, "We'll give you money for the roads you so desperately need, but we'll build them." Thus, one actual stretch of modern highway.

We found a shady little glen alongside the road and decided to stop for a bite of lunch and a cup of tea. Needless to say, we constituted all the vehicular traffic passing through this area. No sooner had we pulled off the road and stopped than three Masaai women, a mother and her two daughters, approached and sat on a log a slight distance from us. They had nothing to sell and didn't seem to be begging. They merely sat there observing us, talking to one another behind their hands and then looking some more.

After a while the women must have lost interest. They got up and walked away, their curiosity satisfied. No sooner had they done so than another group, this time three little boys, replaced them. Again, no one spoke a word or made a gesture. They merely watched with utmost fascination. Finally they spoke among themselves and began giggling uncontrollably. I couldn't help but laugh myself. How strange we must have appeared to them on their turf, these pale-skinned, oddly dressed people. And if not strange, certainly a novelty.

Not long after the boys left, an old Masaai woman walked past on the road. How old would be hard to tell. She may have been thirty and just looked old from the wear and tear of her life. She was doing her chores, carrying what looked like a very heavy load on her back, held there by a leather strap around her forehead.

We finally arrived at the entrance of the Masaai Mara Game Reserve where we were required to show the proper documentation for entry. I was seated behind Lambat with the window rolled down. A young Masaai woman came toward me, her eyes fixed on mine. She was colorfully beaded with necklaces and several varieties of earrings dangling at uneven lengths. She was dirty and smelled very earthy, an intense version of what I recognized as the smell of Africa, and came close enough to me so that I could determine that. But at the same time, she was so fluid and sultry that I couldn't take my eyes off her. She had the confidence of a woman who knows her feminine powers. Her eyes were heavy-lidded and deep, her face beautiful by any standard.

"Hello," she purred, still locking my eyes with hers.

"Hello."

"What is your name?" She said this in a way that instantly engaged me. We could have been anywhere. It was very impressive. I told her my name.

"I Moluta," she said, pointing to herself. She was no more than eighteen inches away from me.

I said nothing even though I was thoroughly captivated by this creature. Her poise and demeanor were confident and sophisticated, not anything you would ever expect to find in the African bush under these circumstances.

"Take my picture," she said in a husky, sexy voice. Her words were "take my picture" but her demeanor said, "Would you like to fuck me?"

I stammered that I had no camera. Before we could exchange any more pleasantries, the guard had stamped the documents and we were waved through the gate.

In any other circumstances, I'd have wanted to jump out of the vehicle and onto Moluta without a second thought. It was pure animal lust. Whatever she had got my attention, just as it was meant to. She knew what she possessed and she knew what she was doing. The exchange was timeless. Because of the circumstances she simply went down in my mind as an interesting encounter, not a lost opportunity, definitely for the best in the long run, but not to be soon forgotten.

We followed the dirt track to a second gate. This one separated the larger park from the land owned and leased out by the Masaai themselves, where our camp was located. The money that was taken in from these leases would be added up and divided among the entire tribe at the end of each year. I could foresee the time when the Masaai would tear a page out of another indigenous book and build gambling casinos on this land.

We continued along this dirt track for another thirty minutes or so to the northern end of the Serengeti Plain, where there were uncountable numbers of wildebeest. This was the last of the spectacular migration that takes place twice each year: once to feed on the grasses as they make their way north and once on the way back south. This was the northern migration. It's a sight that the world has seen on television countless times but still, I was unprepared for its grandeur.

The Serengeti stretches virtually from one end of Africa to the other. The horizon is endless. You could walk south from here for 500 miles and never see a fence or a house or a hamlet until you reached the Indian Ocean. You could walk north all the way to Addis Ababa. This was Africa. The manmade lines dividing one manmade country from another were meaningless in the vastness and timelessness of this sweep of land.

A secluded little glade came into sight just ahead. This was where the camp had been set up. As soon as we arrived, there was someone there with a cool, damp cloth so we could wipe the dust from our faces. Soon after, while we were still by the vehicle, another man brought each of us a glass of apple juice. It was obvious that I was in store for a proper, unaffordable safari experience.

We were each taken to our tents to deposit our gear and get the layout of the place. My tent and Don's were side-by-side facing a little ravine. Rachel's was behind ours more into the trees. Soon we were all congregated around a casual fire in the main part of the camp. The sound of cowbells came from off in the distance somewhere. A hyena scampered past within sight of the camp, a scavenger after whatever he could steal. A bat-eared fox was shooed away. The huffing of a lion could be heard way off in the distance. A mongoose darted past just on the fringe of the camp. Bell bats could be heard calling to one another. My eyes and ears began to sharpen.

Unlike everywhere else I'd been, where the guards were dressed in some variation of military attire, this camp was guarded by Masaai in their traditional garb, something red and toga-like around the shoulders and carrying either a spear or polished wooden stick, or both.

Each of the guards was introduced and we shook hands. It was a Masaai custom that everyone engaged in, men and women, and even children. Immediately after shaking hands with one of the guards, I couldn't help noticing that he reached under his blanket and started playing with his dick. I didn't take it personally.

To describe my accommodations as a tent is to so grossly understate the luxury that surrounded me that I couldn't in good faith use the word. This outdoor domicile was entirely waterproof. The flooring was one piece with the walls, allowing nothing animal, vegetable or mineral inside. Two outer shells separated it from the nature that surrounded me. The outer one was thick canvas, the inner one screened plastic. Persian rugs decorated the floors and the tent was divided into two compartments: the living area, complete with large double bed, table and chairs, a batik on the wall, a reading lamp, a flashlight and a box of tissues; and a bath area where there was a shower, a drop toilet, two basins for washing with mirrors over them and a lantern always glowing softly during the night. Just outside the entrance were two chairs and a table, under a canvas canopy, a small personal verandah.

As I lay in bed that first night, absolute, deadly silence was interrupted at intervals by the animals' sounds that wafted my way. A lion might grunt. A hyena cackle. A hippo bellow. It was an African lullaby.

Just as dawn broke I heard the zipper slide down and the African staff member whose charge I was stepped through the opening with a smile on his face and a tray in his hand on which was pot of hot, sweet, delicious tea.

"Good morning, suh. Did you sleep well?" His voice had a wonderful timbre and a very African accent.

"Like a baby."

"Good. You will let me know if you need anything, suh."

"Thanks. I will." He started to leave. "There is something."

"Yes, suh?"

"Tonight when I go to bed, I'd like a woman in there waiting for me."

He was caught completely off guard and laughed out loud. "I'll see what I can do, suh." He was still shaking his head as he stepped out of the tent. From outside, he unzipped the canvas and pulled it aside. Now, with only the screen in between, I could see the shrubs along the bank of the ravine.

I slipped into my clothes and took a cup of tea out onto my little verandah. I could hear Don humming next door. In order to keep my back supple, I did some stretching exercises and crunches whenever possible. In the midst of some arm swings, I heard Don's voice criticizing my technique.

"You're turning your legs. You have to keep your legs still, Bwana. No, it does no good to swing your torso like that if you don't keep your legs and ankles straight. No good at all. You mustn't turn your legs and ankles."

"I'm just loosening up, trying to keep my back loose."

"Well, you won't do it that way, I can assure you. You must keep your legs and ankles straight. Otherwise it does you no good at all. Learnt it in the army."

"It makes my back feel better."

"Just the same, when you twist your torso like that, you must keep your legs and ankles straight. Do it properly or don't do it at all, I always say."

By now I was losing interest in his opinion, particularly since he hadn't seen his own ankles from a standing position in thirty years.

It was a quality I had been unable to avoid noticing. Don had an answer for everything, an opinion about everything, a rule about everything and no flexibility in regard to any of them. It was the same quality that he brought to the Scrabble game that first time. He tolerated no disagreement and never shied away from stating categorically his views on any subject, including the taboo subjects of politics and religion. No matter how respectful I tried to be, eventually, if I hadn't capitulated, unequivocally, he remained relentless. I never challenged him on anything that had to do with Africa or its politics. I recognized that his views on the wider subject of race were seen from his own perspective and while I didn't agree with them, I decided it was in everyone's best interest to keep quiet and agree to disagree. But when it came to politics away from the Dark Continent, it became a matter of opinion. Trying to make light of it early in the piece, I stated the cliché, "Opinions are like assholes; everybody has one." But with Don, there were opinions and there were *his* opinions. They were like Orwell's farm animals: some were more equal than others.

His standard reply to any point I may try to make was, "You don't know what it's like. You have no idea. You think you do, but you don't. I've had a lot of experience in this world, I can tell you. I've devoted my life to discipline and duty. Queen and country, Bwana, Queen and country. You'd best learn a bit more before you express yourself so casually. You're ill-informed, Bwana." These nonsequiturs ended the discussion as far as he was concerned.

I had never had a friend who remained so inflexible and dogmatic. It's not unusual to have a lively discussion with friends. If it becomes a serious disagreement, someone always puts on the brakes or walks away to cool off or takes some kind of evasive action. In most instances, a friendship survives these trifles. But I could tell it rankled Don to have someone disagree with him on whatever subject. It seemed that in this case I was not his friend. I was a guest in his home and expected to behave appropriately, which is to say, agree with him, or at least not argue.

I finished my improperly done exercises and joined everyone at the mess tent for a quick breakfast before we took our first game run on this vast expanse of bush. Breakfast consisted of virtually anything one could want or imagine. Don had eggs and bacon, toast, some baked tomatoes and coffee. Rachel had some fruit and muesli. I had my usual fruit but added toast because the bread was freshly baked each day. That with a bit of orange marmalade was too much to resist.

Lambat drove us onto the plain. There was nothing but animal life in every direction. The vista was unimpaired in a 360-degree arc.

This was toward the end of the great wildebeest migration and yet there were what appeared to be thousands in our view, which was shared with other plains animals: gazelle, zebra, warthog, elephant, buffalo. The animals that fed on them were also abundant: jackal, hyena, wild dog, lion, leopard. Bird life abounded. Vultures, Secretary birds, eagles, Maribou stork. The entire panoply, the natural heritage of Africa stretched out before us as far as the eye could see. The vastness of this scene is beyond description.

I remembered returning to New York after my first visit and going to see "Out of Africa," the film version of Karen Blixen's life that starred Meryl Streep and Robert Redford. It tried to show the vastness and vistas of Africa. As wonderful as the film was and as beautiful as the cinematography was, after experiencing the real thing, the movie was like looking at it through a box. The real thing encompasses your entire vision in every direction, from horizon to horizon, from ground to sky. Nothing can prepare you for it. And when you're in it, you still can't believe it.

Don pointed to what looked like a good sized brown rock up ahead. "*Fisi*," he said. I looked and finally fixed the rock in my sight but it didn't look like anything more than a brown rock, certainly not a hyena -- until we got too close and it moved from us in its hopping, limping, loping way. Naturally, I was too embarrassed to admit that I hadn't seen it at first.

But I did spot the group of three or four vultures that were on the ground off to our left. Lambat went over to where they were – or, rather, had been since they flew off when we approached. There was nothing left of what had formerly been there except the contents of the victim's stomach -- probably a zebra.

Lambat stopped again when he saw some activity over to our left. A hyena was scampering away from something. It soon stopped near two other hyenas and the three looked back in the direction from which the first had come, obviously on the lookout for something they feared. They were as still as statues, scanning the horizon, trying to locate the whereabouts of the predator that was moving toward them. We couldn't see anything either.

We arrived at a crossing point on the Mara River where there were a great number of wildebeest carcasses in various stages of corruption resting in the water and on the riverbank. This was a place that nature viewers would have seen on television, where the animals try to ford the river before the crocodiles feed on them. Huge numbers of Maribou stork and vultures picked at the bits of meat that were still clinging to the bones that lay exposed. Many of the predators responsible for this carnage, huge crocodiles, were visible in the water and along the banks, all seeming satisfied and relaxed. Hippos in large pods congregated at several places here along the river, their unique fragrance permeating the air in a way that made your eyes sting.

On our way back to camp, we spotted a small herd of Cape buffalo. Suddenly Lambat began chuckling to himself. Don was seated next to him in front and asked what was so funny. Even though his English was good, he chose to tell this story to Don in Swahili, who then played UN translator and told us this story:

"One afternoon I was out in the bush and had to take a shit. So I found a place that looked out of the way and squatted down. I was concentrating on what I had to do when I became aware of a presence nearby. My pants were around my ankles. I turned to see what it was. Standing five feet away, looking directly into my eyes was the face of a big male buffalo — a very big male buffalo. Our eyes were locked. He didn't move and I didn't take my eyes off him. This went on for many minutes. We just stared into each other's eyes. I decided that if I released him from my stare he might think I was afraid and attack me. We kept staring at each other. The buffalo must have wondered what kind of short animal would be so bold as to try to stare him down -- as large as he was. He began to look confused. Suddenly he bolted into the forest and I was left there, pants around my ankles, sweating. I wasn't able to shit again for more than a week."

CHAPTER TWENTY FOUR

One afternoon we were bouncing along the plains when Don spotted a lone lioness. She was resting in an indifferent way next to a small shrub, looking casually out onto the plain in the direction of a small herd of zebra and a few antelope some distance in front of her. We approached and slowly moved past her. She was unconcerned by our presence and yawned as we went by, still keeping the herd in her sight in an offhand kind of way. Lying in some taller grass nearby was a second lioness. There was nothing intense in her gaze either but it was focused in the same direction as her sister, equally offhand and casual.

Somehow I knew this was no coincidence and asked that we wait for a moment. Lambat stopped but kept the engine running. A short distance away and making a triangle with the other two was a third lioness. She was also noncommittal but looking in the same direction as the other two, sitting on her haunches, low in the grass.

A male impala was walking in the direction of the first lioness. He had separated from the other animals and walked directly toward the lioness, never sensing anything, never veering from his course, almost as if hypnotized. The first lioness rose to an extended crouch, low to the ground, a hunting attitude, and slowly put one paw ahead of the next, freezing after each step, her eyes riveted on the impala. She crept closer. She was every cat you've ever seen stalk a mouse or bird. The second lioness now did the same. She began creeping in the direction of the impala, muscles tensed and controlled, belly nearly touching the ground. Both their bodies were pointed rigidly forward. Then the third moved forward with the same tautness, slowly lifting a foreleg and stepping forward with it as if it were independent from all other muscles of the body, replacing it on the ground with effortless silence. Nothing else moved. Three pairs of eyes triangulated on the unsuspecting impala. He kept moving closer, seemingly unconcerned.

In an instant, the first lioness sprang forward, the other two immediately following. The impala never had a chance. He was knocked down and the three of them were on him, one had him by the throat, the other two ripping and tearing at his guts. He was still alive for a few moments as they shredded him.

We were less than twenty yards from the kill. Lambat put the vehicle in gear and sped around a bush so that we were now within ten yards of the feeding lionesses with a clear view. In the time it took us to move from one position to the next, the lionesses' faces were covered with blood as they tore into the carcass, giving us no thought whatsoever. It seemed as though we could have gotten out and stood next to them for all the attention they paid to us.

Lambat told us that the Masaai believe that impala knew it was his destiny to die on this day. That was why he walked so nonchalantly into the trap the lionesses had set for him. It was God's will and could not be otherwise. The impala knew this and acted accordingly.

* * *

On one of our morning game runs, we spotted six to eight vultures on the ground maybe sixty yards away. This indicated that there had been an early morning kill of some kind and whatever made the kill was satiated. Otherwise the vultures wouldn't be welcome. Don looked around, away from the vultures. Up on a little rise something was barely visible under some shrubs. He pointed toward the rise. "Lambat, *simba, huko.*" "Lions, over there."

Lambat drove us closer. There were three young, maybe four-year-old, male lions lying on their backs, bellies bulging to bursting point, rocking back and forth on the dirt in an ecstasy of gluttony.

Lambat got us within ten or fifteen feet of them and they, too, were totally unconcerned about our presence, hardly looking in our direction. A lion with a full belly is contented indifference itself.

On another occasion we were driving along when we saw a lioness stretched out so close to our track that we nearly ran over her. She was breathing but couldn't be bothered moving out of our path. She appeared to be so completely exhausted that nothing could concern her. Her nipples looked especially large, suggesting that she must have some cubs nearby. We saw no sign of them.

Lambat drove us to a place where we could look down on a little stream, just below where the lioness was lying. There were three little lion cubs frolicking together like the children they were. A short distance away were two more lionesses gnawing on a freshly killed wildebeest. Two more cubs were frolicking near them. The one we passed on the track was obviously spent from the hunt that had provided her and her sisters and their families with a meal.

On any afternoon game run, whenever Rachel spotted any elephant dung in the perfect state of dryness, she made Lambat stop so she could pick it up and add it to the large plastic bag she carried for such occasions.

The first time it happened I couldn't contain my curiosity. "What the hell are you doing?"

"Elephant shit is the best fertilizer in the world," she said. "I never use anything else on my garden." Gardening doesn't get any more organic than that.

As we trundled along one afternoon, we came upon a group of six elephants crossing the plains toward the river where they would drink and cool themselves. There were two large, mature cows, two adolescent cows and two very young calves. One was about two or three months old and the other a little older.

We got to within thirty yards of them and Lambat stopped. He made the mistake of switching off the engine.

Even at what appeared to us to be a safe, non-threatening distance, one of the large cows turned toward us and fanned her ears. Her left ear looked as though a tyrannosaurus rex had taken a bite out of it. Half of it had been somehow ripped out of the middle. She continued looking in our direction. She took a step or two closer, ear-and-a-half still fanned and seemed to be losing patience. To her liking, we were too close, full stop. We didn't move, of course. The engine was not on. She was now registering a great deal of displeasure in a way that only a very large elephant can. She took a few more bouncing steps in our direction, covering a substantial distance with each bounce. She was closing fast.

"*Kwenda*, Lambat, *kwenda!*" Don shouted. "Go. Go!" The elephant was headed right toward my side of the vehicle. It was like a bad Hollywood movie. Lambat tried to start the engine. It didn't kick over. He tried again and again. By now the elephant was closing to within twenty feet of me. The engine kicked over. Lambat jammed it into gear and we got the hell out of there. The elephant continued to keep her eyes on us, turning in our direction with ear-and-a-half fanned until the other members of her herd were safely away.

One morning Lambat drove us to a place that looked across a narrow part of the Mara River. Above the fifteen or twenty foot embankment, the flat plains spread into the distance. We could see tourist buses filled with camera-carrying folks from all over the world. But below them, out of their sight, in the embankment, was some brush in which a beautiful female leopard was dozing on a sort of ledge in the dirt, shaped like a little bed. The noise of the people in the buses eventually stirred the leopard and seemed to annoy her. She rose and crept through the light bush and into a small cave that was carved into the embankment.

The tourists above made me think of the two Germans yelling "Yumbo! Hier! Yumbo!" The carryings-on of the tourists then disturbed a large male leopard that was now visible in the brush to the left of the cave. By now the tour bus was directly above the male, even though they could not see him. We watched as he slid along eluding their gaze but in our full view, until he crept quietly into the cave with his mate. Word must have spread that there were *chui* around. Every tour bus in town must have come for a look. But only we saw the animals and the drama unfold.

* * *

Don had suggested one morning that we each buy a sheep to give to the staff as a thank you for the wonderful service they were providing us. Lambat drove us to a Masaai boma which was located on the plains.

When we arrived, there seemed to be a great deal of activity. This village of forty to sixty people was similar to the abandoned one I had entered on my previous visit, except this one was alive with color and people…in addition to the flies, of course.

All the women and girls were decked out in reds and oranges and yellows. All wore the delicate and intricate beadwork that the Masaai are famous for on different parts of their bodies. Some wore layers and layers of multi-colored necklaces. There were others with wide armbands between the shoulder and elbow. Bracelets adorned wrists and ankles. Earrings hung at varying lengths from all parts of the ears, some hanging heavily from stretched out lobes, others pierced into the top and middle of the ears. The atmosphere was festive.

The men all wore their red, toga-like garment knotted at the shoulder. But perhaps as a sign of status, other more familiar articles of clothing were also worn. One may have modern-looking shorts on under the toga. Another a Hard Rock Café tee shirt, another a pair of Reeboks. It was an fascinating sartorial clash to say the least. Many of the men also had stretched-out earlobes but rather than have a beaded earring in them, the earlobes were pulled up and draped around the top of the ear, creating the effect of no earlobe at all.

The chief of the village came up to us in a very friendly fashion and shook hands with us all. He spoke to us in English but it was soon abandoned when Don answered him in Swahili. This was always an interesting scene to observe. Don's Swahili language skills were only equaled by Rachel's and the Africans with whom they spoke.

As Don and the young chief chatted away, I scanned the women to see if there was another Moluta in their midst. Before long each of them was standing in front of me in a queue to shake my hand. The Masaai all shake hands as a way of greeting. It's not one of those robust, knuckle-crunching, Aussie bloke affairs. It's delicate and fleeting, just enough to make contact and acknowledge the greeting. But they all do it, old and young, male and female.

After shaking my hand, two women returned to the sheepskin that they were pegging to the ground in order to stretch and dry it. Like all indigenous people, these Masaai knew the value of everything in their world. This sheepskin would one day be like the one draped around the boy, soon to be a man, who was the center of all the attention. The skin he wore was dyed brown, thin as chamois and uniquely decorated with a beautiful and subtle abstract bead pattern.

It had been made by the chief's hollow-eyed, wrinkled mother for this boy, her younger son, on what was the Masaai equivalent of his Bar Mitzvah day. That she could have birthed both the chief and this boy seemed unlikely. It would have been easier to believe she was their grandmother. Nonetheless, it was true. The boy was having his head shaved when we arrived. Later he would be circumcised and declared a man. Then the party would begin.

Well, that's not quite true. The party had already begun for some of the men who were inside one of the mud-and-cowshit manyattas just in front of me. After coming out to shake hands, they went back to their revelry, slapping hands and laughing together like a bunch of street brothers.

Don was finishing up his business with the chief and asked me for my share of the money for the sheep we bought for the safari staff. The chief turned to Rachel and me.

"We are going to have the ceremony this afternoon. Would you like to stay?"

I was fascinated by the prospect of attending an authentic Masaai initiation ceremony as the guest of the chief. But neither Don nor Rachel had much interest in it. When we returned to our vehicle, they tried to placate me by saying that it would go on endlessly throughout the day and the actual ceremony may not take place for hours to come, hours that they had no interest in spending in this environment. I wasn't convinced and still felt it was a lost opportunity until they told me that as a special guest it would be rude of me not to drink some cow's blood. That helped me lose some interest in the ceremony.

CHAPTER TWENTY FIVE

One final, magical sunset where the clouds separated long enough for the enormous orange ball to sink slowly between them and the endless horizon and cast its brilliant rays onto the now red, now purple now blue now dark gray sky. Our last night here. I stepped out onto my little canvas covered verandah, feeling a gentle breeze and looking up past Orion to the moon that had been full two nights before but which still illuminated the ravine and surrounding trees and shrubs like special effects lighting.

How many times and in how many places have I looked up at Orion? It's the only constellation that I recognize that is visible in both the northern and southern hemispheres. I've looked at it from Amish Country in Pennsylvania, from a hotel balcony on the Black Sea, from an empty beach in Bahia, from Tambourine Mountain on the Gold Coast of Australia. Whether upside down or rightside up, it sparkles up there like a beacon, connecting me to the Universe and eternity.

One night while looking up at Orion from a balcony in Noosa, it occurred to me that even though those three identifying stars appear to be in a line from Earth, they might easily be countless miles from each other in depth, when seen from another angle, Orion could easily be a three-dimensional constellation, perhaps even unrecognizable.

The small plane that brought in the New Jersey couples for the experience of their lives carried us back to Nairobi. From this fairly low altitude, the plains and the floor of the Rift Valley are dotted with the ringed Masaai bomas and a carpet of brown with patches of soft green that covered gentle bumps and sprawled in every direction for as far as the eye could see, as though a giant quilt had been thrown over the undulating earth below.

It had been a wonderful safari. No disagreements or unpleasantness had marred the pure splendor of observing all those exotic animals in their natural surroundings. But the civilized behavior that characterized that primitive setting turned into primal behavior when we returned to civilization.

A difference of opinion easily morphed into a clash of wills. Don was inflexible when his view differed from anyone else's. He was charming and engaging and witty until he was disobeyed or challenged. Rachel had told me that Don and Jungle Bob had had a falling out some years before which was based on Don feeling slighted somehow. It had never been resolved and, according to her, would never be. Friends for all those years in a place where you would think friends were at a premium, and yet they were now estranged.

"He is a very complex man," Rachel told me one day. She was never entirely disloyal but she also never missed an opportunity to point out his shortcomings to me. They both did it, as if they expected me to take sides. I've never liked being in the middle of peoples' private lives. But in these circumstances, it was unavoidable. I got the feeling that working with her son and running her own household compensated Rachel for all the rest she endured. Contact with her husband was strictly a formality.

That night, after our return to Nairobi, Don and I were discussing something, I don't remember what. Whatever it was fell squarely into differing opinions. There was no right or wrong. I had merely refused to accept his point of view. As he ridiculed my opinion as being ill-informed or naïve or however he characterized it, I grew more frustrated and heated. I had reached a point where his bullying was intolerable, eventually matching his obtuseness with my own. It had gone beyond agreeing to disagree. One of us had to be wrong, preferably me. Neither of us was willing to back down. Changing the subject and moving on to safer ground was no longer an option. We had reached a stalemate.

His part of the conversation was patronizing. Mine was vehement and incredulous. Reason had long since departed the scene.

When it was clear that an impasse had been reached, Don looked at me calmly. "I think that when you leave here, we should forget about trying to continue this friendship."

I was stunned. How many times have two friends had a difference of opinion and still managed to keep the friendship alive? We hadn't argued about principle. We had argued about differing views. It happens all the time. But at this place under these circumstances with this person, it was simply not acceptable.

"If that's the way you feel," I answered.

"I think it would be better."

Needless to say, I felt most unwelcome from that moment on. There were still three or four days left to my visit before continuing on to Heathrow and the European leg of my adventure.

The following day I kept to myself. I didn't eat lunch with Don and Rachel, but instead claimed that I was not feeling well and stayed in my room, only coming out to sit in the sun and read when I knew Don would be taking his afternoon nap. They may have been accustomed to their dance and charade after years of practice. I was not.

I had promised Donny that I would have a look at a brochure that he and his partners were putting together to attract business. For the next couple of days I was able to go to his office and work on the brochure on his computer – between power outages. It was an enormous relief to have a task that would occupy some time and keep me away from the house.

While I was at the office, I was finally able to make contact with the woman I had met in Australia at the Artists Retreat. She was now at university working on her masters in communications. We arranged to meet the next day.

Robert, of the house staff, drove me into Nairobi. Lydia and I met at the Serena Hotel at its poolside café while Robert waited in the car.

After hugs and greetings, we sat down to a large glass of mango juice. It was different meeting her on her turf. In Australia Lydia had been open and carefree, pampered and wonderfully sardonic. Here she seemed more guarded and reserved, not quite as forthcoming as I had remembered. I had wished and even expected to pick up where we left off in Oz, forgetting the sage words of Heracleitis.

"I have been living in a British colony for the last few weeks, with a sojourn into the bush on a couple of occasions," I said. "It's almost as though I haven't been to the real Kenya at all. How about let's go out so I can see the Kenya you live in?"

"Are you sure you want to?"

"Definitely. I've got the money if you've got the time."

"I'll call you this evening after I've talked to a couple of my friends."

When I returned to the car, Robert seemed impressed that I knew Lydia. He had seen her reading sports on television in the past. Celebrity is the same everywhere.

Back at the compound, most of my conversation was with Rachel. Whenever I attempted to speak with Don, he was brief, very correct and entirely superficial. It was hard for me to believe that he could be serious about dissolving our long friendship. But it was clearly out of my control.

In the early evening the phone rang and Rachel called me from my room.

"How would you like to go to a club with me and some of my friends on Saturday night?" Lydia asked.

"It's what I live for," I answered.

"It's probably best if I pick you up or we meet somewhere close to you."

I told Lydia the name of the little village where Rachel shopped and posted mail. I didn't want to put her through the embarrassment of coming to the front gate. She knew the village and how to get there. We arranged a time.

Lydia and her friends were members of the Luo tribe. Making the mistake that most people make when regarding groups of people,

I assumed that Lydia was African first or, at minimum, Kenyan. We all seem to think of groups of people as monolithic, as if all gays held the same political views; all Democrats were pro-abortion, or Israelis all agreed on the Palestinian issue. The notion is absurd yet we try to bunch people together as if they were one demographic.

The dominant tribes and, therefore, political groups of Kenya are the Kikuyu, the Masaai, the Samburu, the Turkana and the Luo. The Kikuyu don't like the Masaai or Samburu. The Samburu don't like the Turkana. And none of them likes or trusts the Luo. The Kikuyu are the largest group and hold the bulk of power. Political alliances are fragile.

I didn't have to wait long in the deserted village before Lydia's little red car pulled up.

"We're going to meet two of my girlfriends and then go to a Luo club."

I felt a kind of freedom that I only noticed was missing after I saw Lydia for the first time a day or so before. This was the African experience I had hoped for. It was coming late in the visit. But better late than never.

We arrived at a walled and gated apartment/townhouse complex that seemed to spread over a large area. The guard recognized Lydia and motioned us through without hesitation.

"This is my friend, Jessica, and this is Jett."

I was looking at two beautiful African women, one lighter complexioned than the other but both stunning and fashionably dressed. It was Jessica's apartment where she lived with her 12-year-old son, a bright and modern looking boy dressed in jeans, a San Francisco 49ers jersey and Nikes.

The furnishings in the apartment were like you'd expect to see in any middleclass home except it had a decided African motif. On one of the shelves of the unit that housed the television set were some small bric-a-brac antelope. There was a large, ceramic African head on another shelf. Giraffe-painted side tables sat next to chairs and the couch. It was the kind of home I'd been in a thousand times, only African.

Jessica and Jett looked like the trendy, African American women I'd known all my life. Jessica had that easy, sassy quality that many attractive women have, the kind that puts a man on notice that she knows what she has and she knows he knows, an educated, cultured and sophisticated version of Moluta.

"Who is this good looking man you brought here, Lydia. He looks like he has some of the devil in him," Jessica said in that lilting African accent, her eyes flashing. It was obvious that she knew the devil first hand. "We'd better keep our eyes on him. Otherwise some hussy will run off with him."

Jett was more subdued, more reserved and, I thought, more attractive. Her flawless skin was much darker than the others, her face naturally beautiful. She must have known that I was immediately smitten with her. Whereas Jessica was more overt and flirtatious, Jett was more coquettish and subtle. In their own ways, they were both playing up to me and I loved it.

In a moment, the volume was turned up on the television which had been on the entire time in the background. The upcoming election was being discussed on a news program. Since 1978 the government had been in the hands of Daniel Moi, whose corruption and iron-fisted policies had become legendary. In each past election, he had won handily and ruled dictatorially. Now there was to be a new election in which Moi would not be a candidate.

The election was to be held in two months. Moi had handpicked Jomo Kenyatta's son to succeed him. But by now the smell of democracy was in the air and the people were eager to reclaim their republic. Rallies were being held all around the country promoting opposition candidates who were reform-minded.

We watched as a woman spoke eloquently about the need for reform. Jessica and Jett high-fived each time this articulate woman made a point. It was exciting to observe this kind of political interest and activism. It was also such a far cry from what I had previously been experiencing on this visit to Kenya. It seemed like a different country. The colonial cocoon that Don and Rachel lived in had no relationship to the vibrant atmosphere I was now experiencing.

When the news ended, Jessica offered everyone a brandy and a modest political discussion followed.

"So, who is running against Jomo Kenyatta's son?"

"Mwai Kibaki. And he will win too."

At one point, Jett turned to me. "You don't sound very Australian."

"That's because I was born in America." It was now inevitable that I would be forced to defend the United States, as if I were somehow responsible for the Bush administration's saber rattling. At this point in history, the US was setting the stage for an invasion of Iraq.

"We don't care much what they do in America," Jessica said. "They do what they please anyway. The rest of the world doesn't count."

I couldn't help being quietly amused. Here these women were, slapping hands like street sisters, with a son wearing a 49ers jersey and complaining about America. However much I disagreed with the policies of the current US government, the influence that the America Empire has in the world is, to mix my metaphors, already out of the tube. I may not even like it but that makes it no less true.

In a little while, the subject drifted to a familiar place: relationships. If there was any doubt about people the world over having the same concerns, it was quickly put to rest.

"I haven't had a boyfriend in five years," Jessica said.

"Men don't want responsibilities," Jett added.

"I always end up with cheaters and liars," Jessica continued.

"Single women outnumber men five to one here," Jett said.

"But tonight we have a man." Jessica jumped to her feet and grabbed my arm. "Let's go, girls, before he gets away."

CHAPTER TWENTY SIX

Lydia pulled into a dirt-packed parking area outside The Green House. This was the Luo club. We walked up the path toward the entrance. It was many cuts above the places we had passed in Shit Creek in what seemed generations ago, but still maintained a very African and, therefore, organic feel.

I followed the three of them into the place and felt many pairs of eyes on me. It was not uncomfortable in any way. I had so often been the only white person among a group of Blacks that by now I was accustomed to it. I had experienced it in New York often, in Harlem and elsewhere. It always happens that once people have had a good look, they sense that you must be cool, otherwise why would you bother? After that, no one cares.

We sat in the back section of the room. The bar and dance floor were in the front part which was divided from us by a lattice-like partition. The structure was wooden and one story, open to the night air and filled with cigarette smoke despite the early hour. It was only about 9:30.

The women ordered beers for us all and we settled into party mode. Before long the band started to play. They had come to Nairobi for a Saturday night gig from the Luo homeland, which is in western Kenya around Lake Victoria.

Any doubt about where Brazilian, Caribbean, Soul or Funk or Salsa might have come from was immediately dispelled when the band began. They were dressed as if they'd just stepped out for a beer and they played on instruments that were handmade, whether skin-stretched or stringed. And did they rock! The rhythms were intricate and multi-layered, at times sounding almost Arabic. Here was pure music in its most simple and sophisticated form.

Jett rose and took my hand. "Come on. Let's see what you've got," she teased. She wove her way onto the dance floor, hips and shoulders moving in that subtle, African way that I'd seen so many times in America. It was mesmerizing – particularly since now I had an enviable view of her gorgeous bootie. This was an African woman with what is known by my New York buddies as a genuine ghetto onion and by Latinos as a down home coulo. I wasn't the only one who noticed. Every man in the place was fixed on her perfectly formed, slightly larger than life, gorgeous ass. It's every movement attracted aficionados from all around the room.

Jett was obviously not unfamiliar with this kind of attention. She was constantly on guard for a man who would come too close and try to put a hand on that goldmine of femininity. When one did, she slapped his hand away and waved her finger in his face, as if to say, "Look but don't touch."

As the night wore on, more and more people came into The Green House until it was jammed to the rafters and rocking with this down home music. It was worth the wait to finally be among African people on their turf on their terms. It was absolutely brilliant.

It was late when we finally left The Green House. Lydia had agreed to drive me back to the compound after we all got a bite to eat at a carryout spot. Jett spent the night at Jessica's. And after dropping them off, Lydia drove me back to the compound.

I was still thanking her for a fabulous time when we pulled up to the outer gate. As soon as the headlights hit the gate, someone was there to allow me in. I felt embarrassed. I had just spent such a wonderful time with these three African women in October of 2002 and now I was returning to what felt like the 1950's.

Lydia and I said our goodbyes and she drove off. I sensed that she was as embarrassed as I was. I walked to the next gate where a guard was waiting to escort me with a torch to my wing of the house. The dogs romped up for a sniff, then wagged their tails in approval.

When I fell asleep, it was with visions of Jett's beauty in my mind and the smell of her perfume in my nose. How I wished I had made contact with Lydia sooner.

* * *

The next day, I was taken to the Karen Country Club for lunch. It was the first time I'd been with Don and Rachel when they were out among their peers. Tables were distributed around the lovely, green grounds, shaded by large umbrellas and overlooking the golf course.

It was a fairly even mixture of Africans and Europeans, with a smattering of Indian people thrown in. All were very expensively dressed, making it clear that this was not your run-of-the-mill joint. Nevertheless, it was the present and future Kenya. These were the people who had the money and, therefore, the control. In this atmosphere, Don and Rachel appeared to be antiques, out of place, out of touch. They had nothing in common with any of these people. And wanted none.

The next couple of days, I spent most of my time at Donny's office working on the brochure and was grateful for it. Conversation was now so limited and "civilized" at the homestead that any excuse to get away was welcome.

There was a little café in the complex where Donny's office was located. I popped in for lunch most of the days that I worked on the brochure. It was open-aired and could have been anywhere in the world. One afternoon, while I was enjoying a leisurely moment, two older women entered and sat within listening distance of me.

From their demeanor and talk, I concocted a fiction about them. They looked like every beer drinking bar hag I'd ever seen. They had dirty, stringy hair, drank their beer from the bottle without removing the cigarette that was stuck in the corner of each of their mouths.

Their bodies were bloated and their faces were thin with unhealthy looking wrinkles and skin color.

I imagined them as longtime residents of the Dark Continent, probably married to some old colonials, whom they had now outlived, barely surviving in a man's world without the man. After seeing the finery and wealth at the Karen Country Club, this was a stark contrast that showed that even white people can have it rough in Kenya.

With the brochure finished, I had to start thinking about leaving. Apart from the unpleasantness with Don, I felt as though I could have stayed in Kenya forever, just as I had felt the previous time. Africa has an aura, a taste, a smell, a presence unlike any other in my experience. Other locations may have their distinctiveness, but none of them saturates your senses like Africa. Or at least, my senses. There is something about being in Africa that feels natural and organic to me. I felt it the first time my feet touched African soil those many years before. It was as if they took root. I felt it then and in every subsequent moment. Perhaps everyone who visits Africa feels the same kind of connection, I don't know. But I do know that it engages my primal being in a way nothing else has. Leaving it without knowing if and when I might return left me with a longing that I have never lost.

Neither Don nor Rachel accompanied me to the airport. Only Robert. As I got out of the car, he said, "I hope you will come back and see us again sometime."

CHAPTER TWENTY SEVEN

As I strolled around Heathrow looking for my flight to Berlin, the next leg of my palindrome adventure, I had the thrill I always have when I'm in an international terminal:

"British Airways Flight 273 to Singapore is now boarding at Gate Number 12."

"Emirates Flight 935 to Bahrain is ready to board in 30 minutes at Gate 23." All passengers flying to St. Petersburg on Aeroflot Flight 901 are requested to proceed to Gate 49." The romance of hearing these exotic destinations spoken of so casually never fails to excite me.

It's as though, if you suddenly decided, you could go anywhere in the world – anywhere. Just like that. You get inside this metal container. They close the door. You have a couple of meals and watch a movie, maybe take a nap. And bingo! They open the doors and you're somewhere else. In the first part of the 21st Century, the somewhere else is on the planet we call Earth. In the future, it might be anywhere in what we call the Galaxy. But the thrill will be no different, nor any less intense.

As I was milling around, loud bells and gongs began sounding, followed by an announcement that caught everyone's attention. "YOUR ATTENTION, PLEASE. THE FIRE ALARM HAS BEEN ACTIVATED IN THIS AREA. STAFF WILL DIRECT YOU TO SAFETY!" People were nervous enough about flying one year after 9/11. The buzz that resulted from this announcement was barely contained panic. People looked at one another trying to find someone to tell them what was happening, while the fire alarm continued to clang urgently. There were no flames anywhere and no smoke. Only the incessant clanging and ringing. No staff or anyone official looking was forthcoming. Universal, mass confusion was the order of the day. People looking at one another, some with fear, some with confusion, some with indifference.

In spite of the noise and confusion, and because no one official seemed to be interested, it didn't have the feel of real emergency to me so I merely observed, looking in vain for someone to take charge of the situation. In a few moments, some men wearing fire-fighting gear came ambling up with absolutely no sense of urgency. They seemed equally confused and roamed around the duty-free area rather aimlessly, sometimes checking something, sometimes not. But mostly wandering around. Eventually one of them managed to turn off the alarm and called the staff back to their shops. I looked around for anything directing people to an exit sign. I saw nothing. There was nothing in sight. No signs. No officials. No more announcements. Nothing. What the result might have been if there were actually an emergency is anyone's guess, but it certainly didn't fill me with confidence.

What resonated with me most was that just one year after 9/11, in this ultra-major world transportation hub, an announcement of this nature was met with such a casual approaching indifferent response on everyone's part: the airport, the shopkeepers, the firefighters, the public. Collectively, we all must have thought for a moment about the gravity of the situation, then decided to ignore it.

Once on board the flight, I began reflecting on the last time I had seen Berlin. I didn't need an ancient Greek philosopher to tell me that things had changed between visits. The entire history of the world had changed since then.

As an intelligence analyst in the US Army during the Cold War, I had made the trip to Berlin with warnings ringing in my ears: "Watch your ass when you get there." "It's better not to go at all." "The fucking commies are everywhere and there's nothing they'd like more than to capture you little CIC ass and turn you into an international incident."

On a previous, Cold War visit to Vienna, just before my first trip to Berlin, while I was walking along the streets in civilian clothes, a very strange looking man approached me. He looked for all the world like a cliché of a musician, with a long fringe of gray hair sprouting from his semi-bald head and overlapping the collar of his non-descript dark gray overcoat, wire-rimmed glasses, gaunt, hollow-cheeked, unshaven face. When he reached my side, he whispered, conspiratorially, "Be careful in the *wein stubes*. There are Russian agents everywhere." Then he melted back into the crowd and disappeared.

When I went to Berlin that first time, there was a sense of excitement about it. Berlin was in the middle of the Cold War, perhaps even ground zero. It was the show place for the Western powers, an island of freedom in an ocean of despair. There was no wall. Only check-points between the Russian zone and all others.

I flew there in a military aircraft. Travel on the road through East Germany would have been difficult if not impossible, particularly since I was a member of military intelligence.

I stayed at a military transient facility but otherwise many of my recollections are foggy. The few exceptions are the remains of a church, which was left standing intentionally as a reminder of the devastation caused by concentrated bombing during WWII. There were new buildings, including a government structure that was called The Pregnant Oyster where the municipal officials of the day met.

There was a stark contrast between the relative bustle and brightness of the Western zone and the monochrome torpidness of the East. I had taken an authorized but unwise bus tour across the dividing line. It was unwise because if I had been identified, I could have been arrested as a spy. In any case, the sensation was like passing from a Technicolor film into a black and white one, like when Dorothy left Oz and returned to Kansas.

There was very little activity in East Berlin. The principal thoroughfare, formerly Unter den Linden, renamed Stalinallee, looked like a bad Hollywood set. The buildings facing the street were a sort of yellowish color. When you could see between the buildings at what lay behind them, there was rubble and a lot of unfinished construction. It was all a façade. And this was the showcase of the Russian sector! The place tourists *could* see.

Another vivid recollection is a nightclub that I visited upon some other GI's advice. Its principal feature was that each booth contained a telephone from which you could call someone in another booth. It was like a scene from **Cabaret**, something from Berlin's decadent past. I was too shy to try telephoning anyone. If I had, the likelihood of getting a wrong number or hang up didn't exist.

It was at this nightclub that I drank a Nicolaschka for the first and only time. It was cognac in a snifter with a lemon slice on top and on the lemon slice two little mounds, one of ground coffee and the other of sugar. To me, it seemed to be the German variation of Tequila, salt and lemon. You popped the shot of cognac and then followed it by chewing on the lemon slice and its accompanying ingredients. It was a festival of flavors and went down very well.

Now, in 2002, I was to be met by an interesting artist whom I'd met and roomed with at the same artists' retreat where I'd met Lydia of Kenya. His artistic claim to fame at the retreat was that he was a Butoh dancer. I had never heard of this style before. It began in Japan in the 1950s as an *avant garde* dance form and is practiced in pockets around the world. It is something that most dancers but few civilians know about. Its essence is freedom and formlessness, movement to music that is always spontaneous, sort of a "do your thing" to any rhythm.

Beta, my soon-to-be-host's name, gave us a demonstration of Butoh at the retreat to the music of Schubert's *Ave Maria*, played by violin and piano, that was intoxicatingly beautiful.

Beta and I had bonded well and immediately at the retreat. Male bonding being what it is, we quickly determined that we both had a healthy curiosity about the women at the retreat. We had many a long talk into the night about these and other things. When I decided to take my round-the-world trip, Berlin and Beta were obvious possibilities. When I explored the possibility with him via email, his response was immediate and insistent: Come.

He was there when I reached the baggage claim area, looking unchanged from our previous meeting. His shaved head, small wire glasses and equally wiry physique gave him the look of a healthy cadaver. We greeted each other with a hug and a big smile. I grabbed my bag and headed for the exit.

I was under the impression, prior to arriving, that he was going to pick me up in a car. Wrong impression. Loaded down with my saturated suitcase and bulging suit bag and small shoulder bag that was stuffed to overflowing, I followed Beta onto a bus which took us to the U-Bahn. He gingerly hopped onto the platform *sans* gear while I lumbered behind *mit* gear, if I may be permitted the linguistic Euro mixture.

I was still in a daze. My brain hadn't made the continental transition yet. I did not yet comprehend where I was apart from not being in Africa. The people were no clue. They all looked alike. I could have been anywhere on the planet.

I was brought back to the moment when Beta sprang out of the train and led the way to his apartment complex in Kreuzberg. This area had been where the *avant garde* lived before The Wall came down. Beta assured me that it had remained thus to some extent. But the real *avant garde* had shifted to the East.

Many of the luxurious apartment buildings in what was the Russian zone were abandoned when The Wall came down. As more and more artists and others flocked to Berlin, they squatted in these buildings, paid no rent and lived in relative comfort for a few years, until capitalism returned.

We walked through the courtyard and attacked five flights of stairs, he bounding ahead like a professional golfer, me dragging behind like his caddy. Though I don't remember the number now, I do recall that in order to endure this climb for the next few days, I counted the steps so I could measure my progress, counting up to the number as I ascended and down from the number as I went to street level. It helped pass the time.

Beta's apartment was also a far cry from the luxury I had recently left in Kenya. It had a large main room, off which was one much smaller room in which he slept. Through a doorway was another very large room that served primarily as a storage space but which, during my tenure, had a mattress on the floor against one wall on which was my freshly made bed.

Once I unloaded, he took me on a tour of the rest of the apartment. This consisted of the kitchen-cum-shower-cum-toilet, all crammed into a relatively minute space. With the exception of an abundance of lemons, the space was sparse. Over a cup of tea, we had a quick catch-up, principally discussing the women we'd lusted after at the retreat.

"I would like to fuck ze Albania girl," he suggested. "She had zo good ze ass. I would smack her ass very hard if I fuck her."

"My European wife always liked it when I spanked her," I added, not wanting to seem square.

"No. I don't mean spank. I mean smack her ass mit ze whip."

I didn't have a response to that.

"You never used ze whip?" he asked innocently.

"I'm not really into that," I answered, quickly adding, "I did have a girlfriend for a short time in Hollywood that was a dominatrix but she never brought her work home."

"Such a pity. Mit S & M, it is not necessary to put ze cock in. Ze cock in ze pussy is not important to me." Discretion forbade me from countering his argument. He was, after all, going to be my host for the next few days. I had learned to be discreet when discussing anything that might be controversial with a host.

In order to demonstrate his enthusiasm for this and other related activities, Beta hauled out volumes of photo books on the subject and insisted I look through them while he busied himself in his bedroom hanging new hooks on the wall in anticipation of a collection of devices his girlfriend was going to bring back to Berlin. There was very little space for new accoutrements. The walls were filled with devices already: handcuffs, chains, leather masks and a few whips of varying lengths.

As I perused the books, he called to me. "Did I tell you about ze new show I do?" Without waiting for a negative reply, he went on. "We do S & M mit ze audience. But not extreme. Only a little bit so zey haf a small taste." He came out of his bedroom and found a program from the show. He handed it to me. "Here is in English ze program. Look."

I read:

FOREIGN INTRIGUE is an interactive dance performance. Its succeeding depends on mutual trust. Therefore, we ask you to carefully read the following rules and adhere to them. We have the right to exclude those deemed uncooperative from the performance. The participation is at your own risk and you are responsible for your own actions. RULES/ LEVEL 1 – 1) For the participation in Level 1 your eyes will be blindfolded. Keep the blindfold on for the duration of your participation, it serves as an aid. Completely close your eyes. Take the blindfold off only when asked to do so. 2) Let yourself be guided and moved by the dancers and concentrate on your perception of time and space. Level 1 is about movement, sensuality and communication. You are not obliged to remain passive. You can interact with the dancers in a playful, sensitive way. 3) If you wish to interrupt the process, you can do so anytime by asking to stop. 4) As any session is created individually according to your reactions, you are free to repeat Level 1. RULES/LEVEL 2 – 1) Only after experiencing Level 1 may you proceed to Level 2. Tickets for Level 2 may be purchased at the bar. 2) For Level 2 you will be blindfolded as well as wear wristbands. We will eventually fix your positions. 3) We request that you take off as much clothing as possible to allow access to your skin. 4) Level 2 focuses on the experience of physical pain and submission. Nevertheless, you can count on encouragement, tenderness and even lust. You should be honest with yourself, whether you are emotionally and physically ready to face this challenge. As in Level 1, you can stop the session whenever you wish. 5) We ask for your understanding that we can only offer Level 2 to a limited number of persons every evening. WE WISH YOU A PLEASANT EVENING!

When Beta returned and saw that I had finished reading, he said, "We haf no performance now. We start again after one month."

"What a shame," I responded with relief.

CHAPTER TWENTY EIGHT

I had arrived in Berlin on a national holiday, *Tag die Deutchen einheit*, Unification Day. A huge celebration was to take place in front of the newly restored Brandenburg Gate and the featured speaker was President Bill Clinton who had been out of office for nearly two years and sorely missed by many people in Europe and America. Even though the actual invasion of Iraq had not yet taken place, Clinton's successor was already into his swagger and bluster and "my-dick's-bigger-than-my-daddy's" machinations for all the world to see. I had vowed to myself that I would remain – at least publicly – politically neutral in Australia. The toothpaste was already out of the tube, however, as far as American politics was concerned. I was a staunch Democrat.

Neither Beta nor I was too big on crowds of people so we opted to watch the proceedings on television. It was a particularly momentous event. The Brandenburg Gate had been the symbol of both the division and reunification of Germany and, of course, a Berlin landmark. For the past two years, it had been covered while restoration took place; some of the damage having been done as far back as World War Two. The Brandenburg was one of only eighteen city gates still standing and had been completed in 1791.

When the huge zipper was undone and the pristine, enormous work of art was revealed with the statue of the winged goddess of victory and four horses at the top, the crowd erupted as only a German crowd can erupt -- massively. They screamed and shouted and hurrahed and yelled and whooped and hollered for five minutes or more at full volume and enthusiasm. This historic symbol had been restored. Berlin had been restored. It was absolutely thrilling.

"My girlfriend is zere," Beta announced as we sipped our tea.

"Your girlfriend?"

"*Ja*. She is mit her husband. Zey came beck to Berlin for ze Unification Day."

"Her husband?"

My incredulous look gave him no pause. "*Ja*. It is not a problem for me."

I was impressed by his ease. Intimacy between consenting adults takes on many varieties and forms. Some men like morbidly obese women. Some like twigs. Some men prefer big breasts or shapely legs or shaved vulvas or forests of hair. Some go for anal sex. Some only oral. Some like being urinated on. Some like to look up into an anus as it drops a load. Getting off is only limited by the imagination of the person or people involved. And, it seemed, Beta got off on whipping someone else's wife. I could hear Henny Youngman's classic line already: *Take my wife . . . please.*

Between this and the program for **Foreign Intrigue**, I began to question what exactly *Ich bin ein Berliner* means. Post World War One Berlin didn't seem like such ancient history anymore. *Willkommen. Bienvenue. Welcome.*

We used the car that didn't pick me up at the airport to drive to a section of the former East Berlin that night to attend the birthday party of one of his friends. Beta pointed out a line of stones that snaked across the road as we traveled.

"Zis is where ze wall was," he said.

I had spoken with a young German woman on a visit to Noosa in Queensland. She grew up in Halle, in East Germany. She was a teenager when they began to hear rumors about The Wall and communism about to fall. The older people could not imagine such things and had very mixed feelings about them. But she and her friends were abuzz. Their network was active. News spread among those young people like an epidemic. They began to leave Halle for Berlin. They wanted to be there when it happened. And they were certain that it *would* happen. When she could stand it no longer, she grabbed her backpack and headed northeast to Berlin.

She was there when people had the courage to approach The Wall. She watched as others joined those defiant pioneers. Soon the unthinkable happened. The Wall was collapsing. No one was stopping them. The more adventurous raced across the artificial line that separated east and west. They were followed by a flood of people, mostly young, but of all ages. The celebration had begun. Just like that – with the snap of the fingers – they were free. Even though the event had happened several years before, she could not hold back tears as she told me about it. These stones on the roadway were a reminder of that gigantic event in German history. Everyone in Germany who was alive at that moment remembers where they were when the news of freedom came.

I often wonder why governments and individuals delude themselves by trying to suppress or deny this most fundamental element of the human spirit, the need to be free. Through human history as it is recorded, these attempts by some humans to control other humans in this way have been effective for a while, then thrown off with vengeance. Whether or not we know or learn the lessons of history, as a species we ultimately repeat them anyway. Some animals will always think they're more equal than others. But no one is. To paraphrase Carl Sagan, *We are like butterflies which flutter for two weeks and think it is forever.*

It is also true that the after effects of this emancipation are predictable and typical. The mentality of the newly freed is often confused. Germany was no different. The people of the East had no history of initiative. Everything had been provided, however minimally. While the atmosphere was now not necessarily what I had seen many years before, the black and white picture was now sepia tinted, not yet full color. The thriving element of an undivided society in the early years is the criminal class, white and blue collar.

It is ever thus. From before Byzantium to the American West and into the future.

The difference in Berlin was that the petty theft that went on was just that. Generally speaking, people were free to wander around their city at all hours of the night in safety. I saw young women on bicycles at and after midnight, pedaling along just as indifferently as you please. Personal safety didn't seem to be a problem. But people's stuff was fair game.

As is often my tendency at parties where I'm a stranger, I found a spot in a corner and watched for a while. The partiers were chattering and laughing and drinking and dancing and generally partying away. They all looked so familiar in attitude and style, like they could easily be transplanted to New York, Sydney, Athens, London, you name it. It was like watching a film I've seen a million times. Only it was dubbed in German.

This was one of those apartments that had been squatted. It was filled with young, creative people who had come to pursue their dreams. There were fresh flowers in vases around the room. Virtually everyone who came through the door, including Beta and me, brought flowers. The condition of the furniture was similar to old Percy's, except where he had snake and leopard skins, this furniture was covered with colorful and imaginative cloths. One wall was bare except for a light at one end focused on a small figure stuck on the wall in front of the light which cast a long, macabre shadowy design across the rest of the wall.

Most of the people were courteous enough to find time for a word with an Aussie Yank stranger, though judging by their questions, it was the Yank thing that got most of the play. The hostess/birthday girl was first.

"Zo, you are American?" she asked.

"Well, actually I'm also Australian. I have dual citizenship."

"But you are American," she insisted.

"Well, originally, yes. But if you go back a little farther, I'm…"

"Zo. You like George Bush?" The expression on her face told me that she was hoping for a negative reply.

"I think George Bush is the worst thing that has happened to America in its history," I gladly assured her.

Virtually everyone who came up to me to say hello eventually got around to the American political scene, usually not with intensity, just curiosity. As I engaged in these various superficialities, my male radar was working and picked up two blips.

The first blip had been in Berlin since she first arrived there as a dancer with a Japanese Butoh troupe, that is to say a Butoh troupe from Japan. I thought this was an interesting coincidence since I had only recently learned that Butoh existed through Beta. Now I had a second Butoh moment. Then I learned that she and Beta had been an item at one time and that he was, in fact, the reason she stayed. Their relationship was now cordial out of necessity.

Kuniko was dressed in that totally original, zany, randomly mixed way of dots and stripes and colors and fabrics of the trendy Japanese. She added a layer of Berlin *avant garde* on top of the Japanese trendiness. She was more attentive to me than most of the other women at the party and before long was nicely flirtatious.

"You will be here long?" she asked.

"A few days," I answered. "I'm on a round-the-world trip." I thought it sounded impressive.

"Ooooh," she smiled. "World traveler." It worked. "This is first place you visit?"

I gained confidence. "No, I was in Kenya before I came here…" That led naturally into the story of the three lionesses' impala kill and allowed me to play each of the major roles: one lioness gazing nonchalantly out across the savannah, the impala ambling innocently, as if hypnotized, another lioness creeping with her belly low to the ground – I didn't do this literally, just simulated – then springing from three different directions onto the kill It was the first of many such performances, each improving on the last until I could do it while playing ping-pong if necessary.

I could already feel her blood on my snout as she listened, rapt, to my monologue. That is, until she said, "I want you meet my boyfriend."

It is ever thus. Timing has to be absolutely flawless – split-second – for a hottie like this to be without a boyfriend. The word slapped me back into reality. "Oh, sure," I said tentatively. "Which one is he?"

"He not here," she said, smiling. "Tonight, you my boyfriend." She took my arm and gave my bicep a little squeeze.

Cooled but not altogether frozen out, my attention wandered to the other blip on my screen. This woman fit every conceivable definition of exotic. Her complexion was dark, not African dark, but more than average dark. She had a mane of long, tightly curled hair piled randomly atop her head. Her eyes were raccoon-like with dark pools around them, but stunning, light metallic blue in color. Big, looping earrings dangled, framing her almond eyes, aquiline nose and sensuous, full lips.

Like all beautiful, exotic women from every continent and probably planet or possibly even galaxy, she appeared indifferent to my attention from across the room. She would glance in my direction from time to time – presumably because mine was a new face and thereby aroused curiosity – but with no apparent interest. Yet she was quite animated and easy and having fun with her friends.

I reverted to my standard party M.O. and took a position where I could go back into observer mode. My thoughts wandered. I could have been anywhere, lost in contemplation. *Wonder what Jett is doing now? Wonder if that club with the telephones is still operating. Hope I can sleep tonight after all this adjustment.* Suddenly, she appeared at my side.

"You like being alone?" she asked in perfect English with a slight, unplaceable accent. Indifference is an aphrodisiac for beautiful women. Not feigned indifference, but real, honest-to-god, I-forgot-you-were-in-the-world indifference. I had achieved this latter state naturally, if unintentionally.

"Jet lag," I offered lamely.

"Beta says you are an actor."

"I suppose you could say that. But I also do other things." I couldn't think of anything clever or provocative or, for that matter, interesting to come back with.

"I am also studying acting."

BINGO!!!

Now, if only she is single, I thought to myself, I might be able to improve the quality of my stay in Berlin.

I heard several people call her by name but I couldn't quite catch it. With the sound of the "R" in the German language, I was confused. In some cases, it sounded like "Hada." In other cases, it sounded like "Rada." I finally asked.

"My name is Arabic – Ghada. In Arabic there are two "R" sounds. One is like the Spanish that trills and one is more guttural, like my name."

"You're Arabic?"

"I am Palestinian. My parents are both Palestinian but I grew up in Saudi Arabia until I was six. Then my father brought us to Berlin."

"Your English is perfect."

"My parents also speak English. I like the language. I like to read books in English…"

Before I could continue my literary interrogation, Beta came up to me and rather impatiently suggested we leave. The look on my face told my story.

"I am tired," he said. "Tomorrow, I haf much to do."

I turned to Ghada. "Maybe we can get together for a coffee," I suggested.

"That would be nice. Beta has my number. Call me."

Kuniko caught up with us at the door. She said a perfunctory goodbye to Beta then turned to me. "We can meet sometime tomorrow?"

"Sure."

"The Roxy Café is near Beta's house. He tell you how to find. I meet you there at 2 o'clock. OK?"

"OK."

In the car, Beta was silent for a while. Then, as if he could no longer contain it, he said, "Zis woman is a snake."

"Which woman?"

"Zis Japanese woman. Kuniko. She is a poisonous snake."

"She told me she has a boyfriend. So I'm under no illusions."

"She always has a boyfriend. Zis means nothing. *I* was her boyfriend. It means nothing," he said adamantly.

"Well, I'm not planning to marry her," I said.

"You won't fuck her too," he assured me. "She will find out zat you are not a millionaire playboy tomorrow and it finishes. I know zis woman. She is a snake."

"Maybe. But I have nothing to lose having a coffee with her… unless you have a problem with it."

"I have no problem. Zis is not a problem for me. For you it could be a problem. Not for me."

We arrived at the apartment and climbed up the nine thousand steps to Beta's floor. Before saying goodnight, Beta said, "Tomorrow I haf much work to do. I don't baby-sit you, OK?"

"Sure. No problem. I'm a big boy."

"But I haf my friend, Gudrun, take you around. She is an artist. She will show you ze city. I tell her to meet you, OK? She will come to the Roxy Café after you meet with Kuniko."

"Whatever. Either way, it's fine with me. I'm easy."

CHAPTER TWENTY NINE

I woke up late. The day before had been a long one and I needed a good night's sleep. Beta was already at his desk when I walked out of my bedroom.

"You slept good?" he asked.

"Like a rock. I'll get out of your hair as soon as possible." I looked at his shaved head and immediately wondered if the expression would have resonance.

"We haf a cup of tea together. Zen I work and you amuse yourself mit ze girls."

I was keen to get my bearings and explore Kreuzberg. It was Indian Summer in Berlin. The days were bright and sunny and fairly warm but you got a taste of what was to come in the breeze which had a decided chill. I grabbed my windbreaker and shoulder bag and went down the forty thousand steps to the ground floor.

Beta told me where the Roxy Café was so that was my first destination. I could drop breadcrumbs from there and find my way back. I soon found myself in a lovely, green park. The paths were lined with enormous old horse chestnut trees. I wondered if these Berliners knew that they were walking amongst a harvest of Ohio buckeyes when they passed through.

In Nairobi, whenever I was on a roadway, there would be countless numbers of people walking along or crowded around intersections or plodding aimlessly. By contrast, these streets were relatively empty. There were people to be sure, but they were walking with purpose toward a destination; city people of the kind I was familiar with. Well-used bicycle paths ran parallel to the street in a protected area. These city people were also of all nationalities and races: Asian, Middle Eastern, African, Caucasian, like every other cosmopolitan city in the world. My eyes were only beginning to adjust to being away from Africa.

I looked at my watch and saw that I'd been moseying along longer than I planned. I hotfooted it back to the Roxy Café and there was Kuniko, looking cool and trendy, sitting at an outdoor table.

She gave me a warm hello and a peck on each cheek. She hadn't ordered anything yet. When the waitress arrived, I asked Kuniko what she'd like. Her look took me aback. Her inscrutable, Asian eyes seemed to be saying, "What do you think I want?" But I didn't believe them since I had been forced to add "snake" to her C.V. However, I was prepared to wait until she found out that I was not a millionaire playboy before deciding conclusively about her reptilian status.

She had tea. I continued my world survey. I had tried cappuccinos at two places in Nairobi in an effort to determine whether or not Australia could be topped in the coffee department. Africa came in a poor third, already, without tasting the Berlin version. In Nairobi, they used instant coffee. When this one arrived, I measured the depth of the milk foam and put this one in the same class as its African counterpart, its only advantage being it was made with real coffee. But it was hot and wet and that was satisfactory for the moment.

"So what are you doing here?" I asked Kuniko.

"I dance," she said, adjusting jacket onto the back of the chair.

"Butoh?" Just saying it made me feel smart.

"Also Butoh. But more modern dance."

"Are you with a dance company? Or just freelance?"

"I am boring. I want to know about you. You are actor?"

"Yeah. Among other things."

"You make good money. You can go around the world and spend much time traveling." She was very coquettish. There was nothing blatant in her demeanor. But I thought I could detect a subtle "hiss" in there somewhere.

"Well, you know how it is in the entertainment business. Sometimes you get lucky and put a few dollars away. Sometimes you have to scrape by. Right now I'm doing all right and I like to spend money when I have it."

I thought I saw her wiggle in a delighted, puppy sort of way. Or was it coiling? I wasn't sure. I couldn't quite read it. Was she wiggling because she wanted to bed me? Or did I look like a contact? Or was she just being friendly? Sometimes it's hard to tell the difference, particularly since she was not only inscrutable but also a woman. I felt an attraction but couldn't determine its nature.

"I never see Australia. It is nice?"

"I like it." I decided to bite the bullet and get this boyfriend situation settled. Ghada was in the back of my mind. If Kuniko was going to be bird-in-hand, fine. If not, I had a Palestinian question to resolve.

"Your boyfriend must be very tolerant."

It caught her off guard. "He…is…Norwegian…" This was said as though his nationality would explain everything.

"Yes, but I mean you were at the party alone last night and today you're meeting me for a coffee…"

"He tell me to bring you for breakfast on Sunday to our apartment."

Now I was the one off guard. "Oh…sure…um…Sunday…sure…"

The rest of our conversation was friendly in the way people who don't know one another can be friendly, and eminently forgettable. After sufficient time went by, I told her that someone was coming to meet me for a walking tour of Berlin. We kissed both cheeks, gave a brief hug and she was off.

"You come Sunday?" she asked.

"I look forward to meeting your Norwegian boyfriend," I said, not entirely without sincerity.

My mind was rehashing our conversation as I watched her stroll away. My conclusion was that here was a perfectly nice human being, trying to make another stranger in town feel welcome. She hadn't done anything overt, slightly flirtatious perhaps, but within bounds.

It was the kind of thing I have done many times with people in whatever city I was living in. Yet because of the faulty intelligence from Beta, I concluded that she carried WMDs in her trendy, cloth bag. One of these days we may learn to make our own decisions based on our own experience and observations instead of paying attention to the words of someone who has a vested interest.

I ordered another mediocre cappuccino, saturated it with sugar and sipped it while I read my book-of-the-moment, a biography of Sir Richard Burton, the African adventurer and explorer. I hadn't finished it in Nairobi where it seemed much more appropriate. Here on Sudstern Strasse was an altogether different environment, but the book was still an interesting read.

Before too long, a shadow stood over me. I looked up into the face of a young woman. It was not an entirely unpleasant face. There were no obvious deformities. All the protuberances were of manageable size and location. But there was something about it that spoke of a face bordering on ugliness. Or maybe it was sadness. Whatever it was, it was markedly negative.

"Hi. You're Chris?" she asked with a bare trace of an accent.

"Gudrun? Hi. Want a coffee?"

"Come on, boy, we have a lot of ground to cover," she said playfully. She glanced at my book. "Did you know that he disguised himself as an Arab and went on a Hajj? If they'd have found out he was an Englishman, they'd have slit his throat."

"Yeah. I read that part on the plane coming here," I answered, noticing that her looks had already begun to mitigate themselves.

She set a brisk pace and as we cracked along, I learned that she was a native Berliner. Her family had enough money for her to be a world traveler and indulge her passion which was painting. Her English was flawless and had a decided American edge to it, rather than the British edge most Europeans learn. She also spoke French and Italian fluently. Our banter was uninterrupted, floating from one subject to another effortlessly. She had a wicked sense of humor and laughed with a delightful spontaneity that made everything that much funnier.

Our safari took us to many of the spots I had seen on my first visit during the Cold War. Unter den Linden was once again so named and the thriving thoroughfare that it had been in the glory days of Berlin before the catastrophe of World War Two. The Reichstag, the Pregnant Oyster, Kufeurstendamm were pretty much as I remembered them, except they were buzzing with people shopping, meeting for drinks, strolling in the sunshine and otherwise going about their affairs.

Gudrun pointed out the glass covering the hole in the sidewalk where the books had been burned during the Nazi era. There was no library there anymore. Just the glass hole to look down into. It was made to look like a library down there.

"Berlin has to be the only city in the world where tourist attractions consist of things that don't exist anymore," I said.

"What do you mean?"

"Well, here's this glass hole looking at where a library used to be. There are stones all over the city showing where the wall once was. I'm a little surprised there isn't a spot pointing to where Hitler's bunker was."

"There is!" she said with great enthusiasm and slapped me on the shoulder. "Come on." She set off in a new direction but stopped after a few paces. "Just kidding," she laughed.

We had been walking for a few hours non-stop and evening was approaching. We were back in Beta's neighborhood when I spotted a Mexican restaurant. "Want to get a bite to eat?" I asked. "Seems like the least I can do. And besides, I have to find out what Mexican food tastes like in Berlin."

"Thought you'd never ask," she smiled. When she smiled broadly, which was not often, it lit her face up in a way that neutralized the negativity that seemed to cling to her otherwise.

My suspicions were justified. The food had Mexican names and the ingredients were, if not identical, similar. But something was lost in the translation. It was nonetheless fresh, tasty and inexpensive.

We said our goodbyes in the courtyard of Beta's complex. I thanked her for a terrific day. Then she kissed me full on the mouth. No tongue. But a full kiss that lingered slightly.

"See you," she said and turned away.

I turned and climbed the ten thousand steps to Beta's floor.

Beta and I talked for a while, then said goodnight. I went into my little corner and crawled into my bed on the floor. I was exhausted. Now I had a very active, walking day to add to whatever remnants of jet lag I still maintained. No sooner had my head hit the pillow than I was lost in a deep, dreamless sleep.

At around 3 or 4 in the morning, still in the blackness of night, I snapped awake with a fright. Something cold touched my back. I jerked around to see Gudrun was sliding into bed with me.

CHAPTER THIRTY

With a surprise like that, it is understandable that I'd be incredulous. Well, it was understandable to me anyway. There hadn't been any flirtation between us, just good-natured joking, certainly nothing compared to my experience with Kuniko or Ghada. Yet this woman must have left me, gone home and thought about it for a few hours, then decided to come back across town to Beta's place and let herself into my bed. Was it desperation? Maybe. Was I so charming and irresistible? Doubtful. Whatever it was, it existed exclusively in her imagination. Nevertheless, here I was in Berlin, minding my own business, with a woman who had climbed, uninvited, into my bed.

During the previous day we spent together, Gudrun had told me about this Spanish guy whom she had been in love with. As cleverly as she phrased it, I, nonetheless, sensed no small amount of obsession in her tone. There was something a bit frantic in it. This apparent romance had taken place more than a year before, had lasted for a few days in Barcelona, not even a week, and may or may not have actually been consummated. They had not been in contact since. Yet she spoke of it as if it were a current affair and the guy had run out on her.

She also told me about her current marriage to an African man from Nigeria. They no longer lived together but he claimed conjugal rights whenever it suited him. It was clear from her description of the relationship that he was a particular kind of true African man, which means that women are to be collected into a small herd and used at will. It's a cultural thing. Nothing personal.

With this information available and noted, my reluctance was perfectly natural. A woman who went bonkers about a stranger for no apparent reason; an African husband having casual sex, most likely unprotected, on the loose among all these adventurous women in Berlin, could easily be carrying HIV. Did I really want to follow that train into the tunnel?

In fairness, however, if it had been Kuniko or Ghada who moseyed into my corral, I may not have been quite so thoughtful about consequences. I'd have looked up for a moment, said, "Thanks," and immersed myself in their womanhood.

Gudrun was another matter. I didn't find her attractive to begin with. I certainly hadn't flirted with her by any stretch of the imagination. She had done all the work herself, conjuring up another unrequited affair, this time with a Yank Aussie who would end up a sufficient distance away to allow her suffering to reach epic proportions that the next guy would have to listen to.

But on the other hand, I was, in this circumstance and all others before and since, a man. Put a naked female body in bed with a healthy man and there will be a chemical reaction. It's no different than Berocca and water. And clearly, this woman was making herself irrefutably available, being as how she was naked in my bed and all.

These thoughts presented themselves in an instant. My decision-making apparatus began blinking **RESOLVE IMMEDIATELY! RESOLVE IMMEDIATELY!**

"Look, Gudrun, I'm really very sleepy. And I didn't invite you here. I need to sleep."

"It's all right," she said. "I'll just sleep next to you." And with that, she turned away from me and, taking up the absolute minimum amount of space, went to sleep.

When I woke up, I was alone in bed. I stretched and lay there for a moment with my hands behind my head on the pillow. It took a few moments for me to remember the events of the previous night. Then they came immediately to mind and I wondered when she had stolen away. I pulled on a pair of pants and a shirt and walked into the living room.

Beta was seated at the round dining table. Gudrun was sitting with him. Her left leg was stretched out so that her foot was on his thigh. They were chatting while drinking a morning cup of herbal tea. Beta's hand never left her extended foot, massaging it, caressing it, playing with the toes, all as naturally as scratching an itch.

"Good morning," she said.

"Get a cup. We haf hot tea here," Beta added.

I got a cup and took the empty seat at the table. Why I hadn't noticed before I don't know, but on one of the bookshelves, where all the sex books were, was a plaster cast of a foot, anatomically perfect, about a size 9, I would guess. My brain light snapped on. *He's into feet too!*

Any time any female acquaintance came by while I was there, she would automatically take off her shoe and thrust a foot in his direction. No request was made. No preliminary. Just foot. He would begin his ritual without skipping a beat in their conversation.

That is why their scene was completely unselfconscious. They barely looked up when I entered. The only concession to my being there was that they switched from German to English.

"You slept OK?" Beta inquired.

"Yeah."

"I tried not to wake you when I got up," Gudrun added.

"I didn't even notice you were gone," I said, rather ungallantly.

After I had my tea, I took my cup to the kitchen sink, washed it out and started toward my room. "I'm going to have a shower and then go exploring," I said. Then quickly added, "On my own. I want to have an adventure."

It was a Saturday morning and Ghada had told me that she worked at an outdoor market on Saturdays. I wanted to stop by and say hello.

As I was finishing dressing, Beta came into my room. "Just so you know, I said to Gudrun that you haf plans today. But I don't know. Do you?"

I told him about Ghada and asked directions to the outdoor market. He just smiled at me. "Good luck," he said.

When Beta and I emerged from the bedroom, Gudrun was dressed and waiting for me to go out the door. It was awkward going down the steps together. Barely a word was spoken until we got to the street.

"I'm taking the U-Bahn," she said. "Are you going this way?"

I was but didn't want to share any more information than necessary. "No, I'm going the other way. Beta told me about a shop that I should take a look at," I lied.

"I can go with you," she volunteered.

"No. That's all right. You must have things to do. We'll catch up later, maybe."

She hesitated a moment, then gloom washed over her face. "*Ja.* Later."

I began strolling in the opposite direction, stopping to look in shop windows and glancing back in her direction to be sure she was going. After a sufficient amount of time passed, I reversed my course and headed for the U-Bahn.

Beta's directions to the open-air market were easy to follow. It was a crisp day but the sun was shining brightly. I wandered around the place for a while until I found the sales stall displaying brightly-colored knitted wool bags. And in the midst of the bags was the Palestinian peace prize. She smiled broadly when she saw me.

"I didn't think you would come," she said, taking my hand and giving me a kiss on each cheek.

"Shows how much you know," I answered. My eyes did a quick survey. In this light she was even more beautiful. Her blue/gray eyes sparkled. Even though she was dressed to be out of doors on a chilly day, I could still see the roundness of her figure, something, oddly enough, I could only guess at at the party. Looking at her now was like studying a great work of art. Each facet was detailed and striking.

"Beta gave you directions?"

"No. I just started asking people on the street if they knew where I could find the most beautiful Palestinian woman in the world and they all sent me here."

She would have blushed, and even made a suggestion of a blush, but she liked what I said too much for false modesty. Instead, she impaled me with her eyes.

"Want a coffee or something hot to drink?" I asked. "You must get chilly out here all day."

"There's a place in this direction where you can get a hot chocolate for me. But tell them it's for me. They'll make it extra chocolate." *I'm sure they will*, I thought.

It was getting toward late afternoon when I finally decided to leave. I didn't ask if she had plans that night. It felt like "slow and steady" was going to win this race. Instead, I asked if we might have lunch together. She invited me to come to the – let's call it the Berliner Markt, where she worked on weekdays.

"I'll be there on Monday. What time?"

"Perhaps at one o'clock?"

"And how do I get there?"

She gave me detailed directions that even I could not fuck up. This time I got my cheeks kissed and a little body press. Not overly suggestive. Just a little naughty.

The U-Bahn had taken me past Alexanderplatz on the way to Ghada's open-air market. I decided to get off there on my way back to Beta's.

It was a huge plaza with shops and cafes around its perimeter. A great fountain was its focal point in the center of the circle. I found my way to a café and waited for a table near one of the convenient heaters. With the sun going down, there was nothing left to mitigate the autumn chill.

As I waited for a table, I watched the most unlikely scene develop. It was like watching a masterful silent film sequence, like something Buster Keaton or Charlie Chaplin would pull off with such aplomb.

At the far end of the platz, a tall, thin man was striding along. His pace was brisk, his head held high, his arms swinging naturally, his mind on something else. In his path just past the center of the platz, near the fountain, was a substantial pile of dog shit, one that I had noticed on my way to the café. It sat there like a landmark, not quite steaming but conspicuous. My eyes cut to the pile of shit, then back to the striding man still some distance away. *No. It's impossible. This can't happen.* I was riveted on the unfolding scene. His trajectory was perfect. His stride seemed as though it was carefully measured, even though it was not. It looked for all the world that he couldn't help but mash into the dog shit. I was on pins and needles. If I were a better person, perhaps I'd have called for him to watch out. But one doesn't call out like that in the cinema. And this was definitely cinema unfolding before me. Stride. Stride. Stride. Stride. Splat! He hit it perfectly in the center. His stride was so wide that it threw him off balance as his shoe slipped over the fecal matter, nearly capsizing him. But his balance held and he continued across the platz, never looking back, never breaking stride, never checking his shoe, seemingly unfazed, as if this were something he did every day. It was a masterful performance. I wanted to applaud. I looked around to see if anyone else noticed so we could enjoy a common moment. But no. It was a private screening.

I was pointed toward a small, round table near a heater and took a seat. Time for another cappuccino experiment. Still inferior. As I sipped my brew, I watched life unfold in the platz. Here was a Muslim woman in a black burqa hauling a child in her wake. Here were two African men in colorful dashikis talking animatedly to one another. Next three boys with skateboards rolled by. They were wearing universal skateboard uniforms. One had a red Yankee baseball cap with the bill over his right ear. Another was wearing a University of Southern California hoody with the hood up. The third had an extreme hair-do that was glued into place and rose to several peaks atop his head like an exaggerated rooster's crown. They all carried backpacks with various international logos on them. I could have astral-projected them to Venice Beach or Bethesda Fountain and no one would have noticed.

A busker arrived, set his sound gear up and began singing Paul Simon songs. Well, actually he only sang one Paul Simon song, *The Boxer*. He sang it well enough for a guy who wasn't Paul Simon. It's just that he sang it over and over again, perhaps six times before he either decided he'd made enough money or wasn't going to make any at all, and packed up. And as if this guy not being Paul Simon wasn't enough, another guy walked by who wasn't Arnold Schwartenegger, however much he tried to look like his idol. And god knows he tried because many a head turned as he passed. He smiled patronizingly at them with lots of teeth and may even have flexed a muscle or two under his jacket. *Hasta la vista, baby.*

While taking in these local attractions, I began to think that it was my first time in Europe since the European Union had been organized. I spent euros instead of deutchemarks. A European Union flag was visible from where I sat. The concept of a financially integrated Europe was remarkable. The pettiness of national chauvinism had been replaced by interdependence – at least in theory. As a person who valued the American glorified but probably unrealistic notion of democracy, I was caught up in this European maturity. There may be a mini-Hitler around sometime in the future. But he'd never get a foothold again, I reckoned.

Three different family groups rotated through the table next to mine, each moving itself a little closer to the heater. It was dark by now and time to call it a day. Tomorrow I was to have brunch with Kuniko and Lars, or whatever his name was. I paid my bill and left.

CHAPTER THIRTY ONE

Beta came staggering out of his room, rubbing his eyes, when he heard my noise in the kitchen next morning.

"You must call Gudrun," he said sleepily.

"Why is that?" I asked.

"She is very upset with you. You tell her you will call and you don't," he said matter-of-factly.

"I told her I'd call? When did I tell her I'd call?"

"I don't know. Zis is between you. She said you said you would call and you did not."

Thinking back on our last parting, I remembered that I said I may call sometime. It was what anyone would say in the circumstance, particularly if one didn't intend to call. I explained this to Beta.

He went Sgt. Schultz on me. "I know nothing…only she is upset with you."

"I'm sorry about that but it's not my problem," I said.

"Zis I know. But if you don't call her, it will be my problem and I don't want zis. My girlfriend comes today."

"Will I meet her before I go to Kuniko's for brunch?"

Before he could answer, we heard a key in the lock. Annalise poked her head around the corner of the entryway. Beta jumped up to greet her. They embraced warmly and looked at one another as if they never thought it would happen.

Annalise came toward me without introduction. "You are Chris," she said and gave me an equally familiar hug. "I am happy to meet you."

Without a word, she went into the kitchen, made tea and served it to us with some fresh croissants and fruit she had bought on the way.

Annalise was taller than Beta and, as the euphemism is, full-figured. This was a big girl. She had a lovely, open face, short brownish hair and a smile that revealed two exquisite dimples.

They were very polite and gave me sufficient attention but I knew they were longing to be alone. As soon as I'd finished my tea, I excused myself.

I showered and shaved, dressed and grabbed my poncho and headed for the door. I got down to the street level and halfway to the U-Bahn when I remembered that I'd left the directions to Kuniko's place in my windbreaker. Back up the stairway to heaven I went, thighs burning by the time I reached Beta's floor. I turned the key in the lock and stepped into the entryway.

Crack! Aahh! Crack! Eeee! Crack! Ooooh! Crack! Aaaaiiiii!

They were already in his house of pleasure enjoying their reunion. As quietly as possible, I stole into my room, found the directions and tiptoed out again to the sound of *Crack! Argh! Crack! Eeee! Crack! Aaaaiiiii!* These were either screams of agonizing pleasure or excruciating pain. I couldn't quite tell. The whip crack, however, was identifiable.

When I got back to street level, I noticed the sound of church bells. It took me back to my time in the Army in Germany when I would wake each Sunday to the chorus of bells from perhaps ten or twenty different churches. It was like the opening to the third act of *Tosca*, only multiplied. It was always the same. At the appointed hour there came a solo bell, light and high pitched. Next came another, slightly richer. Then another and another and another, each contributing its special tone and quality to the ensemble until all bells from all churches were announcing their presence, like a flock of birds at dusk, no single voice standing out, just a cacophony of clangs. It was an unforgettable soundscape.

Rain was coming down steadily. But securely dry under my poncho, I walked the distance from the U-Bahn station to the address Kuniko had given me. It was one of a group of flats in what looked like a reclaimed industrial area.

She greeted me warmly, if somewhat awkwardly, and introduced me to Thor. He was a strapping, outdoorsy-looking Norwegian, broad-chested and slightly bearded. His physical appearance was a ruse. In no time, he proved himself to be almost delicate in his manner. He was genuinely sweet and soft and affectionate.

To my immense surprise, he was also a dancer. He and Kuniko danced as partners in pieces he choreographed. After a quick breakfast of eggs, ham and fruit, we took our coffee cups into their living room. There was a laptop on the coffee table and as soon as we were seated and comfortable, Thor activated a video of one of their performances.

It was brilliant. My exposure to dance, per se, was limited. But even to my untutored eye, the colors and movement were unique and original. He tossed her around like a rag doll and caught her like a feather. It was stunning. The music was equally original, created from what sounded like a combination of pure electronic, live and sampled instruments. The rhythms were intricate and sophisticated.

The performance lasted about fifteen minutes. I was virtually breathless at the end. "Wow!"

"You think it is good?" Thor asked reluctantly.

"I think it's incredible!" I answered. "What are you doing with it?"

"We want to try to get into festivals," Kuniko said with some authority.

"You should," I said.

"You can help us?" she asked.

"How?"

"They have festivals in Australia?"

"There are festivals in all major cities in Australia but I have no connections," I replied.

"But you are big movie star," Kuniko insisted.

"I am a working actor who gets lucky from time to time," I said. "But that hardly makes me a movie star." I felt a little boxed in. "I can get you the names of the people to contact and their email addresses but that's about all." Then I added, "You can send them this video and get their reaction."

Thor gave Kuniko a look that was a combination of disappointment and resignation.

It wasn't long after that that I was back out walking in the rain, snug in my poncho. I thought I heard a hissing sound coming from their place.

Quietly, I inserted the key into the lock of Beta's door. Then walked in listening carefully. No sounds coming from his bedroom. I closed the door behind me and entered.

"Ach. You are already beck?" Beta asked from the dining table. They were seated together with the morning tea cups still before them. Annalise had her foot on Beta's thigh and he was doing his thing. She was wearing a dressing gown. He was in jeans with no shirt or shoes.

"Yeah. Kuniko and Thor thought I could help them with festivals in Australia. But I'm too little a fish," I said.

He looked at Annalise. "Snake woman." She nodded.

"Also, Gudrun called you again. You will call her?" he asked.

"Sometime," I answered.

"Oh, yes, also Ghada called," Annalise remembered for him.

"Ghada called?" That perked me up considerably.

"*Ja*. She wants you to call her." He gave me the number and quick as a flash I was punching buttons.

Another friend was having a birthday party and she invited me to go with her. It was to be in late afternoon, just a couple hours from now. Could I make it?

Duh!

I changed my outfit in a jiffy and started for the door. "You can take zis," Beta called to me as I turned the knob. He handed me a large, brown umbrella. "It fits two," he smiled.

I followed the directions I'd been given like a rat in a maze and finally arrived at Ghada's door. She had a welcoming smile on her face as she opened it. "One minute," she said as she ushered me inside.

As she whirled away from me I caught the scent of her perfume. It suited her. The skirt and top she had on also suited her. She looked elegant, not overdressed, more simple and confident. I realized that I was smitten. She had the looks that always got me. Exotic.

"These are not close friends," she said as we were walking out the door. "Only the girl with the birthday. We worked together for some months. The rest I only know from her. We don't have to stay long." This last remark caught my attention

It was another group of twenty-somethings with a few a little older, perhaps thirty people in all. It was another time when I found myself in a room full of people that I didn't know. It happened so many times before this that I took it in stride. One time I would be the only one of my gender. Another time I would be the only one of my race. Another time I would be the only one of my nationality. Once I was the only one of my sexual orientation. And a few times I was the only one who spoke English.

Ghada was conscientious about introducing me to everyone she knew. A few others would drift over my way once they knew I was a stranger, and particularly a Yank.

I talked to one woman who claimed to have visited a kibbutz in Israel seven times in the past few years. She loved the experience of being self-sufficient and the communal feeling of interdependence that is only found in these frontier surroundings. I listened attentively, not having much opportunity to contribute. When I finally was able to make a comment, it had something to do with the number of Jewish friends I had in the US and Australia.

"I'm not Jewish," she said, as if I had leapt to some inappropriate conclusion.

Before that conversation could deteriorate further, a tall man with an intelligent face and trendy glasses pulled up next to me.

"You are American?" By now I didn't bother with the rest of my identity.

"Yes."

"How did this man get elected your president?" He question was accusatory.

"I wish I knew," I answered. "In fact, he didn't actually." But I stopped short of going through the Supreme Court interference.

"America is going to make war with Iraq," he said a little louder.

"America does whatever it wants and don't give a fuck about ze rest of ze world," someone else chimed in.

"Zis country is a bully," someone else offered.

Before long I was expected to defend the indefensible. "Wait a second," I finally broke through. "I didn't vote for him. In fact, most Americans didn't vote for him. I don't like him any better than you do. And I think you're right. America is going to invade Iraq and not care what anyone else says."

That pretty much ended the discussion. They were all either expecting or wishing for me to defend Bush. Since I wasn't so inclined, it gave them nothing to push back against. A remark or two followed but everyone was already in the choir, leaving no one else to preach to.

"We will have cake and coffee, then maybe we leave," Ghada said close to my ear. "There is a very nice Indian restaurant near. I will take you there."

Beta's umbrella came in handy when we left the party a short time later. The rain was coming down steadily. Ghada took my arm as we walked the few blocks to the Indian restaurant.

Two things are and most always have been true in my life. First, I am a romantic. I don't even try to fight it anymore or try to find reasons to. It's a fact. It's in my DNA. It's my temperament, my nature. Call it what you will, I am stuck with it. The second thing is that it has never been an effort for me to live in the now. For me it is always now. Yesterday can be a day away or twenty years away and it's the same to me. When it's gone, it's gone. The future, life has taught me, cannot be planned, predicted or controlled. Anything can happen to alter seemingly inevitable events beyond recognition. That leaves only now. It's now when I write this. It's now when you read it. A different now, perhaps, but now anyway. This was a clear concept to me a long time ago and continues to be.

The now I spent with Ghada in that Indian restaurant was notable. It seemed to go on forever. It was the kind of now that excludes everything else in Life. It consisted of the two of us, the man and woman who cooked and served the food and no one else. The role of the latter was limited to their chores. The rest of it was this beautiful Palestinian woman and me, eyeball to eyeball in a place called Berlin which could as easily been a place called Stockholm or a place called Chicago or a place called Noumea. Each moment lasted an eternity and also flashed by. The time was completely concentrated, saturated. I have no idea what we talked about but I never wanted the conversation to end.

It must have been obvious to her and everyone else on the planet that the hook was firmly set in my cheek.

"I have to tell you something," she finally confided. I didn't like the tone already.

"What's that?" I asked with caution.

"I have a boyfriend."

I felt like Katisha, *Cursed again*!

"He's a merchant seaman. He's on a ship somewhere. But he's my boyfriend."

One always wonders why information is provided that may or not be relevant. If she is telling me this because she wants to put the brakes on, that's one possibility. If she's telling me this because she wants to say the words in order to soothe her conscience before what is to follow, that's another thing. And, of course, she may be saying these words for a reason I couldn't come up with if I had an eternity in which to do it.

Despite whatever reason she may have had in mind, their effect on me was two-fold. It was ice water in the face and it was the kind of disappointment that can only be costly in the end. My purely romantic soul had been engaged and now rejected. You'd think we knew each other forever by the way my insides took this news, that she was the love of my life, the only woman in the world for me. I was devastated and unable to hide it.

"I like you very much," she said, then repeated, "very much. I am happy I met you, that you want to spend time with me."

Now what was she saying? Unless it's so obvious that even I can't miss it – like Moluta, I never know if a woman is giving me a signal or not. Like every other human being, I try to analyze everything and find a convenient box to put it in. When there isn't a useful box handy, I'm flummoxed. I wanted to rewind the clock to thirty minutes before and stay there. But it's always now and this was a new now.

"I like you too," I said. "I don't know what else to say." I was definitely off my game. "Look…I still want to see you while I'm here…whenever you want…"

"Of course," she said, as if it were obvious.

Thus ended the intense moment that was now…then. I got a sweet kiss goodbye on the mouth and the promise of another moment.

On the way back to Beta's, my mind kept turning over this Ghada situation, trying to second-guess myself, trying to find hidden meaning, looking for answers to questions that weren't asked. We do this, we humans. We go over and over the same ground looking for a different conclusion. What we might have said differently. What she really meant by that. I should have done this or maybe that. We land on an explanation. Then in the next moment we're rehashing it again. The same questions. The same inner dialogue. A maybe-it-could-have-been-this response. Eventually, the explanation again.

And then back to the beginning. I was suddenly Gudrun, obsessing over someone I'd just met.

We do this with meaningless experiences, giving them an importance totally out of proportion to their place in our lives. It's only a moment, not a lifetime. A week ago it meant nothing. A week from now it will mean nothing. *Let it be!* Yet we cling to it as if it were a lifeline. Who is the idiot that invented people anyhow?

Back at Beta's. No one was in sight when I arrived. No sounds were coming from his dungeon – I mean bedroom. Quietly, I brushed my teeth and took two steps toward my room before remembering that I'd better take a leak. No sooner had I heard the first splash in the toilet bowl than it was accompanied by *Crack! Aaaahh! Crack! Aaaiiii! Crack! Eeeee!*

Oh you crazy kids! I thought, and smiled all the way to my bed.

CHAPTER THIRTY TWO

I began thinking about leaving Berlin for London. There was only one real reason to stay longer and that was clearly not justified. But since my highest agenda item for the day was a visit to Berliner Markt to see Ghada, that issue would soon be resolved.

Annalise and Beta were sitting at the table at their assigned stations, that is to say with her foot in his lap, when I entered the room. There was hot tea and fruit on the table. Beta looked up as if to say something when he saw me.

"Yeah, I know. Gudrun called, right?" He nodded. "I'll call her sometime today. If she calls again and I'm not here, please tell her that."

"*Gut*," he said, "because if you do not call her today, she says she will come here. I don't want her to come here."

"We do not get along very well," Annalise added.

I could just see them both there together, each with a foot thrust onto Beta's lap, toes wiggling for attention, heels digging in when it wasn't forthcoming, both his hands busy, fingers cramped.

"What is your plan today?" Beta asked.

"I don't really have much to do – maybe go by Berliner Markt to see Ghada – maybe stop at Alexander Platz and people watch. Nothing special," I answered.

"Zere is a club here in Berlin you should see. Annalise and I talked about it zis morning," Beta smiled at her.

"It was a *choke*," she said. "We don't think you would like zis club."

"Now I'm intrigued," I said.

"It is a S and M club. Zey do everything in zis club. It is ze entertainment…"

"*Ja.* Ze people go and watch each other. Ze people are ze entertainment," she added.

"But you can't go," Beta said. When I looked at him questioningly, he said, "You haf not ze right clothes."

"You must wear leather in zis club – or black, at least. Do you have zis?" she asked.

"No. My wardrobe is rather limited," I said.

I didn't make it to that club but as it turns out, an Aussie mate of mine made a subsequent trip to Berlin, looked up Beta and Annalise, stayed with them a night or two and, at their suggestion, went on his own to that club. His report of the goings-on was graphic:

I walked into this darkened room with my black gear on and thought I needed some alcohol in me before I could really take it all in. I saw the bar and started toward it. By now my eyes had adjusted and to the left, in a corner, was a sheila giving this bloke a head-job. I must have been staring because she looked up at me and winked, with his dick still in her mouth. I order a beer and suddenly a little stage on the other side of the room lights up. A sheila gets up on the stage. She's got a pair of long, leather boots on, heels about ten or twelve centimeters high, black belts crisscrossed across her chest and both tits outside the belts. Then another sheila joins her. She's wearing black lederhosen with nothing under them. You could see her tits from the side and a bush of pubes coming out the bottom and she's got a hat on, like a helmet, with a dildo sticking out the front. All right, I thought, this is going to be interesting. Next thing you know, it was on. The belted chick sits up on a stool and the one with the helmet takes turns eating and plunging her helmet dildo in. If I hadn't seen it with my own eyes, I wouldn't've believed it. Then a bloke comes on stage. And he's ready, believe me. He's wearing one of those leather masks and a leather g-string. He goes up behind the helmet and starts mining her arse. Mate, it was unreal. I wanted to jump up there myself but I didn't. I just sipped my beer and watched…with a boner that wouldn't stop.

Since Annalise's arrival, it had become my habit to make myself scarce as soon as possible. After my ablutions were completed and

I was on my way out, I asked, "You guys want to go out to dinner tonight? My treat."

"I haf a better idea," Annalise said. "I make dinner for us here."

"O.K., but at least let me buy the groceries." I took a Euro note from my pocket. "Will this cover it?"

"It is too much, I think," Beta said.

"Zen we buy wine too," Annalise said and snatched the note from my hand.

"Whatever," I said. "What time are we having dinner?"

"You will be back at six-thirty?" Annalise asked.

"If you want."

When I reached street level, I thought of going back to ask if I could invite Ghada but thought better of it. For two reasons. The steps for one. I couldn't bear the thought of re-climbing them. And it would be self-serving for the other. Better just the three of us.

As the U-Bahn was approaching Alexander Platz, I thought about getting off but decided to wait until my return trip. It was after midday and Ghada had been specific about 1 o'clock.

Berliner Markt was a gigantic maze of gigantic buildings interconnected with gigantic courtyards and gardens and paved throughout. An enormous complex. Each building was designated for a different kind of commerce. One would be shop after shop of leather goods. Another would be shop after shop of women's wear. Another would be shop after shop of toys. They went on endlessly. I needed a map to find my way around.

Finally I made my way to a series of buildings that had the correct identification on them and entered one of them. This building was filled with shops that had what appeared to be more touristy items: key chains, snow globes, trinkets and knick-knacks. One little shop got my attention. It had key rings, coasters, tee shirts, ice cube trays, anything you could imagine, all in the shape of East German traffic signals, Ampelmann, as they were called.

Since The Wall went down, Ampelmann had become kitch. These figures, with their hats on, signified "Walk" and "Don't Walk on traffic lights." I thought: *Some East German designer came up with those symbols. They became ubiquitous and ordinary. The Wall comes down, they become trendy and the poor bastard who designed them isn't making a penny in royalties.*

I found Ghada at her shop. This one was more of the same kinds of touristy stuff. There were tea towels and tea cozies and teapots, all with a Berlin motif. She was more reserved when she greeted me but still pleasant and seemed genuinely pleased I was there.

"I have very little time," she said. "There are supposed to be three of us at all times in the store but one girl is sick so I can't be gone for long."

"Is there someplace we can have a coffee nearby?"

"Come," she said and took my hand.

In one of the courtyards was a café. I ordered a cappuccino for myself and a hot chocolate for Ghada. We found a table.

"I'm thinking about leaving Berlin and going to London."

Her look was noncommittal.

"There's not that much more for me to do here. I've seen Beta and revisited some of the places I'd seen before…" Then I dropped the bait. "…unless you give me a reason to stay longer."

Her look now told me everything I needed to know. It was sympathetic and kind but not enthusiastic. She finally spoke. "I told you I have a boyfriend. You are a nice man and I like you, but…"

"I guess that means going to Paris with me is out," I blurted.

"You want me to go to Paris with you?"

I hadn't thought of it before that moment but the sound of it appealed to me. "Why not?"

"When?"

"Now. I don't know."

"I can't just go like this."

"Could you get a day or two off?"

"Maybe," she said.

"Would you go there with me?"

Her look was now less sympathetic and approaching interest. "I have to think about this," she said. "Now I have to go back to work."

"I'll call you tonight," I said.

The Sachertorte was the name of the café in Alexander Platz. I found a table as close to the heater as possible. The last few days were a poignant suggestion that winter was approaching. The sunshine didn't entirely mitigate the distinct chill in the air anymore. In spite of this, however, there were a number of people passing by licking ice cream cones in defiance of the weather and the inevitability of the months ahead.

Today's entertainment by the fountain in Alexander Platz was a classical clarinetist. He had set up his speakers, positioned his chair, flicked the switch and began playing a Mozart concerto for clarinet and orchestra, the backing track supplying the orchestra. This was not a young music student looking for a way to make a buck. This was a mature man, dressed similarly to the guy who warned me about Soviet agents in Vienna. He played brilliantly. Either that or the whole thing was a recording and he was lip-syncing, as it were. I was sufficiently entertained that it didn't matter.

Young lovers passed by. While they wouldn't rank with the French for displays of public affection, they held their own nevertheless. Some would stop and smooch in earnest for a few moments. Others would kiss in full stride. Only in this environment did I realize how inhibited their American and Australian counterparts were by comparison.

At another café nearby a flash of Africa came to me in an unusual display. Why I now made this connection in this way was interesting to me. But the large umbrellas that were opened around the café to shield patrons from the sun were advertisements for The Ubiquitous One, Coca Cola. When we more or less live in one location, we sometimes forget that what we regard as indigenous to our own turf, like Coke, is actually a world brand. Go to any airport and see if you can find a shop that has local goods, like newspapers or magazines. Coke will be there. After the billboard in Nairobi, I couldn't look at that logo without prejudice anymore.

Sitting there, watching this passing parade, I realized that my days were indeed numbered in Berlin. It felt like time to go, Ghada notwithstanding. I would have dinner with Beta and Annalise tonight, then plan for my departure in the next day or so. Traveling around Germany alone wasn't something I considered. My resources were budgeted to stay with friends on this palindrome adventure. A little side trip to Paris under special circumstances I could find a way to justify. But in general, European travel was out of the question.

Two tepid, frothless cappuccinos later, I paid my bill and headed for the U-Bahn. It was about 5:30 when I began my Jungfrau ascent. Five exhausted minutes later, I put my key in the door and was greeted by Annalise wearing an apron over her jeans and sweatshirt.

"You are just in time. Beta is buying wine. I am surprised you did not see him. We haf a special, Annalise dinner tonight. You are angry?"

"What would I be angry about?"

"You want food?" she answered, as if I were stupid.

"Oh, yes. In that case, I am very angry."

I dumped my stuff in the bedroom, picked up my book and headed back out. No sooner had I settled than Beta returned with two bottles of chilled Rhine wine.

"We get drunk tonight," he said and put one bottle of wine in the fridge. "What time do we haf your feast, Annalise?"

"I say in twenty minutes. Chris is angry."

"Why? What is the matter?" he asked.

"I'm not angry. She asked me if I was angry, meaning am I hungry and I didn't want to correct her."

"Shame for you," Annalise said. "How can I speak good ze English if no one help me? OK, pour some wine, please."

While Beta was pulling the cork from one of the bottles, we heard a knock at the door. We all looked at each other with the same thought: Gudrun.

"Oh, shit," I said, "I forgot to call her."

"Now is too late," Beta said, moving toward the door.

When she entered, her already doubtful beauty was further distorted. It would have wilted me if I had any semblance of guilt about how I'd treated her. But I did not feel any such guilt. Whatever was going on between us was going on in her head and nowhere else.

"Why have you not called me?" she began, completely ignoring Annalise and Beta.

"Actually I was going to later tonight," I answered calmly.

Stone silence.

"We are having dinner soon. You would like to haf dinner with us?" Annalise said graciously.

"*Ja*. Sit down. Relax, Gudrun," Beta added.

She took a deep breath and looked around. "OK, I stay."

For the next couple of hours, the meal that might have been so *gemutlich* turned out to be a Shakespearean tragedy. Gudrun was miserable. She was wallowing in her misery. She found new ways to share it with every bite of Annalise's delicious hot chicken salad. It started with me and what an irresponsible, thoughtless, arrogant prick I was and segued into her African husband and the guy in Spain effortlessly. It went on to include some relatives and others unknown to any of us who had wronged her over her lifetime. It was a doctoral thesis in disappointment and self pity. Her poor, distorted face became darker and darker as she spewed out her sorrow. It was like watching a scorpion turn its tail on itself. No matter how she vilified these people who had conspired to fuck up her life, the brunt of it all fell back on her. You could see that she took no pleasure in this self-immolation but she was helpless to do anything about it. You could almost feel her self-hate with each insult she hurled at someone else.

First Annalise would try to change the subject. Then Beta would try. Then Annalise again. But Gudrun was undeterred. She kept me in her sights the entire time and then shotgunned away at every man who had ever crossed her path.

At around coffee time her anger began to cool. It was then that it all really crashed down on her. She stopped suddenly, looked into each of our eyes and burst into the most pathetic, childlike tears. Until then I had been able to remain fairly aloof but that ultimate weapon broke down my resistance.

Beta was already at her side trying to comfort her. He looked at me. I looked at Annalise. Annalise motioned with her eyes for me to go to Gudrun. I sucked it up and put my hand on her shoulder.

"Nobody hates you," I said, in response to her statement just before the tears erupted.

She looked up at me. Her eyes were wet but my words had given them a sparkle that had long ago left them. Before I knew what was happening, she rose, threw her arms around me and buried her face in my neck.

The shock on my face made Annalise have to turn away so that she wouldn't laugh out loud. Beta was still being sympathetic. I felt like a wolf that just stepped into a steel, leg hold trap. If I thought it would have done any good, I'd have started gnawing away at my own ankle to free myself.

"Please let me stay with you tonight," she pleaded.

Annalise conveniently started picking up the dishes from the table. Beta grabbed wine glasses and cutlery. They entered the kitchen and left us alone.

"Gudrun," I started to say, "you have made…"

"You don't have to fuck me," she said, quickly adding, "but you can if you want to. Just let me be in your bed with you again."

How many times in a guy's life would he have prayed for a woman to say these words to him? It's a fantasy. It's like hitchhiking and having a gorgeous redhead with big tits stop and ask if you'd like a ride and mean "a ride." If I could only have done a quick switch and replaced Gudrun with Ghada. Oh, the possibilities. But no. I had this situation and only this situation to deal with. No time for fantasy. And I was torn. I had already heard myself referred to as every kind of prick in the world, in several languages. At a certain point, you figure at least letting her stay is a way to end this insanity. I was going to be leaving Berlin soon and that would be the end of it. At least, I assumed it would be.

"Look, Gudrun," I said firmly but gently, "I am really not attracted to you. You're a good person. And bright. And talented. And probably perfect for someone else. But for me…"

"Please. Just for tonight. I promise." Then she must have thought about what she had said for the previous few hours. "I know you are not like the other men I have known. Just let me stay with you tonight. I'll be a good girl." Her eyes lit up with humor as she said this.

I looked down at my bleeding ankle and stopped gnawing. "OK. But you understand how things are between us, right?"

"I understand," she said.

"I'm really tired," I said. "I want to go to bed soon."

"Whenever you want."

"Go into my bedroom. I want to talk to Beta and Annalise for a moment."

I joined them in the kitchen as Gudrun went into the other room. I must have had a look of resignation on my face because they each smiled a knowing smile. Words were not necessary.

I took plenty of time brushing and flossing. Took a piss. Tightened up my belt, figuratively speaking. And eventually crawled into my bed with my under shorts on, something I never do.

My back was toward her, of course. She pulled herself behind me so that I could feel her naked body spooning me.

"Oh, fuck!" I said aloud.

"What?" Gudrun asked, moving slightly away.

I had just remembered I was supposed to call Ghada. It was too late now. "Nothing," I said. And went to sleep.

CHAPTER THIRTY THREE

The next day was unspectacular. I spent it wandering aimlessly from one known haunt to another. I couldn't call Ghada because she was at work by the time I awoke and got rid of Gudrun, which turned out to be easier than anticipated.

My wanderings allowed me plenty of time to re-think the invitation to Paris that I'd blurted out. Any sensible man would have thought, *I'm thinking with my balls. My funds are limited. If I take this woman to Paris, I'll undoubtedly play big shot and wine and dine her and get a room that I can't afford. And for what? To get laid? When you break it down to its fundamentals, it's about "new pussy".*

When I lived in New York, a bunch of us used to congregate at this writer's apartment. It was when I was known as "the white guy" at a Black playwrights' workshop. All my African American buddies and I would either talk about art or politics or pussy – mostly pussy. One of the guys, noted for his erudition and scholarship, put it in perspective for us one day. His observation has never left me. He said, "It's not about old pussy or young pussy. It's not about black pussy or white pussy. It's not even about good pussy or bad pussy. It's about *new* pussy!"

With that in mind, my thoughts and rationalization and defense mechanisms continued: *As exotic and delicious and voluptuous as Ghada is, what she really represents is a challenge – new pussy. Assuming she comes to Paris with me and we have a great time fucking our brains out, it will still end and she'll return to Berlin and her boyfriend, albeit with another notch on her gun, just as I will return to Oz with a notch on mine. Empires have been sacrificed just because someone thought they just had to get laid with this particular partner. Ask Catherine the Great. It's not as if genitalia could tell the difference. My equipment merely wants to feel that warm, soft wetness around it until it explodes with delight. She no doubt wants her version of the same thing. The rest is all in the mind. Change your mind, stupid, and save yourself some money! If you're in love with her, that's different – well, not really, but it's a way of justifying irrational behavior. But nobody is in love with anybody. It's just sex.*

I talked myself around in circles the entire day, always concluding that I didn't really have any reason to call Ghada again, much less invite her to join me in Paris. My mind was made up. I'd return to Beta's, get the first flight available to London and say *Auf Weidersehen* to Berlin.

I charged up the million stairs, resolute, firm in my conviction, confident that nothing would stand in the way of good sense. I didn't even hesitate about entering the apartment with the sound of whips cracking and accompanying screams in the background. I went directly to the phone, made a reservation for the next day at around midday and opened my book.

Before long, Beta and Annalise came out of their sandbox, her face flushed, his serene. No one was in the slightest embarrassed or uncomfortable.

"I make us some tea?" Annalise said, moving toward the kitchen. I thought she was walking with some difficulty but it could have been my imagination.

"Your day was good?" Beta asked.

"I didn't do much. But I've decided to leave Berlin tomorrow."

"What about Ghada?" Annalise called from the kitchen.

"She's a fantasy," I answered. "When I leave here, she will be a pleasant memory, nothing more."

"You don't fuck her?" Beta asked.

"Not likely," I answered.

"Maybe tonight," Annalise called from the kitchen.

"I don't think so. Tonight I'll get to sleep early and be rested when I get to London."

Annalise brought in the tea and some cookies. Beta and I joined her at the table. She sat down carefully, maybe even gingerly, then raised her foot onto his knee.

"You will call her at least?" Annalise asked. "You must call her."

"Of course. I'll call her later, when she gets home from work."

* * *

"Oh, hello. It's you," she purred. Right away I knew my best-laid plans might well go astray. But I was determined that I wouldn't veer from my thoughtfully reached conclusion.

"Look, Ghada, I've decided to leave Berlin tomorrow. I made a reservation for London at noon."

There was a momentary silence from the other end. I couldn't imagine what was to come next. It could have been anything: fuck off, tears and please don't leave me – though probably not, have a nice trip, drop me a card sometime, who knew?

She broke the silence. "Will I see you before you go?"

I hadn't planned on this response. It never occurred to me that after all my solo deliberations, anything I hadn't put in the imaginary conversation was left out. *Hmm. What could this mean? If I saw her tonight and she responded positively, the unaffordable Paris would be back in play. If I passed up the chance to see her tonight, I would never forgive myself. Now is now.*

"What do you have in mind?" I asked cautiously.

"Nothing. I just want to see you before you go."

"Are you thinking about Paris?"

"I'm thinking about you."

One of the problems with being a horny male – that may be redundant – is not knowing what is and isn't sincere. This woman was probably just being honest. I kept looking for the "Aha!" moment.

"When would you like to see me? Tonight?" I explored.

"I think it is already late tonight. How about in the morning? We can have breakfast together."

My bags were packed and in the entryway. Beta, Annalise and I had a final cup of tea together. I still had instructions on how to get to Ghada's place. All that remained now were the goodbyes.

"I haf one favor to ask you," Beta said as he reached into his backpack.

"Sure. Anything I can do," I answered.

"Zis is for Annalise a gift." He handed me three one-hundred dollar notes, US. "Please buy for me as many kangaroo whips as possible. Zey should only be about one meter long…"

"…*Und* thin…" she quickly added.

"…Maybe red or green…"

"…*Ja*. I like green…" she enthused.

"Ze fringe can be perhaps twelve centimeters. I leave zat to you…"

"We know kangaroo leather is ze best for whips," she added. "We look it up on ze Internet."

"It is more strong and not zo thick like cow leather…"

That was something I already knew. Major League baseball players used to have their shoes made out of kangaroo leather for that very reason, light and strong. Maybe they still do.

"You do zis for us?" Annalise asked sweetly.

How can a guy turn down a woman who asks for so little? I mean, it's not as if they wanted me to send opals or gold bricks. And where else on the planet could you find kangaroo leather in such abundance?

"I'll be happy to," I said and took the $300.

"Ooo…*danke!*" She was like a schoolgirl who just got asked to the prom. She threw her arms around my neck and gave me a kiss. "I like zis man," she said to Beta.

"Maybe next time we see you is in Australia," he said.

"Are you planning to come?" I asked.

"We don't plan. We see."

I was grateful that I was going down the endless stairs with my load and not up. It was lighter because among the things I had carried from Africa were some gifts for Beta and his hospitality. But there was still enough left to notice that the bags weren't empty.

*   *   *

Ghada greeted me warmly at the door. "I have made breakfast for us here," she announced. "I think it is more cozy. You will eat meusli and yogurt with fruit?"

"Sure. That's fine." I put my stuff down and followed her into the kitchen.

"Also I make for you a coffee if you want," she called over her shoulder. "Arabic coffee."

I was off balance from the beginning. I had no idea where this was going. I couldn't read anything in her actions. Was Paris on or off the table? Was this a "here's-looking-at-you, kid" moment? All I could conclude was that she looked absolutely delicious this early in the morning and wouldn't it be nice to see that face on a pillow in a Paris hotel?

Our conversation seemed forced. At least to me. Or maybe I should say mine was. She was completely at ease. Which is logical since she knew what was coming and I didn't.

I looked at my watch.

"You have time to take the train to the airport," she said calmly. "I will go with you."

"You'll come to the airport with me?"

"Why not?"

That prolonged the agony and at the same time suggested there may be some ecstasy in the offing. Sometimes I wish I could be a gorgeous woman just long enough to know what it feels like to fuck with guys like me.

The train ride to the airport was filled mostly with intense looks, a little touching, but mostly looks. I couldn't read her brilliant, laser eyes. Their piercing blueness riveted me but masked whatever softness they may have wanted to suggest. Brown eyes draw you in and warm you. These eyes pinned you and were enigmatic.

Once I got everything organized for the flight and we were about to part, she came into my arms and kissed me full on the mouth with pressure. It felt like a kiss that could have gone either way. It was either a "this-is-the-last-you'll-ever-see-of-me" kiss or a "this-should-last-you-until-Paris" kiss.

"So…" I said.

"So…" she repeated.

I couldn't help myself. "Paris?" I asked.

"Call me from London," she answered. "We'll see."

Great. Just what I needed. A cliffhanger.

CHAPTER THIRTY FOUR

On the flight to Heathrow I replayed the Berlin adventure in my mind. Already it was fading, just as Africa had on the previous leg. It has often been my experience to be at my destination, psychologically, before actually arriving there, as if preparing myself for a new situation. The recent past becomes the distant past – except for Ghada. She remained prominent, as any obsession would.

But even with her prominence, her place in my life was slightly out of focus, its image blurred, shot through a Vaseline lens. It was as if I needed or wanted to cling to this desperate hope as a way of claiming my life. Everything else is unknown. This was a longing or pain or fantasy I could hold on to in this moment. It may be this way with us humans. We clutch the most unseemly moments, nurture them, give them importance beyond proportion as a way of validating our own existence.

I passed through customs still thinking about Ghada, taking little notice of my surroundings. Eventually my eyes focused on a man holding a sign with my name on it. I had been mentally prepared, according to plan, to call my friend, Gena, once I'd emerged from the terminal. A waiting driver was a complete surprise.

Gena and I had been friends in New York, prior to my launching a new life as an actor. We met through a fellow Brit who answered my phones when I thought I wanted to be in broadcasting. Alexandra – my phone answerer – went into the advertising business, eventually becoming a producer. This is where she and Gena met and became friends.

As often happens, Alexandra's dramas – of which there were ample numbers – became Gena's and my dramas by osmosis. Alexandra would talk one of our ears off, then call the other and do the same. Before long our names became familiar until we met. With so much shared history, albeit it was Alexandra's, we quickly bonded with Alexandra as our linchpin.

There was never any danger of a physical relationship with Gena and me. We seemed to have an understanding from the beginning that it was unnecessary and unwanted. I fixed her up with a writer friend of mine instead.

Alexandra and I, on the other hand, had a more "friends with benefits" kind of understanding. It never reached beyond our mutual convenience and could be taken or left without affecting our friendship. And provided a laugh or two along the way.

On one occasion, a woman from my hometown was passing through New York. She and her husband invited me to dinner. I felt I should have a date and there was no one in the picture at that time, so I asked Alexandra if she was busy. She wasn't.

We had a lovely dinner with lots of drinking and laughing and hometown talk and a good time was had by all. When we left the restaurant, however, Alexandra said she was feeling a bit sick.

"Pukey sick?" I asked.

"Maybe. It might have been the shrimp."

"You're not just drunk?"

"No. I'm definitely queasy. Is it OK if I stay at your place tonight?"

I lived nearby. It was perfectly natural. She wouldn't have to travel across town.

"Sure." I answered.

Once we got to my place, she immediately stripped down to her panties and hopped into bed. When I joined her, she was already asleep.

The next morning, a Saturday, we woke up leisurely, realized that each of us had a naked person of the opposite sex in bed and nature began to take its course. That is, until my intercom rang.

"Wonder who that is?" I said, walking bare ass naked to the foyer where the intercom was.

"Darling," said the voice on the other end. "I am coming up!" And without waiting for a response, she gave the phone back to the doorman.

Anka was a married, Turkish woman that I'd met through another friend. Anka was passion itself. Anka was unstoppable, irrepressible and undeniable. Anka made no bones about what she wanted and when she wanted it.

I rushed back to the bedroom and told Alexandra who it was. Alexandra knew of Anka. Since there was no obligation or commitment between Alexandra and me, she was comfortable about remaining out of sight until the storm passed. She gathered her things and went into the bathroom off the bedroom, both of us hoping that Anka wouldn't have to pee.

I slipped on a pair of shorts and returned to the foyer. As has been my habit, my front door was unlocked. I wanted to be there when she walked in and cut her off at the pass before she headed for the bedroom.

She opened the door and her perfume invaded my nostrils. It was heavy, unsubtle and more like a brand than a scent. She was dressed casually in a loose, flowing skirt and peasant blouse, sandals that revealed sharp, painted toenails and a look on her face that was all business.

Anka possessed one of the most stunning bodies I'd ever seen. She had large, firm breasts, a tiny waist and long, shapely legs. Her features were big. Big nose. Big lips. Big teeth. Big hair.

"Do you have another woman here?" she asked, crossing the threshold.

"Why would you think that?" I asked. Never mind that she was married. She wanted to know if I was cheating on her.

"I want you to fuck me now!" she announced, leaving no negotiating room.

It wasn't an order that I wasn't prepared to follow. Looking at this woman would raise a dead man's cock. But I knew that the bedroom was out of bounds.

"How about right here in the floor?" I suggested, as matter-of-factly as I could.

"Yes! Now!"

She flung off her blouse and skirt. She was wearing nothing under them. Down to the floor we went. She dug her long, strong, red fingernails into the flesh of my back. It hurt like hell but I bit my tongue. She reached orgasm before I did which was as soon as possible. She screamed as if someone was stabbing her. All I could think was that Alexandra must have been laughing her ass off in the bathroom – assuming she wasn't cowering in the tub. And maybe even if she was.

"I cannot stay," Anka said, slipping her clothes back on. "I just wanted to fuck you."

"That's OK," I said. "I have a lot to do today anyhow." I thought I felt blood trickling down my back. I winced when she pulled me to her and kissed me with those luscious lips.

In a moment, she was out the door. I stood there wondering about a woman's sixth sense. From the minute she arrived, she looked around for some clue that another woman was there. Fortunately, there was none – clue, that is. She acted as though she only wanted to fuck me to see if I could, that I wasn't already spent with whomever she suspected was there. This could all have been my imagination. But it made sense to me at the time.

When I went back to retrieve Alexandra, she was splitting her sides. By then, so was I.

No sooner had Alf, the driver who was holding the sign with my name on it, closed the car door behind himself, than he launched into a monologue about American politics.

"You bloody Yanks don't give a toss about what the rest of the world thinks, do you?" He didn't wait for a response. "Naw. You do what you bloody like. The rest of the world can just bugger off. That's the way you see it. Bloody George Bush don't 'ave the sense to come in out of the rain, but the bloody bastard's not hesitatin' about starting a bloody war, is he? I got nothin' against war. Fought in Vietnam myself. Sometimes war is necessary. But to start a war just because you want to…that's not right. The bastard just wants the oil. He wants to do what his old man couldn't. It don't fool me. It don't fool most people. But the bastard's gonna drag us all into it, i'n't he?"

When he paused for a breath, I jumped in. "Whoa. Alf. I may sound like a Yank…" and went on with my disclaimer. It settled him but I could see he, like the others before him, was disappointed that he couldn't pound on a Yank and make him defend the indefensible.

By the time we arrived at Gena's address in Hampstead, Alf and I were old buddies.

Gena ushered me into her luxurious flat with a big smile on her face and champagne on ice. It had been a long time since we'd seen each other. When we knew each other in New York, she had been a waif of a thing. Now she was looking more – let's say – prosperous, even though her hairstyle and color hadn't changed. In New York she had lived nicely but worked her butt off for every luxury she had. Here, it seemed, luxury surrounded her.

The flat was large, ultra modern and impressive, more like a townhouse. The living room was expensively furnished, including a Bang and Olufsen big screen that turned toward you when you turned it on. There was a lovely balcony off the living room that overlooked a large, tree-filled garden, almost a park. The kitchen was entirely stainless steel with not a handle to be found. The floors were polished wood. She led me back through a hallway lined with paintings to what was to be my bedroom. Until my arrival, this room had been where she dumped everything. Now it was a beautiful, fresh bedroom with a brand new, queen-sized futon and flat-screen tv, all of which she bought in anticipation of my arrival.

After I put my things down and pried the large handmade bowl I'd bought for her in Kenya out of my suit bag, Gena and I popped the cork on the champagne and sat out on her balcony, surrounded by pots and pots of growing flowers.

"If I didn't know better, I'd say you found a sugar daddy," I said. I always spoke very candidly with Gena. Even in New York, there was a shyness about her that I merely ignored and steamrolled over. It always got a smile from her, then and now.

"Oh, please," she said, peering over her champagne flute.

"Well, you have to admit, it doesn't appear as though you're just scraping by here. This place is fabulous."

"Thank you," she said demurely.

"Well?"

"You're not going to let up, are you?"

"Gena, you're living in the lap of luxury. I don't know much about London but I know Hampstead is a posh address. What's the deal? Have you been working? Did you discover gold? Are you an expensive call girl? What?"

"It's blood money," she finally said. "I hate it. I felt guilty accepting it."

"Blood money? From what?"

Gena's family had escaped the Nazis. They were a prominent Jewish family in Berlin before Hitler came to power. They were among the lucky ones who got out with their lives and whatever possessions they could carry. Gena and her brother were only young children at the time. As refugees, they shared accommodations with other German Jews in London, all of whom had been wealthy and influential. Gena told me that Jerry Springer's family had been among them.

I knew none of these things in New York apart from her being Jewish. But in New York, everyone is Jewish, as Mort Sahl once said. I knew that she had a rather influential relative with whom she shared her last name. But it was not relevant to our friendship and nothing more was ever made of it.

"My family owned a lot of property in Berlin," she continued. "After The Wall came down and Germany was reunited, the German government made reparations to those Jewish families that had been victimized – to the extent that they could. A lot of art works were never recovered. We had some beautiful pieces that I remember from my childhood."

She took another sip of champagne and lit a cigarette. "Anyway, they finally got around to us. My brother and I are the only surviving members of our family. So…"

"You mean I just came from the town that gave you this?"

"Pretty much," she said. "We had real estate. The Berliner Markt belonged to us. And some other buildings in East Berlin."

"The Berliner Markt? I was there a few days ago."

The randomness of this coincidence is one of the things that makes life interesting. What are the chances of my meeting Beta who leads me to Ghada who works in a shop in the Berliner Markt that was once owned by a friend of mine from New York whom I was now visiting in London?

I learned that Gena had had a few flings along the way but was no closer to marriage than she had been in New York. Now, because of her wealth and age, she could easily be vulnerable to some ambitious young opportunist. We're all looking for love if we don't have it. Gena would be no different.

We sat there on the balcony talking until it began to get dark. I hit the highlights of my adventure so far and she seemed interested. When I got around to Ghada, she laughed out loud.

"I knew there'd be a sweet young thing in there somewhere. You'll never change," she said, draining the last drops from her champagne glass. "You want to give her a call?"

"The thought had crossed my mind".

"Let's go inside. It's starting to get a little cool out here," she said. She pointed the remote at the Bang and Olufsen and I watched it rotate in our direction. "You can use the phone in your room if you want privacy. And just dial. I have a cheap long distance service."

I felt a mixture of obligation and trepidation as I walked toward my room. Did I really want to go through with this? Was I going to ask this woman to join me in Paris as planned? What was motivating me now that I was no longer in her sphere of influence?

I dialed the number.

In a moment I was back with Gena.

"So?"

"No answer," I said.

"Too bad," Gena said with conviction. "I'm not very keen on going out tonight for dinner. How about you?'

We ordered a pizza, cracked a bottle of red and I initiated the queen-sized futon.

CHAPTER THIRTY FIVE

I woke up thinking back to New York. Gena had always walked to her own beat there. She had left home as a teenager and eventually moved to The Apple with less than a clue as to what she'd do there. She started slow, taking whatever jobs that were available, mostly secretarial. Little by little, she sorted things out and decided that advertising was the way to go. Finally, she got a job as a producer at one of the major ad agencies. It was very slow going at first but her tenacity and thoroughness soon came to the fore and, as a result, she excelled.

There was a streak of the Bohemian in her from the start. In New York it blossomed into a life style. While she was respectable by day, she was adventurous by night. One of her long time boyfriends was a musician who worked with Miles Davis. This put her in a unique milieu, to say the least. In any circumstances, jazz musicians are a breed apart. In New York, they were a different genus. It was in this environment that Gena acquired her taste for alcohol and cigarettes, neither of which she would entertain suspending for any reason. Jazz was at the foundation of her early New York life.

I remember one time at her apartment in New York when she played an LP for me of a jazz singer I'd never heard of. His mellifluous, baritone voice was magical, like Billy Eckstine singing through velvet.

"Who's this guy?" I asked. I was mesmerized by the sound.

"Johnny Hartman."

There was a photo of him on the back of the album. "I've never heard anything like this before".

A short time after that I was riding a bus downtown to the Village. Who should I see sitting with a beautiful, light-skinned Black woman but Johnny Hartman. Their heads were together conspiratorially. I approached them.

"Hi."

They looked up. Their faces were friendly.

"I don't want to intrude but a friend of mine recently played me your album, the one you recorded with Coltraine. It's magical."

"Thanks, man," he said.

Those words began a friendship that continued for the next several years, until Johnny died. Gena's foundation had now influenced my life.

Despite this colorful aspect, Gena always appeared to be not just unassuming, but insecure. She seemed to try to hide her intelligence and cultural astuteness, waving off compliments and attention as if they were the source of embarrassment. Her generosity was compulsive. Whenever we'd meet for lunch, there was always a battle over the check. Many's the time that I would go to the cashier at Serendipity on the sly only to find that Gena'd been there already.

And now, here I was on a brand new, Queen-sized futon with beautiful down pillows that she had bought just for my visit, in a room that had been a storage room and was now completely furnished.

Gena was already up and making tea when I joined her in her stainless steel world. I now learned that the cups and saucers and cutlery and utensils were also stainless steel. On the other hand, the glasses were all made of the finest cut crystal and the china was Royal Doulton.

"Sleep well?" she asked.

"Like a baby," I answered.

"Get whatever fruit you want and let's go out onto the balcony. It's much nicer to have tea out there."

A few squirrels constituted the wildlife in the garden, with the exception of a cat that patrolled without much interest. In the distance, one could barely hear the occasional siren and perhaps a distant helicopter but this location seemed to pretty much block out the rest of the city.

With a cup of tea in one hand and a cigarette in the other, Gena told me that she has been a virtual recluse for years. "I don't really see anyone," she insisted.

"How about Alexandra? Is she back in London?" I had lost contact with her years before.

As those things seem to happen in my experience, Alexandra had met the Summers at my apartment in New York and became independently friendly with them, even spending time with them in Africa after she left New York. We had just talked about her when I was there. She had married a French male model who was a little too French for Alexandra's liking, as it turns out. He left her with a broken heart to be sure. But worse than that, he left her with a broken spirit. Neither the Summers nor I heard from her after that.

"She's in London and I know where she lives but she won't have anything to do with me," Gena said, with a touch of sadness.

"Really?" I was incredulous. "You guys were such good friends in New York."

"It was more out of convenience, I think. She has always been a bit of a racist, you know. Very Anglo Saxon, if you know what I mean."

I still didn't get it.

"She's not very fond of Jews. It's part of her Chelmsford upbringing. Once she came back to the UK, and, of course, after her marriage broke up, she reverted to type."

"What a shame," I said.

Gena looked wistfully into the garden. "Yes...well..."

The telephone rang and Gena went to answer it. I heard her giggling and talking in muffled tones and soon lost interest. Instead I looked up into the brilliant, blue sky. The weather was holding. The last thing I would have expected was this kind of autumn day in London. It was comfortable to sit on the balcony in only a dressing gown.

Gena was on her way back to the balcony when the phone rang again. And again she laughed and carried on with whomever she was talking to. This was a shorter call, after which she actually made it to her seat.

She lit another cigarette. "That was my brother," she announced. "The other one was a woman I knew from New York. She wants to meet you."

"I thought you said you were reclusive," I teased.

"Oh, well…" she smiled, "maybe that was a bit of an exaggeration. More tea?"

***

I decided to get out of her hair. There's nothing worse than a houseguest that hangs around and takes up time. Besides, I hadn't been in London in years. I had taken a few days' leave there when I was in the Army. My only recollection was that I had attended a couple of musicals, gone to Madame Tussaud's and taken a train ride to somewhere in quest of an attractive woman I attempted to "befriend".

Before going out on a wider exploration, I would have a look around Hampstead. Gena directed me to the village and off I went. It took a special effort and concentration to get there. The winding little streets must have been goat paths at one time that eventually graduated into proper streets. Their randomness and irregularity were challenging. I kept looking back every block or so, trying to memorize landmarks so I could find my way back to Gena's flat when the time came.

When I finally wound my way to beautiful, downtown Hampstead, I found a mixture of ultra trendy, up-scale, name brand shops – the ones you find in wealthy suburbs everywhere on the planet – and the unique charm of a small village.

I wandered around for a while mostly interested in the charming bits. Gena had told me about a café that she thought I'd like called The Coffee Cup. Creative types hung out there, so the legend goes. It had tables overlooking the sidewalk – or I should say, footpath – that were in great demand.

My patience paid off and soon I was squished between two pairs of women. They were busy chatting about this and that, mundane things, normal things, the things that friends chat about when they meet for a coffee. I opened a book I'd just bought and waited for the cappuccino I'd ordered to arrive.

Eureka! The Coffee Cup scored a homerun, knocked it for six, kicked a goal. Use any cliché you wish. This was a really good, Australian-class cappuccino. I now relaxed, put my book aside and watched the parade pass by.

It was a Beverly Hills parade, a Fifth Avenue parade, populated mostly by women at this time of day, dressed elegantly even in their most casual garb. It smelled like money. Well, it actually smelled like expensive perfume where I was sitting. But in general, it was one of those places where you know whether or not you really belong. I had a temporary visa.

There was one "love at first sight" moment as I sat there surveying the passersby. I saw my first Smart car. This little abbreviation of a thing, nearly as wide as it was long, stole my heart. I am anything but a "car guy" but this cute little, efficient auto grabbed me. Having never seen one before, I had no idea where it originated, whether or not it was a local phenomenon or even if it was mass-produced.

When I'd had my fill of people-watching I decided to take a little stroll along the few blocks that constitute Hampstead's main shopping street. The quaint shops were very quaint. The trendy ones were very trendy. I was soon bored with this safari, wondering what I'd do next to kill more time before returning to Gena's for tea. That's when I noticed a little kiosk where several people were standing patiently on the sidewalk waiting to be served.

I moseyed over and discovered La Creperie de Hampstead. It seemed to belong on a street with Smart cars passing by. It was tiny and gave the impression that it could be folded up and carried home nightly. Each crepe was made to order as the customer watched. It was like watching a glass blower or a sketch artist. Every detail was fascinating, whether it was one of a million varieties of sweet crepes or one of the fewer savory ones. The finished product ended up in a crepe cone, as it were, with all the good stuff securely inside.

When it came my turn, after I had studied the menu for several minutes, I did what I often do.

"Oui, monsieur, what would you like?"

"Make me a crepe that you would make for yourself," I answered.

I ended up with a banana and Grand Marnier crepe with a little fork to make sure I got every last bit of fruit.

If this place had been in Santa Monica, there would be three hundred thousand franchises around the world by now, located between Starbucks and McDonalds. But to my knowledge, this was a one-man operation there to provide his customers with a unique dining experience. It was art for art's sake. Very olde worlde, as it were. Very French. And least likely, very Hampstead as it turns out.

In the midst of all our globalization, how refreshing indeed to find a place somewhere that caters to its local crowd without thinking about a bigger picture. The size of the picture is less important than what's on the canvas.

It is one of the things that makes human beings such an interesting lot. One French creperie in Hampstead is fine. More than one can be construed as some kind of cultural invasion. We are fascinated by other cultures when we see them on a screen. But if people from those cultures move next door, it's a terrorist plot. We seem to be so confused. Narrowness and expansiveness are often in such aggressive conflict that it's no wonder there is fundamentalism, whether Christian, Islamic, Jewish, Hindu or any other variety. With the world literally at our fingertips, we still feel threatened by "them." But to quote the cartoonist Walt Kelly, "We have met the enemy and he is us".

When I got back to Gena's, the day was pretty well gone. She had busied herself with whatever it was she busied herself with and when I arrived and let myself in, she was already on the balcony with a glass of white wine and the ubiquitous cigarette.

"Get a glass," she called. "This is a lovely drop."

When I joined her she asked if I like Indian food. My experience at that time was limited to one restaurant in Australia and the one in Berlin. "Sure. Why not?"

"I've asked some friends to join us," she said.

"From your reclusive days?"

"Don't be cheeky," she smiled.

At dinner, Gena's friends were cut from the same political cloth as she was. That is to say, progressive. Compared to them, I seemed like a fascist.

Once again, the situation building in Iraq dominated the dinner conversation.

"Mark my words," Robert opined. "Those bastards are going to subvert the entire American democracy before they're finished."

"Turn it into another Nazi Germany," Ethel, Robert's partner, added. I got the impression that they were a tag team when it came to political discussions.

"I read in the *Guardian* that they've already subverted the Bill of Rights…" Robert said.

"…and the Constitution," Ethel added.

"And the Constitution," Robert repeated. "They're spying on people willy-nilly. The bloody FBI's opening people's mail…"

"That Cheney is the one behind all this. Bush is just a stupid, innocent bystander. Cheney's the one."

"And that Wolfowitz. Don't forget him. Bloody Nazis, all of them."

"They just want to own all the oil," Ethel said.

"Saudi Arabia, my arse," Robert said. "Saudi Arabia is just an extension of the American oil companies…"

"And the Dutch. Don't forget the Dutch. They've got their fingers in the pie too."

"And the Dutch…"

It was like watching a ping pong game. Back and forth they went. The only difference between this and other, previous episodes was that they didn't try to bring me into the conversation as a representative of the Neo-Cons. And their English was better. Gena must have briefed them on my political leanings.

"Why is everyone so caught up in this," I wondered aloud.

"The sun has set – I regret to admit – on the British Empire, per se. America leads the world. When America sneezes, the world says, bless you. These days it's as if the torch on top of the Statue of Liberty has been blown out…" Robert said.

"…casting the world into darkness, " Ethel finished.

"Darkness. Exactly."

***

Gena and I returned to our haunt, the balcony, after we'd put on sweaters.

"Robert and Ethel are old time Socialists," Gena said. "I hope they didn't put you off too much."

"At least they didn't blame me."

Once we'd poured a cognac and Gena lit her cigarette, we settled into New York frame of mind.

"Have you been back recently?" I asked.

"A couple of years ago," she said. "But most of my traveling these days is on cruises. It's much easier. All I have to do is show up and they do the rest. How about you?"

"Once. I still think about New York but my memory of it is the one I last knew. Knowing that city, it's probably morphed five times since then."

"Do you miss it?" Gena asked.

"No. I think about it but I don't miss it. It's that way with me. I am wherever I am and don't long to be somewhere else. Except for once when I was living in St. Louis. I remember thinking that I'd rather be in New York. And before long, that's where I was. How about you? Do you miss New York?"

"I didn't like it that much while I was there, to be honest," she said. "I had fun. And I learned a lot – mostly about life, I suppose – but no, I'm where I belong."

"What about men?"

"There is one man that I've seen. It's over now but he continues to call me. And email me. And harass me."

"Harass you how?" I asked.

She looked out into the garden for a moment, thinking about what she was going to say and how she'd say it. Finally, she looked at me.

"He got quite a lot of money out of me," she said. "He's younger. We haven't been together for several months. But he continues to call and email, like I said."

"Did he steal from you?"

"Well, not exactly."

I had the distinct impression that I'd hit a nerve. "Why don't you have him arrested?"

"Oh, no. Really. It's all right. He didn't get much money. It's more that I was disappointed in him." She paused again, finally lit another cigarette, then continued. "I think I was a little bit in love with him." There were tears filling Gena's eyes when she looked in my direction. "Isn't that stupid?" She waved her hand as if to brush it all away. "An old woman like me in love with a young man. It's a cliché. And don't say I'm not an old woman. I know I'm not. But you know what I mean. He was very young. To him I'm sure I'm an old woman, at least old-er."

I didn't have any instant philosophy handy. Vulnerability and matters of the heart don't have use-by dates. I remembered a woman in St. Louis who must have been in her sixties. We said hello as I came and went from the residence hotel where I lived. She was at the desk.

She was always a very chipper, happy, pleasant woman, a little flirtatious, if the truth be told. I thought it was cute.

Then one day, as I passed by the desk on my way out, I said hello. She beamed into a smile like no other I'd seen and asked, "How are you doing today?"

"Fine, thanks." I stopped and approached the desk. "You seem to be especially chipper today. Why's that?"

"Oh, it's nothing," she said demurely.

"It's something," I probed.

"Oh, no. It's nothing really." She let the moment build until it was impossible to hold it in any longer. "Do you know the man in 410? Bill is his name."

"Can't say I do."

"Oh, well, it's really nothing," she insisted again.

"What's really nothing?"

"Oh, well. I guess it can't hurt to tell you." She was bursting. "I – I mean – we're seeing each other."

Right before my eyes, this mature, grandmotherly woman transformed into a fourteen-year-old girl with her first crush.

"Bill says we should keep it quiet, what with the neighbors and all." When she said the name, Bill, happy sparks flew out of her eyes. She had probably been waiting just to speak the wonderful name out loud to another human being all morning.

Before I left her, I learned that Bill liked fishing, that Bill had been an engineer before retirement, that Bill had four children, two of each, all four married with kids, that Bill drove a sports car and that Bill loved Italian food.

Love may never come at all. But it *never* comes too late.

Looking at Gena now, I understood very well what the promise of sharing life with another human being meant. With the passing of time, each opportunity has the appearance of being the last. There's no confidence that lightning will continue to strike.

That's where Gena was, clinging to the most recent lightning strike, thinking it might be the final one. The devil you know. Et Cetera. Et Cetera. Et Cetera. Like an abused woman taking one more beating because underneath it all he really loves her. No wonder people get hustled by the unscrupulous. They want to believe that someone still gives a shit.

After a moment, she was keen to change the subject. "How about you? Anyone special? What about the girl in Berlin?"

Ghada hadn't occupied a thought the entire day. The fever had obviously broken. One minute she's the light of my life. The next she's *Who?* At least, I thought, I'm not carrying my obsession across the Channel. But now that Gena had brought her up, the candle popped back to life.

"I thought you wanted to take her to Paris?" Gena probed. She liked this situation better, when she could interrogate me with a little, knowing smile on her face.

"So did I." I thought about it for a moment trying to measure my testosterone level. "Maybe I will."

"You know where the phone is," she smiled. "I'll just have another ciggy."

I went down the hallway, passing the beautiful, modern paintings and picked up the phone. I sat for a moment, trying to decide if I really wanted to do this or if I was just following through out of habit. I had already made all the mature arguments to myself. But, it seems, maturity had no role to play in this situation. I punched the keypad.

"Allo," the voice said.

"Ghada?"

There was a pause. "Zis is Chris?" the voice asked.

"Yes."

"Ghada will be home very late tonight. You can call tomorrow?"

It sounded like she was being coached.

"Yes, I can call tomorrow. Thank you."

"No" is the most powerful aphrodisiac in the world. It sets off a chain reaction of Why Nots that can move mountains. In Hollywood, the ability to say No can turn grown, otherwise monstrously powerful executives into lapdogs.

Ghada's "No" had that effect on me. Now I *had* to take her to Paris. Nothing else would do. My manhood was being challenged. I *had* to. The eternal battle between the sexes was in the balance.

In other words, I had lost all perspective. I thought for that empty, air-headed moment that I had some control in this decision, that I could make an argument that would change a woman's made-up mind, that charm and the Paris bauble dangling in front of her would win the day. On the other hand, I wasn't sure I wanted to risk rejection.

I returned the phone to its cradle and went back out onto the balcony. Gena's eyes were alight with curiosity.

"I'll give her a call tomorrow," I said, trying to salvage the moment. "She'll be out until late tonight."

That night I tossed and turned through fitful sleep.

CHAPTER THIRTY SIX

I finally left Hampstead at around noon, headed for the center of London. Gena instructed me about which bus to catch because I wanted to see where I was going rather than taking the Tube.

When I thought I'd spent enough time on the bus and knew which direction I needed to go in, I got off and started hoofing it. I suddenly found myself on Oxford Street, then New Bond. If I thought being in Hampstead Village was like Beverly Hills, I had to recalculate. Hampstead Village was Wal-Mart by comparison. Here a Versace, there a Gucci, here a Hermes, there a Chanel ad infinitum.

I wondered what Moluta would make of this. It was a Henry Higgins moment. I would love to have cleaned her up and watched her strut her beaded, barefoot stuff on Oxford Street, certain that she would have turned a head or two. Or maybe not clean her up. That'd be more interesting. And what would all this look like through her eyes? Could she even imagine it?

All it takes is to get out of the house once in a while to see the vastness of the human experience on this place we call Earth. The people living in the Boston Mountains of Arkansas know their way of life backwards and forwards, scratch out their existence by whatever means and go on from generation to generation without seeing anything else except on a colorful box in the living room. The digger near Coober Pedy makes his way to the Big Smoke once in his life, then longs to get back to his cave-dwelling life among the opals. Being able to get around and see all this magical and humbling diversity among our species boggles the mind. Each of these individuals sees Life through their own prism.

I looked at the people on this upscale, world-class shopping street and realized that the world consists of those who look like everyone else, whether in London, Paris, Seattle or Sydney, and at the same time, look like themselves. It's like looking in an aviary and at first seeing a lot of birds, then seeing them in their different manifestations: large, small, colorful, dull, active, passive. They're all birds, like we're all people, trying to carve out a place in this moment of existence, creating and nurturing the next generation as best they can, trying to guarantee a continuation of themselves.

The concept seems so simple. It is complicated, in my opinion, by our ability to think. Because our species thinks, we *think* we *know* things, whereas what we're doing is merely *thinking*. All of the discussions I'd already had about politics were differences of opinion. No one is right or wrong except from their individual point of view. And that's always subject to alteration. Think flat earth. Think sun revolving around the earth. Think this is the one true religion. Opinions. Nothing more. Nothing less. Based on *thinking* something is true. My variation on the old "opinions are like assholes" comment is: Assholes are like opinions; everyone else's stinks.

Without trying, I found that I was standing alongside one of Nelson's lions in Trafalgar Square, then bumped into Downing Street. I had been to all these places before but my recollection was foggy, so they were new to me while at the same time being familiar. Previously, I had been able to walk right up to Number Ten and photograph the front door. Now the street was blocked off and there was a police presence that discouraged familiarity. I continued meandering. Then I was looking at Parliament and Big Ben.

Looking across the Thames, I saw the London Eye, something that was obviously brand new to me. Gena has suggested I avail myself of this contemporary landmark and its vantage point. I took her advice and made my way across the Jubilee Bridge.

It was a clear, sunny day. The view from my little glass module was spectacular. It was like an amusement park ride, like Disneyland. I was looking at miniature London, miniature Parliament, miniature Big Ben, miniature Waterloo Bridge. I could have gone around and around, and would have if it was permitted without paying. I thought: *It should be like the day I went to Six Flags Magic Mountain in Los Angeles. It was a sunny, Sunday in October. For some reason, very few people were there that day and I was able to ride every ride until I got sick of it. I repeated Free Fall at least seven times, getting off, walking immediately back to the starting place and boarding the next car.* I would like to have done it with The Eye. But didn't.

Instead, I moseyed toward The National Theatre and The New Globe. Going to the replica of The Globe was like making a Hajj. It was a religious experience to be that close to Shakespeare and the genesis of English-speaking theatre. I genuflected at the thatched roof, bowed to the wooden beams, prostrated myself before the groundlings. My head swam. I was drunk – high – ecstatic. I was an astronaut looking at the Wright Brothers' plane. I was a bricklayer standing in front of the Great Pyramid of Cheops. I was an alcoholic lost in the Seagram's distillery. My mind traveled back to the end of the 16th Century and stayed there while I soaked up this history for an hour or so.

Nothing was performing at The Globe. The only thing for me to do was go to the box office of the National Theatre. I bought two seats for a production in the Olivier Theatre. I didn't care what the production was. I just wanted to experience the place.

Revived and renewed, I found a bus going in the proper direction and wended my way back to Hampstead.

While sitting on the balcony the next morning, sipping tea and reading, I was abundantly aware of the coming of winter. It was more gray (or grey, since it was England). The brisk breeze was decidedly cooler without yet being cold.

"Sleep well?" Gena asked, an as yet unlit fag hanging from her lips.

"Yep. You?'

"I always sleep well," she said, the flame honing in on the end of her cigarette. "What are your plans today? "

"Funny you should ask," I said. "We are going to the Olivier Theatre tonight. You and I. I already got tickets."

"Aren't you cheeky? What makes you think I would want to be seen in public with you?"

"Don't worry. I'll give you your ticket and we'll just happen to sit together."

"Oh, well, I suppose I'll have to. But let's go in earlier so I can take you to the Tate Modern. There's a new installation that I'm keen to see."

With our plans made, I decided to mosey on over to Hampstead village for a while. Like a rat in a maze, I went straight for the Coffee Cup and got a table facing the street. Once installed with a cappuccino, I opened my book and glanced from the page to the passing scene at ten-second intervals. Even though it was basically the same scene, it was endlessly fascinating to watch people sauntering, moseying, charging, wandering and strolling by.

I find that whenever I do this, it's with the expectation, or perhaps hope, that I'll see someone I know – as if this were a familiar hometown where you yell hello from the front porch at the neighbor across the street. There's always that sense with me. I've been in a thousand situations where I'm the only person I know and yet I look for another familiar face, even expect to find one.

It probably stems back to an early experience when I was visiting an army buddy in Paris. His roommate was giving us a lift to my buddy, Nate's, car. But he had to stop on the way pick up his girlfriend who was visiting from the States. When the girlfriend hopped into the front seat, Nate's roommate introduced her to Nate, then fumferred trying to recall my last name.

"And this is Nate's friend, Chris…Chris…"

The girlfriend turned to look at me as if she expected to know who I was."

"Wallace," I volunteered.

"You're not *the* Chris Wallace are you?" she asked, wide-eyed. I looked at Nate, then to her then back to Nate. "Did you go to The University?"

"Yes."

"Did you know a girl named Jane Marshall?"

"Yes."

"I can't believe I've actually met you," she said. Then turned to her boyfriend. "Jane spent an entire summer talking about this Chris Wallace that she had such a crush on…"

"She had a crush on me?" I was incredulous. "I never knew she had a crush on me. We were friends and all but…"

"She was nuts about you," the girlfriend said.

"Gee," I said, "Wish I'd know it at the time."

Ever since that experience, it could be that I'm constantly on the lookout for someone that either I know or who knows me. Whatever the reason, I constantly scour faces. Or, on the other hand, it might just be something we all do as people.

When I'd had enough of the Coffee Cup, I ambled around the village for a little while, then returned to Gena's.

She had the giant television screen aimed at her and was watching some chat show. At the beginning of the commercial break, an announcer's voice said: "Filthy Fortnight is coming!" What followed was a promo for *Sex in the City*.

"Filthy fortnight? They're calling *Sex in the City* filthy?" I asked.

"Oh, you know. It's a bit of poetic license, a bit of hyperbole." Gena answered.

"I know. But filthy is a little strong."

"Don't be daft. Where do you think American Puritanism came from? This is England, lovey."

"Then all the clichés are accurate about English schoolboys and proper English ladies?"

"Of course. Think of how Alexandra always appeared to be so prim and proper when really she had the morals of a strumpet. You think you were the only one she was having it on with?"

"I take your point," I said.

Gena's mind wandered for a moment. Then she looked me squarely in the eye. "Let's go out," she announced abruptly.

"Where to?"

"You'll see."

We went down to the garage and hopped into her red Toyota hatchback. Gena drove like a taxi driver, squirming between cars, darting through openings, breaking hard then flooring it with a cigarette dangling from her lips the entire time.

"You've never driven with me before, have you?" she smiled sweetly.

"I'll answer you after my heart returns to my chest," I said.

She stopped on a little suburban side street. "You see that house? The one with the large, black front door?" I nodded. "That's where Alexandra lives. After I tried calling her so many times without success, I finally came here. But she didn't answer the door. She's probably inside right now, looking out at us."

"Should I give it a try?"

"Suit yourself."

I got out of the car and walked to the big, black front door. There was a bell and a knocker. I tried the bell first. I could hear it ringing. I looked back toward the car to see Gena's eyes riveted on me. I rang the bell again. After a few minutes, I used the knocker and banged it with some conviction. Nothing.

I took a pad out of my shoulder bag, found a pen and wrote: "Hi, Alex. I'm in town for a few days staying with Gena. I was just with the Summers in Africa before I came here. I'd love to see you. Please give me a call at Gena's. Love, Chris." I added Gena's number just in case.

When I went back to the car, Gena was puffing a cigarette. I told her what I'd done.

"She won't call, you know."

"How can you be so sure?"

"Because you've told her you're staying with me. She'll never call my number."

In most fiction, these questions are eventually answered: Why did she stop being Gena's friend? What could have traumatized her to this extent? Had her broken marriage turned her into a recluse? Was she living with a house full of cats? In life, on the other hand, the questions go unanswered.

I had a friend in college, Billy, with whom I was so close that we even got summer jobs together. His problems were my problems. Mine his. His father introduced us to Broadway musicals. When his father died, I was there. We were planning to go to live in New York together after we'd finished our military obligations and tear up the town. But then Billy got married. I was his best man. He and his wife often came to visit me and my wife in New York. On one occasion, after his kids were born and in elementary school, he and his wife came to visit. She broke down on a walk with me in Central Park. He was seeing the female half of their best friends back in their Midwestern town. When I asked him about it, he said he was in love. When I asked him if he'd fucked her yet, he said he hadn't, that their love was too pure for that. I suggested that he get a motel room, fuck her and then see if their love was still pure. When I saw him next, he was still living lovelessly with his wife. I moved to Hollywood. We lost contact. Later, I was back in the Midwest for a visit. My sister had recently seen him and he asked about me. I called him. He was now with the love of his life after a nasty divorce. He was both happy in his life and happy to hear from me. He was coming to California in the next few months. I gave him my number and asked him to call, which he agreed to do. I never heard another word. Fade out. Fade in. A few years later I read in an alumni magazine that he had been dead for some months. Next time I was in the Midwest I got in touch with a mutual friend, who told me that our buddy died a slow death from lung cancer (he chain-smoked Camels). While Billy was dying, this friend had asked Billy if he wanted him to call me. He said no, that I was too much of a downer. To this day I wonder what he meant. I will never know. This isn't fiction. It doesn't get explained.

The same was true with Alexandra. Sometimes you just don't get to know.

***

We took the Tube to the Tate Modern. There was a gigantic installation filling the enormous atrium that looked to me like two ends of "his master's voice" connected by a big, long tube. The artist's name was Kapoor. I wish I could understand what makes this kind of thing interesting art. But I can't. Umbrellas in the landscape. Ribbons festooning buildings. Long tubes with flared ends. None of it resonates with my simple brain. I know it's my own shortcoming because other people get it and think it's brilliant.

Gena nodded knowingly at the humongous installation and led me on to another part of the museum, where I'd be more likely to appreciate what I was seeing even if it was just an appreciation of the colors or design.

She was very much at home in this environment. For her it was like visiting old friends. I could pick out a Rembrandt. I have seen enough French impressionist paintings that I have a familiarity with many of them. I could spot a Caravaggio. But Gena would point to a painting and coo and cluck and gape and gush with an enthusiasm that grandmothers save for babies.

"Are you bored?" Gena asked.

"No. I may not know much but I like looking at art. The creative process always fascinates me. Especially the ones where I don't know anything about the mechanics."

I like to get up close to a painting and see brush strokes. Not because I understand things any better. But because it gives me a sense that another human being held the brush or stick or rag or finger or whatever was used to apply the paint. That a person in their own creative world imagined, then executed this series of swirls or dots or strokes that resulted in what is before me. That they had thoughts at the time this all unfolded, thoughts that could be large, universal thoughts with scope, or small, personal thoughts that were mundane. They could be reaching for reality or escaping from it with each motion of the hand. Ultimately, our fascination is with each other. We are endlessly curious about ourselves and our species, wondering what makes us tick in a particular way, how we can all be so alike and yet so diametrically different in thought, skill and understanding.

We grabbed a quick bite at a little bistro on the other side of the river and headed for the Olivier Theatre in the National Theatre complex. The Olivier is a wonderfully intimate setting for a play. We had aisle seats about twenty rows back from the apron of the stage. But it wouldn't have mattered where we sat. The facility is arranged so that everyone is involved.

The night's offering was the first of a trilogy of plays by Tom Stoppard titled *The Coast of Utopia: Voyage*. It was set in Russia in the 1830s to 40s, during the time of Nicholas I. Everything about it was reminiscent of Chekov. The style. The language. The setting. Another playwright may have stumbled walking so close to that classic line. But Stoppard handled it with finesse and agility. The acting and directing and sets and lights were predictably first class. It's always a special treat to see theatre when it's performed at this level.

On the Tube ride back, I was smug knowing that I had taken Gena out to dinner and the theatre without once having to fight for a check.

CHAPTER THIRTY SEVEN

It was raining when I woke up next morning, the kind of rain that feels as though it intends to stay around for a while. It was cozy in bed so I stretched my hands behind my head and gave myself a moment to reflect.

The people I'd visited so far on this journey all seemed to be so settled, happy to be where they were, happy with their lot. The more I thought about it the more I questioned my own wanderlust. While it is true that I am always happy where I am, it is also true that I don't know where I belong. What do I quest after? Why do I keep searching and what do I expect to find?

My thoughts drifted to Ghada once again. Perhaps I should try to call her and ask her to meet me in Paris. Perhaps I should just do a quick day trip to Paris on my own. I looked at the phone but was undecided.

The idea of having a fling and taking the train under the English Channel to France, with or without Ghada, had its appeal. If Ghada wasn't to join me, I knew I'd go alone because Gena would never consider it. Maybe I'd just go for lunch, get a feel of Paris once again, then take the next train back. But then, why go all that way for a few hours? Would I wish I'd taken more time once I'd immersed myself in those familiar surroundings? Would I be selling myself short, just teasing myself by thinking I could pop over and pop back? The more I thought about it, the less sure I was about it all. I couldn't decide. One of the rules I live by is: If you don't know what to do in a given situation, don't do anything. That's what I ended up doing: nothing.

The rain continued. The freshness of the air came through my open window. I could hear the gentle shower splashing on the leaves. I inhaled the purity of the positive ions and felt them cleanse my mind and spirit.

The speculation began anew. Perhaps I could borrow an umbrella and take a leisurely walk around Hampstead. Perhaps I could take a quick trip to the London suburb of Mortlake and see the Arab tent-shaped tomb of the African explorer, Sir Richard Burton. In the midst of these thoughts, I dozed off again. When I opened my eyes, as peaceful as I was, I still felt compelled to do something, go somewhere, *do* something.

"Are you awake yet?" Gena asked, tapping on my door. "It's bloody eleven-thirty."

"I am. Be right out."

The air seemed even fresher on the balcony where we had our tea. The shower was steady but light. An occasional raindrop would splash on the floor and ricochet onto my bare ankle. We sat quietly for some time, each of us lost in thought.

"Do you remember a woman named Alice? She was a friend of mine in New York." Gena asked.

"Alice? What did she do?"

"She worked as a secretary at an insurance firm. But you wouldn't have known that. I'm just wondering if you remember her."

"Not off hand. No. Why?"

"No reason."

"There must be some reason, otherwise you wouldn't have asked," I said.

Gena looked at me for a moment before continuing. "Well, she claims she can't remember if she slept with you in New York."

"She slept with me?"

"Well, that's just it. She isn't sure," Gena said, pulling a cigarette from its pack. "She wants to see you while you're here to see if either of you remembers."

This was an intriguing notion under any circumstances. I couldn't imagine the possibility of not remembering having had sex with someone. It wasn't as though I had been a swinger at any time in my life, or had so many partners that they had all become a blur. I never drank enough to have forgotten what I did. The adventure of it was irresistible.

"Sure. Why not?" I said.

"Good. I've already arranged it. She's coming here and we're all going to Kenwood Garden together."

"When?"

"She'll be here in about thirty minutes. You'd better get a move on, you lazy bastard."

I hurried my ablutions and was dressed and ready when Alice arrived.

She was a walking time warp. Her figure was trim and her face attractive, hardly showing her age. Her dress was pure Carnaby Street. Here was a Hippy, living and breathing. She greeted me with a hug and a kiss and looked long and hard at my face and into my eyes.

"So, Chris, did we get it on?" she asked innocently and openly.

I looked back at her with equal intensity. "I have no fucking idea."

Gena looked from one of us to the other with a smile on her face.

After a pause, Alice laughed, "Oh, well. Let's say we did and it was the best shag of our lives,"

"Suits me. But if it was the best shag of my life, I'm really sorry not to remember it."

"Me too," Alice said, slyly. "Me too."

"That's enough, you two," Gena interrupted. "Let's go to Kenwood Garden and act like ladies and gentlemen."

Kenwood Garden was at one time an enormous, rambling estate, the prototype for a thousand British films about the upper classes. Now it was a public park. When we arrived, the rain had slackened to a sporadic spritz. As we emerged from the car, the sun began to peek out from behind large, white, billowy clouds, revealing patches of a clear and brilliant blue sky. The wind continued to blow through the huge trees that lined the estate, sending large drops of water onto anyone passing below. The sunlight on the moist green of the lawn and colorful flowers gave it all a stunning sparkle.

Even with the precariousness of the weather, there were a number of people there, some carrying umbrellas, others walking unconcerned along the footpaths.

Alice took up the middle position of our little promenade. In my mind, at least, there was something delicious about not knowing whether or not we'd had sex. As I looked at her, I tried to put her back into my New York world and imagine what she must have been like then. Given her current appearance, she would have been very attractive. She would certainly have had sex with abandon. It was what was done at that time. A one-night stand had no negative connotations.

Something nagged at me. Had we actually had sex and I'd forgotten? Or had we had sex and I remember vaguely? Or was I trying to remember that we had had sex when we actually hadn't? Nothing registered.

"You don't really remember, do you?" Alice asked, as if reading my thoughts.

"I'm trying to."

"Didn't you live on the upper Westside? In a third or fourth floor walk-up?"

"Yes," I answered cautiously.

"Separate bedroom? Just a little cupboard of a kitchen?"

I stopped walking. "Gena put you up to this, didn't she?" I said.

"Leave me out of this," Gena said. "This is too much fun. The only thing I'll take responsibility for is introducing you, assuming I did. Otherwise, I had nothing to do with it."

Both Alice and Gena looked at me, waiting for a response.

"Well? Did you have a little cupboard of a kitchen and a separate bedroom?" Alice finally asked.

"Yeah, that's what Stalag 17 was like," I answered.

"Stalag 17! *That's* what you called that apartment. There were big cork letters on the wall!" Alice exclaimed.

"Oh, shit."

"I knew we fucked," she said a little too loud for Gena's liking.

"Alice!" she scolded. "Behave yourself."

"Now I'm embarrassed," I said.

"Don't be," Alice smiled. "It's no big deal. Buy me a cup of tea and we'll be all square."

"Really. I'm sorry."

"Forget it," Alice insisted. "It's ancient history. I just wanted to know that I'm not demented."

"You're not. But the evidence says I might be," I said, recovering slightly. "Tell you what I'll do. When we've had our fill of Kenwood Garden, we'll go somewhere for a drink and I'll take us all out to dinner."

Over drinks, I couldn't erase the idea of a repeat performance. I know it's a male chauvinist, pig/dog thing, but I qualify. Why is it that virtually every man believes in his heart that once he's "been there," he can do it again by merely wishing to? The male ego says to itself something like: *If I was such a stud then and she found me irresistible, and I've lost none of the old juice, what's to prevent an encore? Never mind that that was then and this is now. She let me in before. That's all my genitalia have to know.* Genitalia being the operative word. No thought whatsoever is involved. No brain. Just testicles.

Our harmless flirtation continued through dinner at a restaurant near Gena's called Walnut. "I can't believe you don't remember," Alice said repeatedly.

"Actually, I think I do," I lied.

"No, you don't." She turned to Gena. "Don't you remember every man you ever slept with?"

"Every one," Gena said with conviction.

"There. You see?" Alice turned back to me.

She was clearly having fun toying with me. Gena was quietly pissing herself with laughter. I was completely off balance. Sometimes you just have to bite the bullet and take one for the team.

Back at Gena's flat, we all said our goodbyes. It had been an interesting and informative day. Everyone got something out of it. Alice got the satisfaction of knowing she still had pulling power. Gena got a laugh to last a lifetime. I got a lesson in humility.

***

The time had sneaked up on me. This was the day I was to leave London. When I got to the balcony, Gena was visibly upset.

"What's up?" I asked.

"Look at this," she said, pointing to the front page of *The Guardian*. The Bali bombing had taken place killing a number of Australians in a nightclub terrorist attack.

I had been in Australia when the Twin Towers were destroyed. I was now in London when Australia was traumatized. In both cases, I had avoided the immediacy of those horrendous events. They were news events that played like pieces of film fiction to me. I observed them from a distance.

Gena, on the other hand, was extremely upset by this latest incident. Her own experience as a child no doubt wired her differently where these kinds of mass killings were concerned. I was embarrassed by my own reaction. I didn't boil over with emotion in either instance.

As I watched the World Trade Center event unfold, my first reaction was a sadness that those young Arab men had been duped into thinking they were doing good by creating such havoc and killing so many innocent people. In my mind, it was all about oil from beginning to end. I wrote an untimely and unwelcome letter to the editors of the *New York Times* to that effect.

This Bali event seemed even more remote. I had no history with the place or the relationship with the people. I knew it to be a destination for Australian tourists, like Americans from the east coast going to the Caribbean or Americans from the west coast going to Hawaii. I had been to no countries in the immediate proximity of Australia. They all seemed the same to me: Indonesia, Malaysia, New Guinea, Vanuatu, Bali, Kuala Lumpur. I, the world traveler, was essentially ignorant of my own geographical neighborhood.

I packed with a sense of displacement. Gena and I said our sweet and sad goodbyes. I took one last look into the garden off the balcony. The leaves were suggesting that they would soon explode into color. My load was slightly more manageable as I walked out the door and toward the awaiting car.

As the car approached the airport, a Concorde ripped into the sky and vanished in an instant.

Waiting for my flight, I was again seized by the romance of hearing flights announced to Moscow, San Francisco, Cairo and mine to New York.

The flight was delayed for an hour due to some security problem, never identified. The cabin crew dismissed it as unimportant and nothing more. We took off. Now two-thirds of my trip was behind me. A familiar and at the same time unknown portion lay ahead.

CHAPTER THIRTY EIGHT

I had been back to New York for a brief visit a couple of years after I moved to Australia and not since. It was a place where I had made lasting friendships, friendships that stayed alive over the time and distance. Larry Klein and I were particularly close. We had shared an office when we both produced on-air promotion at WWWW—TV (that's not the name but it will do).

Along with our colleague, Bill Goldman known to us as Goldy, we also created several television concepts that were ahead of their time, just as my idea for Jungle Bob was. One incident was especially painful.

We had created a game show which everyone loved playing and watching. We got to pitch it to an important television producer who had invited a program guru to observe our demonstration. After a smashingly exciting game, the guru said, "This is a terrific game. It's fun to watch and obviously fun for people to play. But no one will ever buy it." I was stunned into silence. Goldy asked, "Why not?" The guru's answer was simple, to the point and the story with lots of tv ideas, "Because nobody's ever seen it before. It's too original."

It was overcast when the plane arrived in New York. No view of the harbor. No Statue of Liberty. No Empire State Building. No visibility.

Larry Klein picked me up at JFK and drove me back to his house in the New Jersey suburbs. Up until now, every place had been exotic, unfamiliar, even though I had been in each location before. Now I was crossing bridges in a landscape that had been my home at one time. And yet, I felt oddly unconnected. My consciousness hadn't caught up with me physically.

Larry's wife had cooked a lovely dinner, the first real home-cooked, American meal I'd had in a long time. The combination of the good food, the long trip and my disorientation took most of my energy. Conversation was limited and I was soon excusing myself and isolated in my bedroom.

If I had felt disoriented before, waking up in this room was the Twilight Zone. I hadn't noticed anything but where the bed was located the night before. Now, as I opened my eyes, it took me some seconds to realize where I was.

The room was a frozen memory of a boy, Larry's son. He hadn't lived at home for some years but the room looked as though he had just left to go to the corner for an ice cream cone.

It was a teenager's sanctuary. Mementoes that could only mean something to the occupant filled and cluttered the place. A portion of a pant leg was stuck onto the wall. Trophies of youthful successes sat atop a bookcase cluttered with all manner of books, from comics to old textbooks to classic novels. Miniature busts of Mozart, Beethoven, Mendelssohn and Brahms were placed among the books. A signed New Jersey Nets basketball rested in a corner next to a keyboard that was standing upright, which was, in turn, next to yet another keyboard that was properly set up. Stacks of CDs and cassettes and a globe sat in and on a second, smaller bookcase. The walls were covered with movie posters and bunches of photos taken at birthdays and other high school functions, showing kids skylarking and making faces and caught in the midst of uninhibited laughter.

I tried to think back to my own teenage room. Even if I no longer lived in it day to day, if someone had trespassed on it and violated its sanctity in the way I had this one, I'd have felt violated. Larry's son would probably never know the difference so I became sensitive on his behalf.

Larry was in the kitchen when I got there. His wife had gone to work in Manhattan. Larry worked these days as a free-lance writer from home. He and I hadn't seen each other in a long time. But like all close friends, we resumed our conversational ease as if we were still sharing an office as we had done in a previous lifetime. There were some old, staple references of those days, references which we made repeatedly at the time, the kind that are always good for a reflective laugh or at least a smile.

When those essentials were sufficiently dealt with, Larry got up from the kitchen table. "You'll have to excuse me," he said. "I've got a couple of deadlines that are fast approaching. Have what you want for breakfast. There's cereal. There are eggs, toast, whatever you want. Just help yourself."

"I'll be fine," I said. "I'm just going to have another cup of tea and then I'm going into the city." Larry gave me instructions on which bus to catch and a front door key.

"See you tonight?" he asked.

"Yep. Don't know what time though."

"Whenever. *Mi casa, su casa.*"

Sitting at the kitchen table alone, I began taking in my surroundings. Just beyond the kitchen window was a wooden deck with two lawn chairs and an outdoor table on it. The yard beyond was lined with full, lush trees, through which you could see fragments of the neighbors' houses. One squirrel and a small bird constituted the visible, suburban wildlife. Not a warthog or baby elephant in sight. The morning sunlight filtered through the leaves of the trees brushing them with light and dark patches.

I got lost in my thoughts. Everyone lives inside their own head. I had been accumulating these various experiences over the past weeks. As I sat in this New Jersey kitchen, these recollections were in my head alone. I was reliving my own movie, seeing the various characters, hearing their voices. It was an experience of my mind. Larry was upstairs in his office with his thoughts, perhaps thinking of his children or his wife or immersed in the project that was his alone. A friend back in Australia, whom I had just learned had been hit by a car and badly injured, was focused on her accident, perhaps reliving it or blaming herself for not being more careful crossing the street or maybe thinking about the upcoming surgery. Gena and Ghada and Beta and the Summers were all in their worlds at this very moment, thinking their thoughts. The assumption is always that things are as they were when we last observed them. But, as metaphysicians say, the Universe is omni-active, constantly in motion, continuously unfolding. We can only be where we are, not where we were and never where we will be. We can share our world for a moment with others but never experience it as they do, even during the sharing.

I thought about a neighbor I'd had in Australia. She was a much older woman whose parents were originally from the UK. Her husband had died long ago and her children were all married with children of their own. She had a wicked sense of humor and we often teased one another. Often I'd make myself a cup of tea then go to her flat and talk with her as I drank it. I sometimes used language that I knew she would blush at, while she secretly enjoyed the naughtiness of it. On rare occasions, mostly when she was referring to other neighbors, she would use an uncharacteristic word herself. She was a believer and went to church regularly but she questioned life nonetheless. We often discussed large matters and her views were always thoughtful and interesting. We were non-judgmental friends.

One day, I noticed that she was not around. The building manager told me that she had gone to the hospital for some tests and was at her daughter's for a few days. When she returned to her flat a day or so later, I popped in.

"I have cancer," she said matter-of-factly. "They've found a little tip of my liver is where the problem is. I'm going in in a couple of weeks to have it snipped off. They do it all the time." She was calm and spoke without any sense of drama.

"Sounds like they've caught it in time," I said. "I thought you looked a little worn last time I saw you."

"Yes. Well, that's what it was."

She went in for the surgery and was back in a few days. She and the manager were standing outside her door talking when I walked by.

"Are you psychic?" she asked me.

"Not that I know of," I answered.

"Well, come in here for a minute. I want to talk to you."

I went in. She looked as healthy as at any time in the past. Once we sat down, she looked at me with a curious expression.

"You knew it was serious, didn't you?" she asked.

"What?"

"The cancer. You said it was serious when I told you about it. I was thinking about what you said last night and I thought he must be psychic."

"The only thing I remember saying is that you looked a little tired," I said.

"No. You specifically said you sensed that it was serious. I'm sure of it."

"If I did, I don't remember."

She paused for a moment. "Well, it is serious. When they opened me up, they had a look and closed me right up again. They said there was nothing they could do."

I was silent.

She continued. "I could have five years left, they told me. I think that would be all right. I'm 82 now. Eighty-seven is a pretty good innings, don't you think?"

"Very respectable," I said. We each entered into our own thoughts for a minute or so.

"You know," she finally said, "I've got some old books and other memorabilia that were given to me by my father and mother. Who's going to want all that junk?"

"I'm sure your grandchildren will find it interesting,' I said.

"Oh, rubbish. They couldn't give a damn about all this old stuff! But what do I do with it? It means something to me. Maybe I should just sell it. It might be worth a bob or two."

"I'm sure your children would want it," I suggested.

She may not have heard me. She was already staring vacantly into space, consumed by the enormity of her upcoming journey.

Without the information that her situation was hopeless, she might have continued battling. Ignorance might have been bliss. But with it, she was confronted in every waking moment with her own mortality, the imminent reality.

A few days passed. I popped in to see her. She looked ashen. All her color was gone, but not her mind. We talked about the medication she was required to take. She told me that a nurse came in daily to administer it and see that she was comfortable, and that her doctor is scheduled every fortnight. With the exception of the subject matter, it seemed like every other chat we'd had.

A few more days passed. I popped in again. Her face was colorless. She was in her pajamas and dressing gown, sitting in a recliner.

"Excuse me for not being dressed," she said. "I just don't feel much like it today."

"I hope the neighbors don't see us," I teased, hoping for her usual gesture of slapping the air in my direction.

Her eyes barely acknowledged my joke. I noticed that her ankles were swollen. The radio that normally would be tuned to a classical music station was quiet. There was no talk of five more years. I imagined that she spent her time thinking about dying. What else would one think about in this situation? It had been decreed by the authorities. You're alive at this moment, but thinking about death, trying to imagine what it will be like. Consciousness attempting to conceive of unconsciousness.

She broke the silence. "I've always taken this certain pain reliever. All my life. Now they say it can have a side effect of damaging the liver. I wonder if that could be it? Imagine. All those years I could have been damaging myself, taking those pills, thinking I was doing myself good..."

Stupidly, I said, "That's why I stay away from anything but plain aspirin." No sooner had the words escaped my lips than I knew they were inappropriate. She wasn't the least bit interested in how steadfast I was about pharmaceuticals.

"Are you in any pain?" I asked.

"No." Again, she removed to her internal world. Her eyes were looking in the direction of the wall but seemed to be staring through it into eternity. It was quiet for a long time. I made an excuse and left. She did nothing to stop me.

In my world, I was observing her, thinking whatever thoughts I had about how she looked and how she responded to her surroundings, any of which or none of which may have been actually in her mind. We were both experiencing the same moment in time but I couldn't understand, with all the empathy in the world, what it meant to be her.

A few days after that, the manager knocked on my door. "They've taken her to the hospital. She won't be coming back. She'll be needing palliative care for however long she has. I knew you'd want to know." A few days later, she died. It hadn't been three weeks from her first visit to the doctor to her death. In the blink of an eye, she was no longer.

At any given moment in time, we are where we are, absorbed in what we are thinking or doing in our own consciousness. One person in Australia might be reading a book. Another in San Francisco might be having an orgasm. Another in Congo might be taking her last breath from starvation. Someone in Samoa might be pulling in a net full of fish. All at the same, shared moment of time on the Planet Earth. None aware of the other. But all connected, nevertheless by that tick of the clock.

***

From the bus, on the way to Manhattan, I got a full view of the New York skyline from across the Hudson River. It was a crystal clear, bright, sunny day. My eyes went to the place where the Twin Towers were supposed to be in lower Manhattan. The Empire State building no longer had any competition. It rose proudly, as if compensating for New York's loss.

I had lived in New York before the World Trade Center was built. I was so attached to the Empire State building as New York's premier skyscraper that I resented those dual interlopers at first. Little by little, I began to accept them as complementing, not competing. There is a picture etched in my memory of going around Manhattan with a friend in his small boat. We were on the East River going north. The setting sun was perfectly placed between the towers as we drifted along. A great, orange dot halfway between enormous, shadowy pillars. It was a spectacular sight and removed all my prejudice in an instant. Now as I looked, I could only see them in my mind.

I emerged from the Port Authority bus terminal and immediately made my way to Times Square. Very little was the same as I had left it. But it was still as familiar as yesterday. It was odd, knowing my way around without recognizing much of it. Forty-Second Street was as clean as a whistle. No junkies nodding against the walls of the trashy cinemas. No hookers parading around. Nothing to mitigate the squeaky cleanness of what was before me.

Times Square looked like Disneyland. It didn't have any of the seediness and grit anymore that had characterized it for so long. When I first arrived in New York to live, one day I was in the Times Square area. A fat slob of a guy came up to me as if he was going to ask me something. But as he approached, he came too close, violating my space. I took a step back. He closed the gap, still not saying anything, just looking at me.

"What's your fucking problem?" I asked.

"Hey. You can't blame a guy for trying," he said with a slight smile and walked away.

That New York seemed to be non-existent. Now, everything sparkled like a toilet bowl commercial.

I walked up Broadway leisurely, very un-New York-ish. When I lived there, I would walk with speed and purpose, weaving in and out of the masses of pedestrians like a running back, barely scraping past some sideways, but never losing my momentum, always looking ten or fifteen feet ahead, looking for openings.

Now I strolled, pausing to look at the Broadway marquis, remembering where a restaurant or bar had been. I was in no hurry. I had no place to go. I was in my former hometown but no one knew it except me.

When I got to Columbus Circle, I remembered that in the wintertime, it seemed like all the winds on the planet converged there and swirled around together in a freezing frenzy. Every other place in the city could be relatively calm. But at Columbus Circle, you got blown around like a plastic bag. You could never dress warm enough for that onslaught.

As I neared Lincoln Center, I remembered how, when it was built, it looked classic already. I used to imagine it a thousand years hence as spectacular ruins, like the Coliseum in Rome or the Treasury of Athena in Delphi.

I saw a familiar landmark, Fiorello's, a restaurant where I'd had many a conversation with friends over lunch or a coffee or a glass of wine. I decided to stop for lunch and found a table on the sidewalk in the sunshine.

The song of New York filled the air as I sat there. Endless sirens blared from all directions. Heavy construction clanged and rang. Cement trucks whined as they dumped their loads. Busses roared by. In other times, I may not have even noticed these sounds. I would have been so accustomed to them that they would never have intruded on my serenity. They weren't objectionable to me now, just present.

After lunch, I continued walking uptown. New names graced some of the streets: Gershwin, Bernstein, Duke Ellington. These were all new to me. I liked that they were there. In the midst of all the turnover that is inevitable in New York life, the past still lives.

The Ansonia Hotel still stood at 72nd Street. I remembered seeing a psychic there who told me that I had done something recently that would impact the rest of my life. Two things came to mind. It could have been either of them, assuming, of course, one wanted to take that leap of faith. I had produced a big gala at Lincoln Center. I had never done anything like it before. It was a huge success. That could have been what the psychic meant because it led to other similar shows. Or it could have been that I put a song I wrote in the show. After that, I went on to write more songs for more shows. But I'm more interested in the coincidence of it all than taking it too seriously as a sign. To me, it's like religion: at a certain point, it gets dangerous when you don't view it as a possibility instead of a truth.

I decided that was enough nostalgia for the day. The thought crossed my mind to go downtown to see the hole in the ground but I couldn't bring myself to do it. It felt too voyeuristic to me. I didn't have to see the result to know that an enormous tragedy had taken place. For others, it might have been a pilgrimage, a way of paying respect. For me it was maudlin.

I was also surprised by the number of flags and the preponderance of red, white and blue. Everywhere you looked the city was awash with flags. They flew everywhere. Umbrellas were stars and stripes. Shopping bags were stars and stripes. Flags flew on car antennas. They were plastered on the side of trucks. They were on billboards, on the top of buildings. They were stuck on bus windows.

The cynicism that characterized the New York I remembered was lost in this patriotic fervor. And understandably so. New York was traumatized by the events of the year before. The unthinkable had occurred. Manhattan had been violated in the most extreme and spectacular way. I had felt it in Australia and requested that my sister send me a flag since American flags were all sold out where I was. But I was still unprepared for this maximized expression. I hadn't realized how deep it really cut.

CHAPTER THIRTY NINE

Larry took the day off and we drove to Scarsdale in Westchester County to have lunch with another of our old friends. Brig, as we called him, had been my replacement when we all worked at the same television station.

The only thing I really knew about Scarsdale was that it was hoity-toity, where, according to Sky Masterson in *Guys and Dolls*, "Galahads, the breakfast-eating, Brooks Brothers type" hung out. Brig was a natural fit. He grew up with a major symphony orchestra, as it were. His father had some administrative function with the ensemble. It left Brig with a comprehensive background in music. The television station may have introduced the three of us but it was music which bound us together. Larry's father had been a Tin Pan Alley songwriter. I was a Broadway musical maven from way back. We pulled up to Brig's house around midday. It was a lovely frame affair, white with blue trim. Nice front yard. Manicured lawn. Brig came out as soon as he saw the car drive up.

"Well, well, well. If it isn't Crocodile Dundee," he said with his hand extended.

"Brig, you old son-of-a-bitch," I said, clasping it. "You realize, of course, that Sky Masterson would never approve."

"I don't eat breakfast," he said defensively. "Come on in a minute. There's something I want you to hear. The Mrs. isn't quite ready yet."

Brig's wife, Lonny, had the most open, engaging smile of anyone on Earth. "Come here, you big lug," she said, "and give me some of that Australian lovin'."

"Why don't you dump this loser and come see the kangaroos," I said, taking her in my arms and exchanging a big hug.

In Australia, because of the time in my life that I went there and the limited number of years that it had been my home, I had no old friends. Often I'd be with Aussies who had history with everyone else in the room, sometimes going back to primary school. They'd known each other through lots of thicks and lots of thins. Watched hairlines recede. Watched facial hair come and go. Watched hair color go through a rainbow of changes and a variety of lengths. Watched children born and grow. They could refer to the past with a familiarity that removed all bullshit. When they knew you *when*, they knew you. My frame of reference with my Aussie friends began with me being an adult of some accomplishment. No one "knew me when" in Oz.

Here I was with people who had seen me through numerous incarnations. Before I was a producer. Before I was an actor. Before Hollywood. Before my first divorce. Before everything after leaving Smalltown and the army.

"You gotta hear this," Brig said, leading the way to the den. "This is unbelievable." He put a CD in the stereo.

Even before the sound came out, I knew it was going to blow my socks off. Brig always had the very latest, highest tech, most pure sound system on the planet. Years before, he played for me the first CD I'd ever seen. In fact, I hadn't even heard of a CD until Brig. I remember asking him how it played, if there was some kind of needle under there somewhere. When he tried to explain it to me, he might as well have been speaking Mandarin. It meant nothing to me.

The opening strains of the Overture to *The King and I* began.

"The King and I," I said, showing how smart I was.

"Yes, but who's singing it?" he smiled wickedly.

When it got to the first song, "I Whistle a Happy Tune," I knew I recognized the voice but couldn't place it. Brig just smiled smugly. "Give up?"

"Wait a second. I know the voice," I said.

"I soitainly hope so," he said.

The light went on. "Julie Andrews," I said, leaving out the nyea -- nyea, nyea – nyea nyea. "But when did she do *The King and I?*"

"Aha!" Brig said. "Exactly. And who plays the king?"

He skipped forward to "Is a Puzzlement."

I listened to the entire song. "I have no fucking idea," I confessed.

"Ben Kingsley," Brig announced triumphantly and handed me the album cover.

"When did they do this?" I asked.

"It was not on stage, just done for the recording. Pretty good, huh?"

"I want a copy," I insisted. "Where can I buy it?"

"You can't," Brig said. "Maybe Klein can make you a copy." He took the CD out of the tray, replaced it in the cover and handed it to Larry.

"This is against all my principles," Larry said.

"Mine too," I said.

"And mine," Brig added. "However, under the circumstances, seeing as how they ain't got no culture down there with the dingos…"

"Watch yer tongue there, mate," I said in my best Aussie accent. "Yer insultin' me homeland."

"Yeah, yeah, yeah. Let's go throw a shrimp on the barby and have lunch," Larry said.

"For your information, it's prawn, mate. We don't have shrimp in Australia. We have prawns."

We went to a restaurant on the main drag of Scarsdale. Brig was well known at this establishment and was greeted appropriately.

"Hi, George. I think we have a reservation," Brig said.

We were shown to a table against the wall. They asked me what it was like living in Australia, if I was dating anyone, was I getting much work, all the usual catch-up questions. But no sooner would I start to answer than someone was reminded of something we had experienced in the past and we'd go off on a tangent until the next question about Australia.

For the next couple of hours we waded through our lives together. The subject matter switched from former wives to former bosses to musicals we'd seen to parties we'd attended to dinners we'd had.

"You remember the time we went to that Chinese restaurant and Brig fell asleep at the table?" I wondered aloud.

"That wasn't funny," Brig said.

"Was I there?" Lonny asked.

"Maybe not," Larry said. "I think it was just the guys: Brig, Wallace, Goldy and me."

"What happened?" she asked.

"We were having this lovely dinner…" I started.

"We were just about finished…" Larry went on.

"And we were laughing and having fun as we always do," I went on. "And Goldy says, 'Would you look at this?' And there was Brig, head back at a 90 degree angle, mouth gaping wide open…"

"Snoring…"

"I was tired," Brig said defensively. "I needed a nap."

"So we hushed each other, got up, told them he'd pay the bill and left," I concluded.

"I never thought that was funny then. And I don't think it's funny now," Brig said smiling. "You guys have no class. And you still owe me for that dinner."

My history with these people, what we shared culturally, the shorthand we used, the reference points that needed no explanation, all this gave me such warmth and comfort during the time we had together. I knew, however, that it was only to be captured for a moment. My life was in Australia now. I didn't live in their world anymore. I loved being with them and seeing them and being able to joke and touch and laugh with them. But they were yesterday.

Once again I felt out of place.

I took my time getting the next day started. Larry had work to do but we spent an hour or so chatting before he gave me some time to check emails, then hustled me out of his office.

I caught a bus for the George Washington Bridge and when it got to the Manhattan side, I caught a subway downtown. From

Times Square I shuttled to the East Side to Grand Central Station, still without having a specific destination. I started walking uptown from there.

The weather was getting serious. A chilly rain fell intermittently and the wind whipped up every now and then just enough to surprise people carrying umbrellas and turn them inside out. Abandoned, twisted, mangled umbrella leftovers protruded from bins all along the midtown streets. I still had the poncho that had served me so well in Berlin. And besides, by the time the drops negotiated their way through the high buildings of midtown Manhattan, the effect was minimized.

Like that Impala that walked, mesmerized, toward its death on the Serengeti Plain, I found myself walking as if drawn toward Serendipity, near Bloomingdale's. It was lunchtime anyway, so I went in.

Just entering this unchanged world brought back a flood of memories. Gena and I had often met here for lunch or sometimes dinner. But that wasn't what settled in my mind. It was a lunch I'd had here with my second wife, who was European.

We had been legally separated for some time through her instigation. Losing her caused me the kind of pain that you don't wish on anyone. But time passed and, as it always does, put a patch on my heart. The legal separation had been filed in California, the stated reason for which was irreconcilable differences. At some point, I realized that I had to move on and finalized the divorce, which was within my legal prerogative after six months of legal separation.

It was after that that she returned to New York and insisted we have lunch together. I suggested Serendipity. After catching me up on all the family gossip and telling me how her son was faring, and generally being charming and engaging and cute and sexy, she got around to her "Oh, by the way…"

Now that the blinders were off and I could see beyond my pure animal desires, I had expected an "Oh, by the way…" There had to be an important reason for her to contact me after all this time. Important to her, that is.

The "Oh, by the way…" was that she wanted a green card. She hadn't bothered to get one when were together but now thought it would be useful.

"I can't help you get a green card," I explained.

"You can!" she insisted. "You are my husband. You are American. You can do this for me." It wasn't a question or a request.

"No, I can't," I insisted with equal vehemence.

"I am your wife," she said a little too loudly.

"See, that's the thing," I said. "You're not my wife. Not anymore."

"We are not divorced. Only separated."

"You'd better check again. We're divorced. I got the final dissolution about eight months ago."

The charm went. The friendliness went. The gossip went. The sexiness and cuteness went. And soon after, she did too. I sat there looking up at the Tiffany lamps.

I looked up at the lamps as I made my way to a table. At this time of day, most of Serendipity's clientele were female except for the little kids they may have had in tow.

I became aware of the loud voices around me. A woman at the next table was telling her dining partner what sounded like way too much information about her intimate family details, then laughing way too loud at her own story. People sometimes seem to forget that they're not at home. Someone else, a little farther away but still within earshot, told about her "deadbeat fucking boyfriend." *More New York music,* I thought. Across the room a little girl, smartly dressed and cute as a button, went out of control and began using her silverware like an Alcatraz inmate. One of the ubiquitous gay waiters finally came to me and announced the specials as if he were in the Amphitheatre in Athens. I could still barely hear him above the din.

I looked up at the hanging Tiffany lamps. *Too bad they can't talk,* I thought. *They could undoubtedly tell some interesting stories.* Mine would have been just one of hundreds, or perhaps, thousands of New York dramas played out in these kitch surroundings, featuring the over-botoxed, the broken-hearted, the happy birthday celebrant, the out-of-towner, the jilter and the jiltee, as many stories as there are people in *The Naked City.*

With my Serendipity jones satisfied, I paid the check, stepped out into the real world again and went toward the subway. I knew what was in store for me in Brooklyn.

Punkin, as I called her, had been one of the few American friends I had in Australia. We met through an Aussie whom I'd recently met at a showcase event at one of the local acting schools.

Punkin was an original. She was attractive without being beautiful. She had one of the most efficient, thorough, organized, comprehensive minds I've ever known. Whatever the situation, Punkin would find a no nonsense, totally organic solution whether she had any previous knowledge of it or not. She had dabbled in several entrepreneurial enterprises in Oz that ranged from show business to food business and was definitely not someone who could work for someone else. However, her Brooklyn abruptness was over-balanced by a generosity that could make you cry. If you were on Punkin's good list, the sky's the limit. If you were on the shit list, as a colleague of Tony Soprano's might say, *fa-ge-da-ba-dit.*

She had taken a trip to visit her mother, grandmother and brothers. While she was in Brooklyn, the World Trade Center was destroyed. She suffered the trauma, along with every other New Yorker, as a personal loss. Because of this strong sense of being, at heart, a New Yorker, her life in Australia was essentially over, despite the fact that just before this trip, she had taken citizenship. She needed to be at home and home was Brooklyn.

When I told Punkin that I was going to be passing through New York on my round-the-world trip, she said I had to come to Brooklyn for dinner. But not just any dinner. Thanksgiving dinner.

One of the things that Punkin and I did, once we'd become friends, was wrapped around Thanksgiving. This is a non-existent holiday in Australia, one of the great shortcomings of the society, in my opinion.

If ever there was a culture that ought to be in a constant state of appreciation, it is Australia. From the very beginning of white Australia's history and for at least 40,000 years before. Can you imagine? A boatload of criminals is taken farther and farther away from the cold, crowded, filthy misery of the London slums and deposited in the never-ending sunshine and naturally welcoming purity of the Australasian continent. *And this was their punishment!* Everyday ought to be Thanksgiving for white people in Oz. And that's not even taking into account the stability of the government, the prosperity of the economy, the egalitarian, multi-racial, multi-cultural, multi-ethnic, multi-religious composition of its population or the "she'll be right, mate" philosophy that permeates everything from the ground up. When you factor in all that is Australia, plus the high penchant for taking time off, it's amazing that someone hasn't suggested Thanksgiving as yet another public holiday, like Melbourne Cup day.

Punkin and I got into the habit of celebrating Thanksgiving in Oz. My contribution was the turkey and the mashed potatoes. Hers was everything else, including the house.

Having been in the food business, when she was in the kitchen, Punkin was Br'er Rabbit in the Briar Patch. She whipped up gourmet treat after gourmet treat to accompany the traditional bird.

The first year I went to my local poultry place and asked for a big turkey, they asked how big.

"How big can you get?" I asked.

"Mate, we might be able to find one around six or maybe eight kilos," he answered. I did the quick calculation in my head. *Eight kilos is sixteen pounds, plus another pound-and-a-half, seventeen-and-a-half pounds.*

"Do you have any bigger?"

"Bigger?!!?"

"Yeah, something like ten or eleven kilos?"

"I don't know. I'll have to check with my supplier."

"And make it organic if you can."

He answered the way most Aussie merchants answer. "Leave it with me," he said.

When I went to pick up the turkey, there were several people in the shop being served. He brought out my twenty-plus pound turkey. It stopped all conversation. One of the larrikins waiting to be served said, "What're ya cookin' there, mate, a bloody emu?"

There were never fewer than fifty people at our Thanksgiving dinners, most of whom, logically, were Aussies. Not one failed to suggest that Thanksgiving needed to be put on the Australian calendar.

So now I was on my way to Brooklyn to have yet another Thanksgiving dinner with Punkin, despite the fact that the actual holiday was more than a month away.

I got off the F-train and followed the directions she'd given me to her house, a brownstone on a nice, clean Brooklyn street. Punkin greeted me with a big smile and a bigger hug. She was wearing her battle gear, viz., an apron with a wooden spoon in the pocket.

"Come on up and meet Grandma and the gang," she said, retreating back up the stairs.

Grandma was already legendary. We knew about Grandma in Australia. Grandma was the one who taught Punkin how to cook. She was the master. She was also African American, Punkin's father's mother.

Punkin's mother was the cookie cutter from which Punkin was made. They looked like twins except Punkin's mother was white. Punkin's father had been from the Caribbean and long since departed the domestic scene. This left Punkin a gorgeous *café au lait* version of her mom.

Before long the other dinner guests began to arrive. Larry Klein and his wife had been invited. A couple now living in New York who had met and fallen in love in Australia rocked up a short time later. Punkin and I had known them in Oz and the three of them had been in touch since she returned to Gotham. He was African American from the Midwest; she was half Aussie and half Polynesian. Another breathtakingly stunning, female, African American friend of Punkin's was part of her extended family. A gay friend whom Punkin had worked with in a restaurant in the Village years before showed up. A gathering at Punkin's wouldn't have been complete without at least one gay man. She had some terrific friends in Australia that rivaled her in both the kitchen and on the Scrabble board. Punkin's brother and Latino wife rounded out the party.

"You must be pretty special, honey," Grandma said to me. "This girl hardly let me in the kitchen."

"Yeah. That'll be the day," Punkin laughed.

Between mouthfuls of heart-stoppingly delicious food, and because of the makeup of the crowd, a lively discussion of race in America ensued.

"See, people don't understand that about Australia," Punkin said. "Everyone here either thinks that kangaroos are hopping around in downtown Adelaide or that the whole country is just an extension of the United States. A kind of southwestern suburb of California. They think that the same worldview exists there. I've told any number of my African American friends here that they should spend one day in Australia to feel what real freedom from prejudice is. People don't give a crap if you're black…"

"As long as you're not aboriginal…" I added.

"As long as you're not aboriginal," she conceded. "But even that's changing."

"True," I agreed.

She continued. "But you can wear a Taliban burqa, be a blue-black African, a Greek, a Turk, Lebanese, whatever, and as long as you don't break the law, nobody gives a shit. For me, it was an advantage to be my color. I stood out."

"Even I am exotic in Oz," I added. "I walk around here expecting people to notice my difference and it's like, 'Yeah. Right.' Nobody cares when I open my mouth and an American accent comes out."

It was true. I had become accustomed to being noticed. Even on this trip, everywhere else I went I stood out, either as a Yank or an Aussie, or both. Here, with the exception of having no problem with immigration, there didn't seem to be a personal advantage to being American. Australia has no US Constitution or Bill of Rights, per se, but the forms of government were similar, a kind of hybrid between the British and American systems.

The biggest difference is race. In America it was still a problem to be dealt with. In Australia, it didn't have the same resonance. Slavery made the difference.

Punkin had conceded the pumpkin and pecan pie making to Grandma. The only thing missing from the meal was the traditional NFL game with the Detroit Lions. Everything else was perfect.

I made a modest attempt at a toast, thanking Grandma, Punkin and her mother for such a special treat, loosened my belt and had another look at the white meat.

CHAPTER FORTY

I was to spend one more night with Larry and Barbara Klein. As a thank you, I took them to a Thai restaurant in the city that they especially liked. Then we went to see a new musical that they had freebees for. The Thai restaurant was excellent. The musical was so eminently forgettable that all you could do was scratch your head when it was over and wonder why anyone bothered. Hence, I suppose, the freebees. My comment at the time was that it was a bore, illiterate and un-musical. Enough said. I can't even dignify it by stating the name.

My new digs were to be on the upper Westside, with the couple that had come to Punkin's for Thanksgiving dinner. A little background. He was African American from the Great Plains. By now the bloodlines were so mixed that to call him African American was for convenience and not for accuracy. He had Comanche, African, Portuguese, French and Swedish in his recent ancestry and only god knows what farther back. It's probably fair to say that with the exceptions of Australian Aboriginals, some Pacific islanders, African tribesmen and Eskimos, very few people on the planet have pure bloodlines anymore anyhow. All right, maybe it's not fair to say but it's clear that the human race is pretty much mongrelized, one way and another. But I digress. Her background was half Polynesian, originally the Cook Islands. The other half was pure, fair dinkum Aussie.

They met when he was on tour with a show in Australia. He was in his forties, she in her late teens. In fact, nineteen. More April and October than May and September. I was one of his groomsmen when they got married, more because I was a Yank in Oz than because we were such close friends. I was a default choice. Nevertheless, their nuptials placed us in a relationship and so when I was going to be coming through New York, they insisted that I spend a couple of nights with them. I accepted for two reasons. The first was because I didn't want to burden the Kleins any more than necessary. The second was because I would be in Manhattan and not have to get there by bus.

When I lived in New York, their address would have been in the heart of Harlem, 114th Street. Now it was just a part of the extended, gentrified upper Westside. It was one of the things I didn't like about this newest version of Manhattan. To me, it had lost a lot of its charm and heritage. I remember one Saturday afternoon when I ventured into this part of town for the first time for a tryst with an African American woman I knew from the television station. Despite the fact that it was broad daylight, I moved cautiously along these unfamiliar streets. I wasn't so much expecting trouble as I was watching out for it. And it wasn't because I was in any danger. It had to do with the exotic nature of the place. It was like being in a foreign country. Eventually I was as comfortable in Harlem – the real Harlem, not this gentrified, yuppie version – as I was anywhere else in New York. But on that first safari I moved with less confidence. Now, every other shop on the avenues was a Gap or a Kinko's or an organic food store or any of a thousand other brand spanking new franchises.

It was a beautiful, sunny afternoon when I arrived at my new digs. Bruno, as I called him, was at home. Blanche was at work. Unlike Larry Klein, who worked at home, Bruno tended to laze around the house when he wasn't either working for a caterer or singing, mostly the former. Bruno liked his sports and if there was any athletic contest being contested anywhere on the globe, Bruno was likely to be watching it with expert concentration. It didn't matter if it was Rugby, badminton or a bunch of Norwegian guys throwing telephone poles around. Bruno was on the case.

With each new stop along my journey, I got rid of another gift. The load kept getting lighter and was now very manageable. For that reason, Bruno didn't really have to budge from his reclining chair after he buzzed me in.

"Just put your stuff down anywhere," he said, refocusing on the netball game from Christchurch that filled his enormous television screen. "Blanche is working for the caterer this afternoon. She'll be home in time to make supper."

I found a spot to deposit my bags in the hallway. There wasn't really any room but a couple of bags weren't going to add much to the existing chaos.

"I'll make us a cup of coffee in a minute," Bruno said. "It's almost halftime."

"That's OK," I said. "I'm going to take a walk. It's a nice day."

And with that, I walked around the neighborhood. It was mostly brownstones that were either in need of or recently renovated. It was the New York story: reclaiming a part of the city that had been neglected. The problem was that these days, there was less and less to reclaim. People were forced out of their homes and neighborhoods by landlords or new owners that could hear the distant sound of a cash register ringing.

The same had been true years before when I left the Eastside for an adventure in the West, as it were. When I bought a co-op in the west seventies, people used to jokingly say, "The only time I go to the Westside is take the Circle Line cruise." There were abandoned brownstones, entire brownstones, for sale by the city for as little as $25,000. Those days were long gone. That's when they were begging people to come to Manhattan. Before I bought the co-op, I had an apartment on East 79th Street that gave me three months free rent on a two year lease. These places that I was looking at now were not abandoned or empty. They had been the homes of poor people, scratching out an existence in a part of New York only they cared about or knew.

When I got back to the apartment, Blanche had just arrived. She was pretty well exhausted. Bruno hadn't moved from his recliner. A soccer game between Arsenal and West Ham was on the big screen.

"I'll make something to eat in a little bit," she said, cheerily. "My feet are killing me. I'm gonna sit down for a minute."

"I've got a better idea," I said. "Why don't we go out for dinner, someplace nearby. Maybe go to a movie. My treat."

"What do you think, honey?" she asked.

"Yeah. Whatever. Let's go to that organic place. Chris'd like that," Bruno grunted.

And so we did.

When we got back, we had a cup of tea and chatted into the wee hours. Neither of them had to work the next day until late afternoon. When it came time for bed, Blanche brought out an air mattress. Bruno pushed the furniture around to make room on the floor in front of what had at one time been a fireplace.

"You'll sleep like a baby on this," he said. "It's the most comfortable air mattress I've ever slept on."

His words were ringing in my ears when, at about 3 a.m., I awoke with a thin layer of plastic the only thing elevating me from the hardwood floor. Little by little, the most comfortable air mattress in the world had deflated until bones and board were making much too serious contact. I couldn't find any part of me that liked the feel of that floor, however often I tried. I finally obtained some semblance of consciousness. In my stupor, I climbed into Bruno's recliner, wrapped myself in a blanket and attempted to sleep. But by then the immediate city sounds serenaded me wide awake. Empty trucks banged and clattered and echoed every pothole and bump as they sped up the street. A drunken argument between two people in some kind of loving relationship, which was taking place on the sidewalk just outside the window, suggested that murder may not be far behind, her voice being far more threatening than his. Someone in a nearby apartment must have been having difficulty hearing their television. On the other hand, I was having no trouble at all hearing it. And the final straw was what could only have been the entire chorus of tap-dancing Rockettes in full rehearsal on the floor above me.

I found myself longing for the screech of a tree hyrax and footsteps on gravel.

I heard Blanche's voice ask, "How'd you sleep?" She said it as she came out of the bedroom and before she saw me wadded up in the recliner. "Oh…" She looked down at the airless mattress and started laughing.

"Very funny."

Bruno staggered out of the bedroom. "What's so funny?" He looked at the mattress lying limp on the floor. "I'll be a son-of-a-bitch. It did it again."

We had some toast and coffee together, then I decided to have a Sunday afternoon stroll down through Central Park. There were glimpses of the New York I knew and loved along the way. I passed a card table that had been set up on the sidewalk with four Latino men sitting around it, smoking cigarettes, sipping from cans wrapped in brown paper bags, playing dominoes.

As I entered the park, I saw old and new Westsiders intermingling. A young couple was sitting on a bench watching their kids with iPods plugged into their ears. A professorial looking gentleman was sitting on a bench reading Kafka, his legs intertwined like a pretzel. An older, blue-haired woman was clopping along inside her walking frame, smiling pleasantly at anyone who looked her way. Men were playing checkers on concrete tables. A soccer game was in progress in one open area. A softball game was going on on another of the many fields. The leaves on some of the trees had started to turn. Soon it would look like that shot from *When Harry Met Sally*. As I walked along, I heard French, German, Chinese, Italian and several languages that I didn't recognize at all. There were people everywhere doing their weekend thing on a sunny afternoon. I was happy to be in New York. I felt at home again for a brief moment. How many times had I come to the park on a Sunday afternoon for a touch football game or to shoot hoops or a bike ride or just a stroll?

Without a specific destination, I meandered all the way downtown through Central Park. Across the street, on 59th Street, I saw a restaurant I'd never seen or heard of before: Mickey Mantle's. Out of respect I had to stop in for something. He had provided me with thrill after thrill during his years as a New York Yankee.

The young waitress came up to my table.

"You have any birthday specials?" I asked facetiously.

"Hey," she answered, "if we did that, everyone would come in and say it's their birthday."

"No," I said, "today is Mickey Mantle's birthday." It really was.

There was a long beat before she said, "He's dead."

"Well, it would have been his birthday," I said.

She thought for a moment and smiled. "Well, we ought to all have a shot of whiskey. He'd like that." She was probably right.

But instead I had coffee and a danish. On the check, she had handwritten, "I Love New York, God Bless America and Happy Birthday, Mickey."

I moseyed on over to Sixth Avenue. Here was definitely something that had developed in the years since I'd lived in New York. The street was blocked off from 57th Street down to 42nd. Hundreds of booths lined the street with virtually anything you could imagine for sale. A lot of the stuff was for tourists. But one place sold furniture and another had authentic African artifacts, many like the ones I'd seen at the Masaai Market. It all had a kind of community feel to it, like a big block party.

As long as I was this far downtown, I decided to walk the rest of the way to Washington Square Park where I was to meet Punkin. I walked along 42nd Street to 5th Avenue. When I got to the corner, it was like running into an old friend, the New York Public Library. The lions in front made me stop and think how important lions appear to be as a symbol. There are lions everywhere. At Nelson's monument. On the MGM logo. In front of SAE fraternity houses. The Detroit football team. The Masaai prove their manhood by fighting a lion on the plains of Africa. On this trip, it seemed like I couldn't turn around without running into a lion.

Being in front of the library made me think about the days I'd spent in there researching a project that I thought would make me a millionaire. It required that I look through copies of old newspapers. It was a tedious process and before long I got distracted by other information on the page. One front page blended into the next so that over fifty to a hundred years, all you saw were reports of corruption, natural disasters, war, famine, untimely deaths and various other disasters. You could substitute one for another without being concerned what the date was. The headlines were all the same. It made me stop reading papers for a long time. I concluded that if the news had any effect on me, I'd know about it. If it didn't, I wouldn't be missing anything by not knowing the specifics of someone else's misfortune. Somehow the world would continue to turn and life would go on without my assistance, observation or direct input. *"Art and music will thrive without you. Somehow Keats will survive without you…"*

There was a demonstration in progress on 5th Avenue. I stopped to see what it was about. It may not be very generous of me but I was actually pleased to see that the object of the protest was The Ubiquitous One, Coca Cola. The Global Access Project and Act Up were passing out flyers with a headline that read, "Coke to workers with AIDS in Africa: Drop Dead." It went on to say that because Coke was one of the largest private sector employers in Africa (about 100,000 people), it had an obligation to look after their health needs. According to the protesters, it wasn't. But that could have been because, according to the flyer, Coca Cola only made a mere $620 million in Africa the year before and $20 billion worldwide.

Like lions, Coke kept popping up. And to think it all started with legalized cocaine at a soda fountain in Georgia.

I got to Washington Square Park a little early and saw a huge crowd watching an unbelievably acrobatic performance by a group of young break-dancers. They whirled and spun and balanced and flopped around as if suspended on wire. It was amazing. This act would have been a crowd pleaser anywhere. If it came to Oz, it could demand top dollar. Yet here they were busking for a buck in a New York park.

The chess players were at their assigned stations going at it. One game in particular had attracted a larger crowd. A young Asian boy and an older, Eastern European-looking man were in the final stages of an aggressive match, moving their pieces with lightning speed and whacking the timer as if to punish it. Before the match concluded, Punkin tapped me on the shoulder.

We went over to the East Village and walked around for a while, stopping in to say hello to one of her friends, then making our way to one of her favorite bistros, The Café Loup.

"I didn't think you'd ever want to eat again after Thanksgiving," she said.

"Me too," I said. "What's this place known for?"

"You've got to try the clams."

After dinner, Punkin and I said our goodbyes, promising to keep in touch. I'd done enough walking for the day so I hopped a train uptown. This day made me savor being in New York again. While staying in New Jersey, I felt like a tourist. Now, riding the subway after dark, I felt at home again. I knew I wasn't at home anymore but it was fun fooling myself for a little while.

Bruno and Blanche were at home when I walked in. To no one's great surprise, Bruno was in his recliner watching sports news. Blanche was sitting at the little desk in the hallway writing checks. Both were exhausted and it wasn't long before everyone hit the sack.

In this instance, mine was three sofa cushions lined up in front of the would-be fireplace with a sheet holding them together. The world's greatest air mattress was in the garbage can.

I began thinking about leaving New York. Staying without purpose was like treading water. I couldn't fool myself into thinking I belonged there anymore. I decided to spend the day walking around places I hadn't seen in years. I took a train down to Spring Street. I walked east to Soho, which was only beginning to be reclaimed when I left New York for Hollywood. It had every feeling of New York but nothing about it was familiar to me. My wanderings took me to Canal Street, then back up to Mott, up through Chinatown, Little Italy to Houston.

It was impossible to be in this area of Manhattan and not have songs spinning through my head. "*And tell me what street compares to Mott Street in July…*" It also reminded me of another of our famous dinners.

Brig, Larry Klein, Goldy and I decided to have dinner at one of the famous restaurants in Little Italy. And for kicks, idiots that we were, we decided to dress the part. So we rock up to the restaurant wearing dark suits with dark shirts and white ties and hunching our shoulders in a bad Jimmy Cagney imitation. Brig had made the reservation under the name of Noodles Boyardee. We thought this was a riot. The maitre d' wasn't laughing. He showed us to a table pretty much away from everyone else. I looked around the room. It looked a set for a Coppola movie. All that was missing were the camera and lights. Against the wall was a table with three men – Italian looking men – engaged in serious conversation. At tables on either side of them were two guys each who did nothing but look around the room, no doubt prepared for trouble. This place had the reputation it had because there had been a Mafia hit here a couple of years back. The smartass, college boys thought it was a joke. No one else did.

When I got to Broadway I decided to walk uptown for a while. It always impressed me that I could keep walking to Albany on this street if I wanted to. Broadway is like the Serengeti Plains of New York. It goes on forever. I made my way through to Union Square, Madison Square, where the original Garden had been, Herald Square, where I'd attended a Black Playwrights Workshop, Times Square and past Columbus Circle to a restaurant named Josie's for a vegeburger. Punkin had recommended it. I still had time to kill so I found a movie house and spent a couple of hours there. It was really a nothing movie but the day was a nothing day, making it all a push.

On my penultimate day in The Big Apple, I had social engagements lined up with people whom I'd been friendly with when I lived there. I met an old flame, Brenda, who, it turns out, was also a friend of Bruno's. Hence our hooking up. We had had a very brief fling once upon a time. But our flirtation lasted a lot longer prior to the actual consummation.

We met when I was producing a show at the television station. She was a member of a choral group that was featured on the program, the only African American member. We "noticed" each other from the beginning and the flirtation began. We saw each other for a while, going to a movie, going out to dinner, going here, going there but not "going there," as it were.

It was with Brenda that I experienced my first moment of reverse racism. We were on a subway on our way to Queens. The car was mostly filled with other African Americans. Brenda and I were holding hands and occasionally exchanging a quick kiss. At one point I looked away from her at a pair of eyes that were drilling us. They belonged to an African American woman in her thirties or forties. She had a look of terminal disgust on her face as she looked from one of us to the other.

Brenda saw her too. "Don't pay her any mind," she told me. "She doesn't like that I'm with a white boy. It's her problem, not ours."

Finally, one night, I saw her up to her apartment, prepared for another "No we shouldn't" or "I can't" or "I think we should wait." Instead, when I made my customary move, she said, "Oh, hell. I don't know what I'm saving it for." And she didn't save it any longer. Being the natural born dog that I am, the challenge had been met and the movies and dinners grew scarcer until we naturally drifted apart. No animosity. Just different directions.

I met Brenda at Fiorello's for lunch. She was now happily married to a man with a considerable reputation in the music business. Her face hadn't changed at all. I always thought it should have been on a Nubian coin. Her complexion was a medium brown. Her eyes slightly almond shaped, just a hint of a Roman nose, full, rich lips. She was dressed casually but elegantly. She would have been very much at home in Hampstead.

She kissed me hello warmly, nothing perfunctory, as though she wanted to remind me of what I had missed. If this was her objective, she succeeded. *La donna* wasn't the only one who is *mobile*. My fickleness was beginning to worry even me. We spent the entire lunch remembering the good stuff and updating the new stuff.

"How do you like living in Australia?" she asked.

I went through my standard reply. After so many inquiries, I began to wonder if people were asking out of interest or if they were wondering when I was going to come to my senses and return to the USA.

"I'd like to see it." Those were the words she spoke. But the words I heard were, "I'd like to come there and pick up where we left off."

"You should." I answered my version of her words.

We lingered for as long as possible, then Brenda said she had to get home to her husband. This reminded me that it was no longer then. It was now.

She pressed her soft body against me as we said our goodbyes and kissed me sweetly. Nothing more was said.

That night I was to meet an Army buddy and his wife for dinner, one of the few I kept in touch with. We went to a Greek restaurant around the corner from Carnegie Hall on Seventh Avenue. I had never even noticed it when I lived there. It was one of their favorite spots. The restaurant was gigantic. Not noticing it was like not noticing the Rockefeller Center skating rink.

Again, it was catch up time intermixed with nostalgia. I had known Barry's first wife better than this one. But it was clear that Naomi made him much happier than her predecessor had.

"You boys must have been real scoundrels back then," she observed.

"I wasn't so much. But Chris has always been a scoundrel," Barry said.

"It's true. I wish it weren't. But it is. Barry was a goody-goody. I'll bet you don't remember this," I said. "When we were in the army, I had been hounding my roommate to take me to a Jewish service at the post chapel. He kept procrastinating and I kept hounding. This went on for a few months. Then he finally gave in. Yom Kippur was coming up and he said he'd take me then.

"So we arrive at the chapel and Barry is standing out front with a couple of other guys, ready to go inside. He sees us and comes over. Does he say, "Glad to see you? No. Does he say, *Shabat Shalom?* No. Does he say, *Shana Tova?* No. He looks directly at me and says, 'Very nice. The only time you come to services is on the high Holy Days? You should be ashamed!'"

"My roommate was the Jew. He didn't say a word to him. Just me, the *goyim.*"

"Is that true?" Naomi asked.

"I'm afraid it is," Barry laughed.

More "war" stories followed before we called it a night and exchanged email addresses.

When I got back to 114th Street, Bruno and Blanche were cuddled together on the couch watching a movie on the big screen.

"Brenda called," Bruno said. "She wants you to call her back tonight. The number's on the desk."

I called. She answered the phone.

"I just want to tell you that it was wonderful seeing you today," she said.

"Same here," I answered.

"And…" she paused a moment. "And that now that we have rebonded, I want you to know that you will be in my life forever."

I didn't know how to respond to that. It seemed so profound, so uniquely expressed, not to mention so off the wall. I couldn't fathom how I could possibly have been so seemingly important to her, particularly since so much time had passed, during most of which she had been married. Wouldn't it be wonderful to know what this magical substance is? I'd like to bottle it and get rich. I'd like to have asked what she meant. Instead, I just said, "Thanks. That's really very sweet. Thanks."

CHAPTER FORTY ONE

I woke up an hour before the alarm was to go off. This next leg of the journey was a question mark. I was going to stop in my hometown in Ohio and pay a surprise visit to my family, at least that portion of it that was still alive and speaking to me.

When my mother was alive, it was something I often did. I loved just showing up. From right after college, with the exception of one year, I was always somewhere else, either St. Louis, New York, in the Army or Hollywood. Now I was in Australia. Also when my mother was alive, no matter where I lived, I would receive phone calls from her. She and I had always been in the habit of calling every couple of weeks; one time I'd call, the next time, she'd call. On those occasions, I'd talk to whoever else was there too. Now if I didn't call, there was no contact. I had decided not to call or let them know I was coming this time.

At the airport, I was once again in that romantic atmosphere. Every airport looks essentially the same. It's only the announced destinations that change. Johannesburg becomes Jacksonville; London becomes Los Angeles; Dubai becomes Detroit. And the people at this airport looked like most of the people I'd seen in the last couple of airports. The difference was that I didn't need subtitles.

I had arrived in ample time to find my gate, have a coffee and danish and open my book. I had already traveled around much of the earth but I was most apprehensive about this trip.

I grew up believing that family was the most important relationship one could have, blood thicker than water, the only people you could trust, etc. etc. etc. I have since decided that dysfunctional family is redundant. My mother, who never used any kind of profanity, ever, once said, "I'll kiss anyone's ass to keep this family together." I was shocked at the way she articulated it, but not by its sentiment. When she made that statement, there was no reason to think she'd ever have to kiss anyone's ass because, perhaps due to her resolve, there was no disharmony of any kind. Oh, sure there was the usual stuff that any family dynamic experiences. My brother's wife liked to gossip. My uncle's wife never stopped talking. But we were always together for Christmas, New Year's and Thanksgiving and often at other times as well. We all got along, teased and laughed, played cards and ate, watched sports and played games. We were an extended, cohesive, normal, happy family, just like on tv.

When I got my first divorce, I felt as though I'd let everyone down. Both my brother and sister married people who had been married before but only my uncle had been divorced. He was considered the black sheep of the family. I thought he was the coolest of them all but the divorce tarnished his image for some of the others. When I followed his example, in my own mind, I had added a blemish to the family's reputation. My mother was quick to disabuse me of this notion.

Now that she was gone, through circumstances totally out of my control, I was responsible for a gigantic rending. That's not true. I wasn't responsible. I was a scapegoat.

In brief, here's what happened, as best I can piece it together. My niece was responsible for a traffic accident that took her husband's aunt's life. She was traumatized and went for psychological counseling. That accident may also have been responsible for the problems she was having with her marriage. For whatever reasons, she needed help sorting things out.

These events were unfolding unbeknownst to me since I was always somewhere else and only around for the occasional holiday or other visit. I knew about and responded to the accident but that was all. At first, well into my niece's counseling, I was given excuses why she, her husband and children weren't around when I showed up. It usually had something to do with their church of choice, The Church of Jesus Christ of Latter Day Saints. I accepted the excuses without question, only sorry that I hadn't seen them. I had always had an active, loving relationship with my nephews and niece when they were kids and now with their kids. Plus, it was the only family I had and according to my mother's admonition, my closest relationship.

It was my habit to call other members of the family from time to time just to keep in touch, even when my mother and I spoke regularly. One day I called my niece's house and her young daughter answered. It was the first conversation I'd had with her family in a long time. The girl and I caught up on what she was doing in school and I learned that she was studying the trombone and singing. I asked if she'd like to have the sheet music for some songs I had and she answered with an enthusiastic yes.

A short time later, I received a letter from my niece. I hadn't heard from her directly for a long time. We had, at one time, exchanged letters on a more or less regular basis.

I was living in Hollywood at the time. I opened the letter immediately, saw the first sentence and stopped dead in my tracks. It read: "Don't ever contact me or anyone else in my family again." The letter went on to accuse me of having molested her as a child and causing her no end of trauma and grief.

As soon as I got home from the post office, I called my brother.

"I just got a letter from your daughter," I said, my voice shaking. "She said that I molested her when she was a little girl."

"I know," he answered.

"You know?"

"Yeah. We've known about it for a while now," he said.

"You've known about this? And you didn't say anything to me? Do you believe her? How long have you known?"

"She told us about three or four years ago but we didn't believe her. You weren't even here when she said it happened."

"And you've never said anything to me about it? What the fuck is the matter with you?"

"I know. I should have said something. That damned psychologist put it in her head," he said, absolving himself of any responsibility.

"Does anyone in the family think I could even do something like that?"

"We talked about it. But like I said, we figured it out and you weren't even here. I told her not to say anything to her grandmother about it. It would break Mom's heart," he said as if he had taken charge of the situation.

"Mom doesn't know anything about this?"

"No. We didn't think she should know about it."

That was the beginning of the cleft in the family's stiff upper lip. I made one attempt to end the madness when Mom died. I was in Australia and couldn't make it back for her funeral. Instead, I wrote a letter to my niece which contained a poem I had written for my mother, asking her to read it on my behalf at the funeral and end this insanity. Her husband wrote me the most vile, insulting, treacherous letter in response that I've ever had the unpleasant misfortune to receive. It accused me of using my own mother's death as a way of "weaseling" my way back into the family, as if it were his family and I wasn't a part of it.

Through this my brother maintained that he and his wife never believed it, particularly after they did the math and realized I wasn't even there. Yet they never lifted a finger to do anything about it. My sister, who had always been loyal to me, was going to be complicit in getting the addresses of our niece's children so I could write to them and, at least, let them have a look at the truth. But my brother-in-law didn't think she should get involved. No one made any attempt to un-poison the minds of those children toward me. The only person who would have, Mom, was now dead, never knowing that this horror had taken place. She'd have straightened it out in a heartbeat if she were still alive.

I had asked my brother to tell his grandchildren the truth and he promised that he would. He never did.

This was the background when I arrived at the nearest airport and caught a taxi to my sister's house.

265

CHAPTER FORTY TWO

When the taxi rolled down her driveway, my sister came out of the house. The taxi didn't have the usual markings so all she could see was a Black man driving toward her in an unfamiliar car. The look on her face was defensive and suspicions. But when I got out, she burst into a smile and approached me for a hug and a kiss.

The first thing that I noticed was how much she had aged. Since I had last seen her, eight years before, our mother had died. My mother and sister never lived apart. When my sister got married, she and her husband lived in my mother's house. When they built their own home, my brother and brother-in-law insisted that Mom live with them.

I took my bags up to the spare bedroom, withdrew a carved, African animal and returned to the kitchen, where Sis was busy cooking. Her house was situated in the middle of a woods. In this part of America the trees were farther along in their explosion of reds, rusts, golds and browns. The spectacle was brilliant. It was familiar to me, just as walking down 5th Avenue had been, but no longer a part of my world. I was both completely comfortable and utterly displaced.

I poured myself a cup of coffee from her never-empty coffee pot and sat down at the kitchen table. I told her where I'd been and what I'd been doing for the last few weeks. My travels were never a big surprise to my family. I had already seen much of the globe one way or another. My sister took it all in without comment. After the initial shock of seeing me in her driveway, she took my presence very much for granted. I always had the feeling, when I returned to my hometown for any length of time, that nothing had changed, that I had accomplished nothing, that they had all indulged my absences and once I'd returned, accepted everything as back to normal. Statistically, I had spent a mere fraction of my life there. Yet, they always assumed that this was my home and everything else an aberration.

"Can I use your car?" I asked.

"It's in the garage," my sister said. "Keys are in the front hall on that little table."

I started for the front hall. "Don't tell anyone I'm here," I said

"OK. You going to have supper with us?" she shouted after me.

"I'm not sure," I called back.

"Doesn't matter," she said. "There'll be leftovers if you want 'em."

I drove to my brother's house. His wife answered the door. "Oh, for heaven's sakes. Look who's here."

"Who is it?" I heard my brother's voice ask.

"It's your brother," she replied.

"What the hell are you talking about?" he asked with a hint of impatience. Then he came into frame, as it were. I had seen him five years before in Greece, which our parents had always called their place of origin. I had convinced him to join me there to visit where the folks were born. At that time, he was having trouble with one of his legs but was still fairly mobile.

As he approached the doorway now, he looked frail, almost feeble. He walked without aid but slowly and cautiously, as if he could lose his balance or stumble at any time.

Christ, I thought, *he's an old man.*

This was my big brother, the guy whose approval I had always sought, whose comradeship I quested for. He was the measure by which I judged my youth. This was the guy who never refused me the use of his car and never complained when I brought it back to him with dented fenders. This was the guy who took me to my first wrestling match and my first nightclub. This was the guy that I always looked up to. And this was also the guy who, when he got caught with his hand in the cookie jar, and all the women in the family chastised him, called me in New York and talked for hours because mine was the only sympathetic ear. What stood before me now was a mere shell of the idol I once knew.

I stepped inside the door and gave my sister-in-law a hug and a kiss. My brother extended his hand.

"Jesus Christ," I said, "didn't you learn anything in Greece?" I grabbed him, nearly pulling him off balance, kissed him on both his cheeks and held him in my arms. He felt as frail as he looked. He had been diagnosed with diabetes a while back and lost a substantial amount of weight. Too much, I thought.

"You want a cup of coffee?" my sister-in-law asked.

"No, thanks. Just had one at Sis' place. I want to go out and see Kleeze," I said. This was their younger son's family nickname. I looked at my brother. "Why don't you come with me?"

"Yeah. I don't care," he answered. It was his standard answer to virtually any question and had been for a very long time, as if indifference was his default position.

He struggled making it down the two steps from his little front porch but angrily refused my assistance.

We had only driven a block or two when I forced myself to bite the bullet. "You know, you promised me that you would tell your daughter's kids that no one believed I did that."

He stared ahead, through the windshield, at nothing.

"Did you?" I knew he hadn't but I wanted him to acknowledge it to me in person, face to face.

His eyes teared up. He still didn't look at me. He reached his hand toward my leg and rested it there. "I'm sorry," he said. "I thought it would all blow over. I should have done it. But I didn't." And he repeated, "I'm sorry." Then, unsolicited, he said, "I promise I will."

"Don't promise me unless you are going to do it. I'd rather just leave it than have you promise me and not go through with it again."

"No. I promise. I will."

I had been prepared to do battle, to confront him with all his shortcomings, to admonish him for his spinelessness. Most of my motivation for stopping in Smalltown on this trip revolved around this moment. Now that it had arrived and I saw how defenseless he was, I had no stomach for it. I realized that there was no point in trying to make someone do something of which they were constitutionally incapable. He knew. I knew. Nothing more needed to be discussed.

"OK. Let's forget about it," I finally said.

Kleeze had just arrived home from work when we pulled into his driveway. He saw his aunt's car and his father get out of it but it wasn't until he saw me that he broke into a huge smile and came running.

"Unc!" He yelled back to the house. "Hey, Unc's here!"

Kleeze and I never had any problem showing our affection. In this regard, the acorn had fallen miles from the oak tree. We grabbed each other and hugged each other and slapped each other on the back with smiles and laughter.

Kleeze had always been the closer of the boys with me. His older brother and I had had some good times in the past. But his second marriage put him on a different course in life and his new wife had less tolerance for me than she had for upward mobility. His heart was no different but it seemed that he had inherited his father's backbone.

Kleeze, on the other hand, had always been salt of the earth. He wasn't formally educated beyond high school and he used Smalltown vernacular when expressing himself. But he was shrewd and honorable in business and in life. He married an equally solid woman and they had two great kids.

Back in the day, when the family would go to my uncle's lakefront house for a holiday, the kids always slept upstairs in what was actually a big, open bar. I always woke up early when we were at The Lake and used to tiptoe up the stairs to where the kids were sprawled out on mattresses. I'd bend down close to Kleeze's ear.

"Kleeze," I'd whisper.

His eight-year-old eyes would snap open. "Yeah?"

"Want to go fishing?"

"Yeah."

He'd pull on a pair of shorts, a tee shirt and take his shoes in hand. In five minutes we'd be in a rowboat on The Lake with our lines in the water.

Now, not only was Kleeze a champion fisherman, he had put a pond on his property and had it stocked with his catches. He could go out the back door and go fishing any time he wanted.

When I was visiting my hometown one summer, Kleeze and I hauled his boat to a private lake where he was a member. He had bought a small lot never intending to build on it, but knew this was a great place for fishing and only people who had property there could use it. We had to get up before dawn in order to be there when the fish woke up. It was a Saturday. We made a compulsory stop at the bait store where we picked up some crickets and night crawlers, and which conveniently had hot coffee and fresh doughnuts also available.

Like all fishermen, Kleeze had an instinct about where they'd be. He knew this lake was full of bluegills and bass. We slid the boat off the trailer and into the water and jumped aboard.

"Let's see if we can find us some bass," he said confidently, and aimed us toward a spot where his gut told him the fish would be. Once we got there, he moved to a seat in the bow of the boat that allowed him to control it from there while trolling. "I ain't been here before but if I was a bass, I think I'd be right over there along the bank near them roots."

He picked up his rod and plopped a perfect strike about fifty or sixty feet away into an area no more than a foot in diameter. Six inches either way and he'd have snagged. "Why don't you give 'er a try over there, Unc" he said, pointing off to the left. He had wisely chosen a much more open area for me to apply my limited skills with a casting rod.

It seemed that no sooner had his lure entered that circle of opportunity than a bass hit it. He eased the hook into the fish's lip and began reeling it in.

"Feels like a pretty good one," Kleeze said with a smile on his face. We hadn't been there 50 seconds and he had already bagged a nice, two to three pound bass.

Before the sun got very high in the sky, he caught another two and even I caught one.

"These'll be real good eatin'." He dropped his last bass into the live box. "Sun's probably come up too much for more bass. What do you say we get us some bluegills?"

Again he knew where to go. As we approached his chosen spot, he saw some kids in a smaller boat headed in that direction. "Like hell you will," he said, and accelerated so that we coasted into the spot ahead of them.

"You sure they were headed for this spot?" I asked.

"Maybe they was and maybe they wasn't. I didn't care to find out," he answered. "Drop your anchor, Unc, and let's catch us some bluegills."

What follows is a fish story. Except this one isn't about the one that got away. Hardly. There must have been some very sexy bluegill-ettes down there or maybe even a bluegill whorehouse, something that definitely attracted some big, old boys.

We got settled, baited the hooks with cricket and tossed them in toward the bank. In an instant, Kleeze said, "Hell, I think I got one already."

"Me too," I said.

We tossed our catches into the live box and re-cast.

"Son-of-a-bitch!" I said. "Got another one!"

"Me too," Kleeze laughed.

We could hardly get a fish off the hook and the bait back in the water before another big bluegill was in line for a taste of cricket. We laughed our asses off as we hauled in one after another of these bluegill monsters. It was a fisherman's dream come true

When we went fishing at The Lake, we often caught little bitty bluegills, maybe three or four inches long that we threw back in. But on this day, we never saw any less than eight or nine inches long. And all of them were big and fat and healthy. The live box was filled and they were still biting.

"I'm beginnin' to feel uneasy," Kleeze said. "I've never caught so many bluegills in my life. We sure don't want to fish this place out. Gotta leave some for next time."

As we headed back to where the car was parked, I took a moment to look around at my naturally beautiful surroundings. The lake was large enough that all shorelines were distant from its center. From where we were, you could see the trees that were in pockets around the lake. All sizes and shapes of lush, leafy, green trees. There were evergreens, oaks, maples, all the many indigenous varieties that I'd grown up with and taken for granted. Beautiful deciduous trees that were beginning to burst into crimson and pink and brown and gold.

We stopped in the south end of town, where most of the African American families lived. "I gotta give some of these to my buddy, Roscoe. Come on up with me."

Kleeze didn't bother knocking on the front door. He just opened it and yelled in. "Hey, Roscoe. You here?"

A gray-haired man in his sixties came into view. "Hey, Kleeze. Whatchu doin' here? Been fishin'?"

"You ain't gonna believe this," Kleeze laughed. "We caught us about — well, let's put it this way, we stopped countin' at around seventy."

"Bullshit!" Roscoe laughed too. "Whooey! Looks like I'm gonna have me some fish for supper tonight."

Kleeze dumped a quantity of bluegills and two of the bass into Roscoe's kitchen sink.

"Who's this stranger, Kleeze?"

"Don't you know my uncle?"

"Don't believe I do. You from around here?" Roscoe asked.

"Used to be," I said. "I just come back now and then to go fishing with Kleeze."

"Me and Roscoe usually go fishin' down by the river," Kleeze said.

"Got us some mighty fine catfish. I likes me some catfish. If it's cooked right, it's damn near better 'n bass."

You'd think that was the end of this fish story. But it isn't. That night, after we munched our fried bluegill dinner like popcorn, we went to see my brother. When you have that kind of day fishing, you'd like to put an article in the *New York Times*. But we had to settle for just bragging to everyone we knew that ever got a fishing line wet.

The result was that my brother insisted on getting in on the action. So next day we took him and Kleeze's young son, Chris, out with us. We went to the same spot but didn't have to beat anyone to it this time.

The identical thing happened. The only complication was that in his zeal, my brother continually got his line tangled and needed rescue. And one other time, when he jerked his line a little too quickly and forcefully, he nearly hooked me in the cheek. Fortunately for me, the hook was facing away when it hit me. When I brought it to his attention, with a certain amount of in-your-face brotherly love, his reaction was predictable. He said, "The hell with it" and stopped fishing, preferring instead to sulk.

Little Chris caught his share, chip off the old block that he was. My brother caught the fewest owing to the fact that he quit fishing. This made him the butt of my jokes for the rest of the day. Kleeze landed the most, as usual. And we ended up with another haul nearly equaling our previous record. Now *that's* a fish story! And it's absolutely true.

CHAPTER FORTY THREE

The next morning, when I woke up, it took me a few seconds to once again adjust to my new surroundings. I was in a proper bed, a definite improvement over either the greatest air mattress in the world or sofa cushions held together with a sheet. I was also upstairs in a real house. Until I left for the great world beyond, I had just assumed that people ate and entertained downstairs and slept upstairs. It was normal. So many of the things we grow up with become the standard by which everything else is judged.

The Masaai children I'd seen on their land near the Mara River, grew up thinking that you walked miles across the plain to go from one place to another, that you slept in a hut made of mud and cow dung and ate whatever meat you could kill or food you could grow yourself. It was normal.

I stretched myself awake and went downstairs to the kitchen. My sister was sitting at the table reading the morning paper with a mug of coffee next to her. Her husband had already left for work. I poured myself a mug and took it into the living room.

The house was an A-frame, built in the style of a Swiss chalet. The main wall of the living room was glass allowing you to look out into the woods. I stood there watching Nature's activity. There were a number of bird feeders of varying sizes and configurations scattered around and about the yard. Finches and sparrows and other small birds darted back and forth from tree to feeder in a flurry of activity. Now and then a blue jay would announce his presence and try to intimidate the others but they paid no attention. Robins had already begun their migration, otherwise they would have contributed their orange-breasted presence too. As these birds whirled around before me, my mind went back to the little garden where I had my breakfast in Nairobi. The birds there would be out of place here, just as these would be there. Yet they all were in perfect balance with their own habitat.

As I looked out, I remembered a stunning scene from one of my winter visits. Snow blanketed the ground. It was a wet snow so it also stuck to the naked tree limbs creating an ocean of pure, nearly blinding whiteness. On one of the trees, standing out like a bloodstain, was a lone cardinal, its redness even more brilliant against this colorless background. I wished for the ability to capture it somehow. It begged to be painted or, at least, photographed. I stood watching it for as long as it stayed there.

"You watching the pigs?" My sister's voice interrupted my reverie.

"Pigs?"

"That's what I call them. We buy birdseed in those great big bags and it seems like we never have enough. You wouldn't think those little things could eat so much, but they sure as hell do."

"Sure are pretty though," I said.

"They are that," she said. "Mama used to love sitting here watching them. Sometimes she'd go out on the deck but mostly she stayed inside because she didn't want to disturb them."

We hadn't talked much about our mother. This family wasn't much for talking about anything. I always wondered how my sister really felt but whenever I attempted to find out, I would get monosyllabic answers that warned me onto another subject.

On one occasion, some years before, my sister made a reference to "that woman," indicating toward Mom's bedroom with her head. It was the only time she expressed anything, one way or another.

It made me speculate on what their relationship must have been like. From the time my sister was born, she and Mom always lived under the same roof. When I came along, years later, it all seemed quite normal. But as years passed, and my sister became a woman and remained in that house, it must have taken on an interesting dynamic.

I wondered if they ever had "that" talk. When my sister fell in love and got engaged with a guy who turned out to be married already, did Mom comfort her the way she comforted me in my escapades? When my sister began drinking and smoking, did Mom have an opinion? She never would have said anything to me or my brother or any man. But to her daughter, another woman, would she?

When my sister finally got married, she and her husband turned the upstairs of the house I grew up in into an apartment for themselves. Mom lived downstairs. They had separate kitchens and lived separate lives. But it was still under the same roof and they entered through the same door. After a few years with both my sister and her husband working and not paying rent, they saved up enough money to build this chalet in the woods.

Mom insisted on staying in her own home. She had her yard and her flowers and vegetables. She had nurtured and loved them for years, since the first time she put her hands in the earth and felt energy flow into her body. She had no intention of leaving them. But my brother and brother-in-law, who had been my brother's best friend and a part of the family long before he and my sister hooked up, would not hear of it. They went to Mom and told her in no uncertain terms that she was going to live in the chalet in the woods.

As the story was always told, it was my brother and brother-in-law who insisted Mom live in the new house. What was my sister's view? Would she have preferred to be free of "that woman" or would the separation have been too much for her after all those years? My brother and I both knew what kind of mother Mom was to her sons. But my sister never spoke about their relationship.

When Mom moved into the woods, the situation was reversed. It was my sister's house. She made the rules. If she wanted to plant the roses here and the tomatoes there, it was her choice, even though Mom pointed out that the sun was better for them if they were reversed. It was my sister's kitchen too. She was the queen of this castle.

It may have been awkward at first to adjust to the new dynamic, but Mom was always an adaptable and accommodating person, the kind who loved being alive and didn't sweat the small stuff. *OK, it's your house. Where can I plant some roses?*

Before Mom died, she had had a series of accidents and broken bones here and there. All of them mended amazingly, given her age. But on the last occasion, she fell out of bed and lay there for some time with a broken hip before my sister discovered her. After surgery, Mom was taken to a nursing home in Smalltown where she had served on the board for years. They looked after her as she convalesced. When the time came for her to go home, my sister decided she was not capable of looking after Mom and suggested she go into a facility that could.

I was told of this decision by my brother. I was in Australia. My honest reaction was that it was unfair to this wonderful woman not to let her die at home, if that's what she wished. But I felt that because I was not there and hadn't been there for years, I had no vote. I kept my opinion to myself.

Mom, when she was told she was not going home, decided to die. She stopped eating. She stopped drinking liquids. She stopped talking. She just died. She was not going to go to some facility. She would just quit living. It was one month short of her 100th birthday.

How did my sister deal with all of that? I have no idea. She never talked about it. Or the guy who jilted her. Or the baby she lost after carrying it to full term. It's no wonder that when my niece accused me of molesting her, no one said anything. It was this family's modus operandi. No one talked.

CHAPTER FORTY FOUR

One of the genuine highlights for me whenever I visited my hometown, something I looked forward to almost as much as seeing my mother or Max, when they were alive, was The Pinochle Game.

Whenever I visited back in those days, my priorities were always the same. First I'd spend a little time with Mom, usually have a cup of coffee and some Toll House cookies that she always had on hand for my arrival. She was far less interested in what I may have been doing with my life than she was to see me and see that I was properly fed. After we'd had a catch-up, I'd get on the phone and see if Max was at home.

Max and I grew up together. His mother took us both to school on our first day. Mom had to work at the family business. Max and I went through twelve years of school together, in the later years on separate trajectories, but never lost our closeness. When I went to The University in Smalltown, Max worked in a grocery store as produce manager. I'd stop in from time to time and catch up. When he got married, I was his best man. When I left town for parts unknown, I never lost touch with Max. He'd receive many a late night or early morning phone call from me whenever something was bothering me or if I had good news to share. Max was as much a constant in my life as my blood family and probably even more so.

After the first box was ticked and I'd spent some time with Mom, I'd set a time to catch up with Max. Often I'd drive my sister's car out to his house just outside of town after dinner and we'd spend hours talking about everything in our history to that point. We also managed to log an impressive amount of time talking baseball and the Yankees in particular. We were baseball outcasts though. No one there would root the Yankees out loud except us.

I watched Max become one of the most impressive fathers to his three daughters that I'd ever seen. His patience and tolerance and unconditional love and support were monumental. I marveled at his open-mindedness in racial and other social issues. He was uncharacteristically liberal compared to the rest of the citizens there.

He was my anchor. His friendship grounded me as I floated around in the ether of my life. When he died – any loved one always dies too soon but in Max's case, it was way too soon – I drove to Gettysburg with my brother to scatter Max's ashes on the battlefield where Pickett's Charge took place, per his request.

So catching up with Max was the second box that got ticked whenever I went back to Smalltown. The third box was always The Pinochle Game.

Pinochle was the card game of choice at our house, a house where card games were even more important than elections. It started with Pop. He was a card player – not a gambler – but a card player. Pinochle was his game of choice and therefore the family's game of choice. If you couldn't play pinochle in our house, you must have been adopted.

For years, as a kid and even a young adult, I could never break into the big leagues. Pop and my brother were always at the table in a three-handed game, my brother-in-law often making up the third. When my brother wasn't around and family friends were visiting, it would be a fourhanded game, the men against the women. I have a permanent picture in my mind of Mom holding her cards in one hand and her head in the other, trying to stay awake between tricks when the women were forced into this pinochle servitude.

As a kid, maybe eight or nine, Pop taught me the fundamentals so that even as I was the designated spectator, I knew the game. One of my proudest moments in life was soon after I learned how to play when I challenged my brother to a two-handed game. He laughed at me but it was a happy, proud laugh. Bar Mitzvah may be the sign of manhood in the Jewish faith, or a circumcision for the Masaai, but at our house it was pinochle.

When I got to my later years of high school, the rookie got his chance. Pop, my brother and brother-in-law gathered around the table for a game on a Sunday afternoon. "Let's play fourhanded," I blurted out.

They looked at me, at first scoffing, then incredulously, then with gentle good humor. Their expressions said, *Why not?*

"Draw for partners," Pop said. "Two highs and two lows."

I had arrived. From that moment on, I was in the pool. If I was around and a player was needed, I moved ahead of all the women, to our mutual delight.

But let me stop for a minute to explain a pinochle game at our house. It wasn't some little baby, regular-deck, according to Hoyle, chicken-shit pinochle game. We played *double* deck pinochle, two full pinochle decks. When you played fourhanded, each player held twenty cards. When you played three-handed, each player held twenty-five cards, almost half a normal deck. The five cards left over constituted the widow. However you slice it, this was a fist-full of cards. It was no wonder the women were glad to be relieved. Most of them couldn't even hold all the cards in one hand.

The other thing about this game was it was played for a modest wager. But far more important was the scalding you took if you lost. The winner became a bullhorn of abuse to those whom he vanquished. The last thing you wanted, if you were me, for instance, was to leave Smalltown having lost to either my brother or brother-in-law – especially my brother. Fuck sportsmanship. You'd rather be castrated. In fact, for all practical purposes, you were.

So, with both Mom and Max gone, the remaining tradition was The Pinochle Game. After dinner, my brother came over to Sis' house. The ritual was always the same. Everyone put on his game face. The jibes were gentle. No one wanted to be too provocative in the beginning. You didn't dare. It would make the agony of defeat that much more unbearable. My brother took a place at the table. I took one. My brother-in-law got the cards out, counted them and placed them in the middle of the table. He then took out a pad and pencil. He was always the official scorekeeper. I was seated between them with my brother on my left and my brother-in-law on my right.

"High card deals," my brother said and picked up a few cards, revealing the bottom one of his stack. We each did the same.

"You boys want anything?" Sis asked. "Otherwise, I'm going out in the yard."

Each of us looked at her with disdain, without response. She had contaminated the atmosphere with something non-pinochle.

The game was on.

The key to winning was beyond skill. We were all skillful players at this time in history. The keys were luck and guts -- and the guts were only validated if you were lucky. If you were dealt the cards, you were quietly laughing on the inside. No one laughed on the outside until the score sheet said you could. But if you weren't dealt the cards, it was all about what cards were in the five-card widow. These cards were separated from the others by the dealer in whatever way he chose. These five cards in the widow could make or break you. If you needed help and one or more of those cards improved your hand, you were laughing, usually out loud – vociferously – tauntingly – obnoxiously – and adding any ad libs that came to mind, equally obnoxious. If not, and you were fucked, the other two players showed the same quality of compassion. It wasn't called cutthroat for nothing.

Secretly, my brother-in-law and I would prefer that the other would win if he didn't. That's because my brother was at the same time the worst winner and the worst loser in pinochle history. We never minded when he was in the position of the worst loser. That was only painful for his thin skin and a joy for everyone else. But when he won, he was impossible. He had no grace. No equanimity. No humanity. He became a gloating, pompous horse's ass. None of us was guiltless. We all rubbed it in if we won but he was the master.

But only for a minute because if there was still time, we'd start another game or there'd always be tomorrow. The ribbing was unending throughout the games. The same jokes and expressions used year after year. The Pinochle Game was its own comfort zone. For those couple of hours, the world stopped. There were no injuries or insults. There were no broken promises. There were no cares or hurts. Only the game.

As we played this game during the Palindrome Adventure, at one point, I looked up from my cards. Each of them was lost in concentration. I took a moment to study them. They were old men. I could see it. Even though, while they were in the game, they had no age. It played as it always had. I was nevertheless conscious of their frailty, their vulnerability, their mortality. I wondered if I'd ever see them again. I wondered if these would be the last pinochle games we'd ever play

As the days passed and I relaxed in the warmth of familiar surroundings, I felt the inevitable tug. I was comfortable. I was safe. I was among those whom I'd known all my life. And yet I felt the tug. It said to me that I didn't belong here either, that I needed to keep moving, that my wanderlust was a permanent condition.

My sister prepared meals that she knew I especially liked. I went out to visit Max's wife and daughters. Neither my hometown nor its people had changed. They were still possessed of the same Midwestern values and loyalties and honor they had always been. Whatever they disagreed about, the disagreed about with civility. Rarely did anyone step over the line. Respect and tolerance were the norm. They all knew that at the end of the day, they all had to live with one another and conducted themselves accordingly.

I spent much of my remaining time there alone, mostly seated on the deck looking into the woods. I watched more leaves fall from the trees and more turn color. I watched the birds feed and the squirrels scamper around for food to store.

How had I become so estranged from all this? It was my roots. Why, then, did I feel as if I had no roots? This feeling had taken hold long before the business with my niece. Before I went into the Army, I never wanted to be more than a day's drive away from Smalltown. When the Army told me that I was going to be stationed in California, I protested because I wouldn't be able to drive back to Smalltown on weekends. They told me California was a mistake. I was going to Germany.

Upon arriving in Bremerhaven, I noticed that the stevedores looked different, interesting. Within a couple of months I took a quick trip to Vienna. I had been forced to discover there was a world beyond my hometown's city limits. It was a fascinating, daunting, but at the same time, manageable world. How can you know what your path is in life if you never try anything different? If you never look around the corner or over the next hill? I tried to return after Pop died. I wanted to be a comfort to my mother.

She appreciated it but after a year told me that she could see I wasn't happy. How could she be happy if I wasn't? Where would I rather be? In two weeks I left for New York. Now my home was in Australia. As I sat there on the deck, feeling so nurtured, it was hard to imagine that all my stuff was sitting in an apartment somewhere else, in another hemisphere, on the other side of the globe. But it was.

Assessing my stay was easy. This visit had been balancing for me. Sitting in the tranquility of these woods, I could see that while the cast of characters remained unchanged, my relationship with them had. I had arrived with a feeling of harshness and was judgmental. Those edges were now smoothed. This was my family. The affection ran deep and was abiding. Even though I was not welcomed by everyone, I felt that somewhere down deep, even my niece knew the truth and would confront and acknowledge it one day. In the meantime, my affection was constant.

My brother chose to drive me to airport, rather than letting me take a taxi. We both got out of the car when we arrived at the departure area. He came around to me and embraced me. He kissed me on the cheek and watched as I walked away. I had seen the same expression on Mom's face each time I left. *Will I ever see him again?*

I got to the airport in plenty of time to check in and find a café. The café was crowded with people watching the state university football team in a Saturday afternoon contest. My brother-in-law was an alumnus of the state university and a season ticket holder to all the home games. Since this was an away game, he would be in his recliner in front of the flat screen tv, a beer by his side and no one to interrupt him. I was able to watch the first half of the football game before the flight was announced. No one seemed too keen to leave. But one by one and two by two, the café emptied.

It was impossible to get a flight directly to LAX. We would have to make a stop in St. Louis. When we got to flying altitude, we flew over a blanket of cloud cover that looked like a gigantic snowfield in every direction.

I had been up and down eight times on this journey. This was number nine. First from Melbourne to Johannesburg, then Johannesburg to Harare, then Harare to Nairobi, Nairobi to London, London to Berlin, Berlin to London, London to New York, New York to Ohio. Now to St. Louis, then again to Los Angeles. And I still wasn't finished going up and down.

Each stop had been so utterly different from its predecessor. This was more than a trip around the world. It was a trip around my life. Ahead was yet another taste of the past and present.

It was rainy in St. Louis. I had lived in this city at one time but never landed at the St. Louis airport. All my traveling in and out of St. Louis was by car. Therefore, I had no sense of being anywhere I'd ever been before aside from the advertisements that lined the corridors. It wasn't a very long wait until we were airborne again. I'd like to have had a look around at some of my old haunts but that would have to wait for another time.

It was dark by the time we began our descent into LAX. It always passed through my mind that Thomas Edison would be laughing gleefully if he could approach Los Angeles from the air at night. As far as the eye could see, from horizon to horizon, electric lights of every color and size sparkled below. You could imagine him clapping his hands together and saying, "Goody, goody, goody!" The contrast between what I saw now and what I'd seen between Harare and Nairobi made me think of the photos taken from space with great dark patches interrupted by sparkles of light as the spacecraft orbited the planet.

Once again I was on known turf. The trip into L.A. was one that I'd made often, taking someone to or picking someone up from the airport. Traffic was relatively light, relative being the operative word. It was, after all, Los Angeles. My permanent US address was here. Smalltown could have been. But California was. When I finally had to guts to move to California from New York, it was completely organic. Even though I had grown up landlocked, when I saw the Pacific Ocean for the first time, it spoke to me. I had never developed a fondness for the Atlantic. It always seemed too rough and brown anywhere that I'd seen it on the East Coast. But the Pacific was another story. And it was also the Pacific that linked me to Australia or America, depending on where I was.

CHAPTER FORTY FIVE

There are two things in Southern California that always give me a special thrill. One is the Jacaranda tree. When they are in full bloom, there is no more spectacular sight in the world. I had never seen those trees before moving to Hollywood. They enriched my life. There was one street in Beverly Hills that, for two long blocks, had huge Jacarandas that made a violet arch over the roadway. I used to ride my bicycle up and down that street just to be in that explosion of color and the faint scent the blossoms give off. If any of the neighbors had noticed me, I'd have surely been arrested on suspicion of casing the joint. But it was worth the risk.

The other special thrill is the mockingbird. I have always thought that bird was poorly named. It doesn't mock anything. It's an original. When I first moved to Hollywood and had an apartment in the Flats, there was a huge tree in the courtyard of the apartment complex. Soon after moving in, I was awakened in the dead of night by what I thought at first was a dream. As I gained consciousness, I was aware of a bird song. No other sounds competed with it. No traffic. No helicopters. Nothing. When I was fully awake and able to take it in, the song became an endless riff, never repeating a phrase more than once and even then, with a slight variation, eventually moving on into another motif all together. It went on for twenty minutes without repetition, endlessly melodic in rich, full tones with an occasional, perfectly timed, percussive squeak thrown in. It was like Ella Fitzgerald with feathers.

I was fascinated. What creature was capable of making such original music with such variation? I spoke with a neighbor about it the next day, one who was a native Angelino.

"Probably a mockingbird," she said.

"What do they look like?" I asked.

A dull gray bird with some white markings fluttered into view. "There's one," she said, pointing.

"That's a mockingbird?" I was incredulous. I expected a rainbow of color to match the rainbow of sound.

"Yep," she said.

A mockingbird singing in a full-blooming Jacaranda tree is my idea of heaven.

I was to meet an old flame, Betty, for lunch. This was very unusual for me. With the exception of Betty, I never stayed friends with women I'd been involved with. It may have something to do with my tendency to be here now and not there then. For whatever reason, that was definitely my M.O. But Betty was different. We were lovers for a while, saw it wasn't going to be a ride off into the sunset, and decided we didn't want to lose each other as friends. It was only awkward for a week or so. After that we were like brother and sister.

Betty was from a largish family and grew up in Pennsylvania. The family lived on the edge of poverty most of the time, owing to the fact that their mother was their sole provider and not overly employable. The father was around but of little value. In spite of that history, Betty was like a hunk of alluvial gold. She and her next older brother made their way to L.A. He became a hairdresser and she applied her computer skills at a time when they were in great demand.

Her brother, John, was one of the sweetest guys I ever knew. I never saw him without a smile on his face. He laughed at everything and had a wicked sense of humor. When I met Betty, they were living in a big house above Sunset Boulevard east of Highland. They shared it with three other gay men, one of whom later went into the priesthood.

That was at a time when there was nothing to restrict their behavior. HIV was unheard of as yet. It was soon to come. And John was one of the first of his crowd to contract it. By now, Betty and I were well beyond our sexual relationship and deep into our friendship. I became her refuge as she watched her well-loved and loving brother disintegrate before her eyes.

When he got really sick, she insisted that I not come around to see John.

"He has plenty of friends who visit him," she said. "I don't have anyone else that isn't involved with AIDS in some way except you. I need you to be apart from all that."

It was a role I was happy to play. It wasn't just for her. I have never been able to confront death in an organic, healthy way. When they held up my father's funeral for me because of a delayed flight from Germany, I was upset. I wanted to remember him as vibrant and alive. Instead I had to look at a motionless, plastic copy of him in a box. Somehow I have managed to stay away from corpses since then. It was easy to honor Betty's request.

When she came by to pick me up, Betty looked great. She had a healthy glow and none of the despair of those years before. We decided to go to the beach, grabbing some sandwiches on the way. We drove up to Malibu and got settled near some rocks.

"I've got a new boyfriend," she said.

"Hope he's worthy," I said.

"Oh, he is. Don't you worry. He has a locksmith business. I help him out sometimes. It's great. Everything's done by phone and computer. Say you get locked out of your car. You call us. We call a lock guy who's close to where you are. He opens your car door. Bingo!"

"And you don't have to get off your butt."

"Exactly. I can be giving my boyfriend a blowjob while he's remotely getting someone's lock fixed."

"Sounds perfect. Now, tell me how you're really doing."

She didn't answer for a moment. Then, her mood changed. "Pretty good. I still miss John. Some of his old friends are still around. Some of them are dead too. I hate that fucking disease."

"What ever happened to the guy who wanted to be a priest?"

"He went through seminary and was ready to take his vows and then quit at the last minute. I heard he's doing social work with AIDS victims now. Haven't seen him though."

This was also a part of my Hollywood history: Betty, her brother, her ups and downs with relationships. We talked for a couple of hours until it started to get cool. Since we were unprepared for it, we picked up our garbage and left. There was no way to recapture our closeness. Our paths had grown farther apart. I knew I'd make another attempt to keep in touch once I was back in Oz, as I always do. But I also knew it would be unproductive.

Betty dropped me off where I was staying and waved goodbye. I made a cup of tea and watched the Angels beat the Giants in the final game of the World Series. There was something special about being in L.A. for that game. In my mind, they were still the Los Angeles Angels, not the Anaheim Angels. But that's because old habits die hard. It's kind of a Sixth Avenue thing.

CHAPTER FORTY SIX

The next morning I tried to put myself back in Hollywood as a resident. What would I be doing? Whatever it was, it would be extremely important, whether it was an audition, a meeting, a lunch date or tennis. There was never the surface electricity that you found in New York. In New York, even if you've never been there before, you still feel the energy, the pounding rhythm, the sense of urgency while you're there. Here, the urgency was disguised by the sunshine. Your heart rate is even until the moment of truth. Then, anything can happen.

Some of the most successful people in Hollywood are the ones that can appear not to give a shit. They either have to be convincing at it or truly not give a shit. But only a fool would believe that anyone who goes to Hollywood in the first place, doesn't give a shit. It's Hollywood. The atmosphere is seductive. It's easy to get distracted. But when the slightest little opportunity arises, you jump.

Whether it's true or apocryphal, there's a story that made its way around when I was there about Danny DeVito when he went in to meet with the network people for the series, *TAXI*. He had done a few things, most notably *One Flew Over the Cuckoo's Nest* as one of the inmates, but nothing greatly noteworthy. Normally, these are solemn occasions where everyone is trying to impress everyone else, whether it's the actor being interviewed, the junior network exec wanting to seem creative, the up-and-coming studio exec who wants to show how tough he can be, or the producers, writers, directors and assorted others playing "who's got the biggest dick."

In all these circumstances, that roomful of insecurity is waiting to pounce on the lowly actor who is trying to impress them.

That reminds me of another story. I went in for an audition for an ensemble series, like *TAXI*. Wanting to say something engaging and thoughtful and memorable to the casting director, I said, "It must be interesting for you to create an ensemble. I mean, here are all these different types and personalities that you mix and match and turn into a cohesive acting family." She looked at me for a second like I was nuts. Then she said with poignant sarcasm, "What I do is make fucking actors rich!"

OK, back to DeVito. So the stage is set for this diminutive actor to come in and try to convince all these self-important people to hire him. When his name is called, he gets off his chair, strides into the office, slams the door behind him and says, "I just gotta ask you one question: Who wrote this shit anyway?" And with that he threw the script across the room. All the execs and creative people looked at each other and said, "Louie DePalma!"

That was the character's name and Danny got the part. He became the character right before their eyes. He convinced them that he didn't give a shit. Inside, he was probably wondering if he should be so ballsy, if he would offend someone irreparably. But then he must have thought *Fuck it* and just gone for it.

As I sat there, I thought about the people around Hollywood who were at this same moment trying on different outfits to make the right impression. One could be going in for a series regular. Another could be going to make his or her first national television appearance. Someone else might be in town from Keokuk hoping to land a job in the mailroom at William Morris. A blond with tits out to here might be plotting a way to say hi to Mr. Big (you can fill in any blank you want for that: movie star, studio exec, producer, director, writer, key grip, runner – everyone looks important to someone below them on the ladder to fame and fortune in Hollywood). Somebody else was off his or her head on (blank). You can fill that one in too. Someone else was waking up in a strange bed that he or she thought would give them a leg up with the aforementioned Mr. Big. Someone's heart was broken. Someone's balls were broken. Someone's contract was broken. It was all going on within a ten-mile radius at the instant I put the cup to my mouth and thought the thoughts.

It had been my world. I had thrived in it for a while. Then like everyone else, saw the writing on the wall. The difference between me and most others was that I read the writing. They refused to.

On a previous visit, after living in Australia for six years and not returning to the USA during that time, I called some old friends. They were all good people, clever people, talented people, exceptional people in some way, just as everyone in Hollywood is. In the six years I'd been gone, not one of them had made any significant progress in their "careers." One was creating a website that was sure to attract the needed attention. Another was trying to work her way into a Horror Movie Convention as a Scream Queen. Someone else just had an audition for a small role that might, maybe, could perhaps be expanded into a major role on a television series. And on and on. The only thing I noticed was that they all looked older and weren't doing any better than before. And in Hollywood, looking older is not an advantage unless you're a character actor or a star, but even then, particularly if you're a female star, it can be iffy.

There's another story, perhaps apocryphal, credited to Oscar Levant. He was under contract to MGM during the days of the great musicals. Levant was a brilliant pianist and interpreter of Gershwin's music – and a New Yorker. He was quoted as saying something like, "You get to Hollywood, check into the hotel, go down by the pool for a drink and the next thing you know, you're 70."

***

Since I was going to be having dinner with Hawk, my film editor buddy, I decided to spend the earlier part of the day on more familiar turf, where I'd lived most of my time in Hollywood, roughly between Beverly Boulevard and Highland from Sunset down to Wilshire. The only way I could get there was by bus. If you live in Los Angeles and you're not Latino or African American, this is a word you may not be acquainted with. A bus is a large motor vehicle that has seats for a large number of passengers. You step aboard, ask the driver how to buy a ticket, take a seat if one is available, ring the bell when you've arrived at your destination and want to get off. It's a little like the airplane thing except you can see how fast you're going and what you're passing.

When I stepped onto the bus I immediately felt to see if I'd grown a second head. A thousand eyes coming from black and brown faces looked at me with wonder. I ride public transportation in Australia virtually every day. The trains and trams and busses are populated by the Australian population. There are Asians, Middle Easterners, Caucasians, Africans, Europeans. In other words, the world rides public transportation in Oz without giving a thought to who else is riding. That was hardly the case in L.A.

Some looked at me questioningly, as if to say, *Are you lost?* Others looked at me with pity: *Poor guy must have totaled his car.* Someone else: *What the fuck you doin' on my bus?* But they all looked and kept looking until I finally got off.

Walking around this part of L.A. was like being in a movie. Everyone looked super chic, like characters in *Entourage*. The women took your breath away. The constant sunshine was an aphrodisiac. The cars all sparkled. There were more Rolls Royces on Sunset Boulevard than in all of Australia. Mercedes-Benz? Porsche? Alpha Romeo? Name a year and model. It was there. Classic Thunderbirds. Even cherry Deloreans. Ah, yes, the substitute phallus. When I lived there, I drove a beat-up Toyota Corolla until I could afford a used Beetle convertible.

How seductive this place is, I thought. It's no wonder no one wants to leave. The weather is perfect. The people are stunningly gorgeous. Creativity is the coin of the realm. One lucky break can literally change your life. That lucky break can keep you in chips forever. And it can come at any time. And everybody was on the lookout for it.

I often thought that when Gloria Stuart got the role of the old Kate Winslet in *Titanic*, there would have been at least a hundred older women in Hollywood wondering, *Why did **that** bitch get the job? I could have played it a ten times better.* They would have been waiting for that break since Norma Desmond was ready for her close-up. For most, it never comes. But they wait just the same.

Eventually I made my way down Fairfax toward the Farmers Market. I was torn between finding someplace in the Market to grab a bite of lunch or giving in and going to Cantor's. I hadn't tasted pastrami or kosher corned beef in years. All due respects to the favored Jewish delis in Oz, but they wouldn't know pastrami – or a good bagel, for that matter – from a wombat.

I gave in. After gnawing my way through a pastrami, turkey and chopped liver on rye and washing it down with a cream soda, I wandered up the street to the Silent Movie house just to look at the one-sheets. I had often gone to this cinema to see the classic films of Lon Chaney and Douglas Fairbanks and Laurel & Hardy and Buster Keaton and Charlie Chaplin and all the others. You may have to look long and hard for good legitimate theatre in L.A. but you never had to go far to find any movie that's ever been made. When I lived there, I went to as many revival movies as new ones. Now, with the advent of DVDs, they aren't as necessary as they were then. But at that time, it was like a history lesson.

I checked my watch and saw that it was nearly time to meet Hawk and his wife, Rita. When I decided that I was going to live in Australia, I had an apartment in Hollywood. My departure date was only tentative. So when Hawk made me an offer to stay in his house while he and his family were in New York, where he would be working on location, I took him up on it.

He and I had met in New York. He was a working film editor and director. I was a struggling actor. He was one of several African

American guys I hung out with. Each of them was in an area of show business. Two were writers. Another was an actor. Another was a producer. Another was an Assistant Director. Hawk and one of the writers were the only ones who worked consistently. He was also the only one who was married and had kids that he was still living with.

In New York, Hawk worked on anything he could. His formal education was limited to a high school in The Bronx. But his real education was gained visually on a moviola. He cut documentaries. He cut television shows. He cut short films. He cut the rare feature. And because he was African American, he was one of the first to crack the film editing business, even in New York. But he was so good and easy to work with and such a workaholic that he was constantly employed. In the beginning, it may have been the oddity and socially correct notion of having an African American on the job. But it soon became clear that Hawk could make your film better than you thought it could be. He could tell a visual story with clarity and flair.

Hollywood was obviously where Hawk was headed. He got there a little before I did and went to work cutting very low budget features for a company that would make Ed Wood look like Cecil B. DeMille. But it kept money coming in and it kept Hawk working with up and coming directors and writers.

He was also a novelty in Hollywood. There were very few African Americans in the mainstream business when he got there, even at the level that Hawk operated on. As his career progressed, he never missed a chance to bring another African American into the business, either as an assistant or in some other production job where he may have had some influence.

One of the directors he'd worked with in the early days caught the brass ring for a minute. He started making pictures for the majors. He knew Hawk's value from those early days and brought him along to edit his films. This put Hawk in the inner business, where the real money and opportunity lay.

In spite of his obvious success – and it was significant – he was still a Black man in Los Angeles. I remember him telling me that one evening he had worked late cutting a film. It was starting to get dark out and he had to walk about six blocks to his apartment on Gregory Way in Beverly Hills.

"I ran the whole way, man. The last thing I wanted to be was a Black dude on any street in Beverly Hills after dark."

That reminds me of another of our African American friends who had been a successful playwright in New York and was now writing for the screen in Hollywood. He told me this story:

"I was looking to lease a car so I went to a Lexus dealer in Santa Monica. The salesman gave me the keys and we started to drive around Santa Monica so I could get the feel of the car. We stopped at a red light and a black and white police cruiser pulled up next to us. The cops kept looking over at us suspiciously. It got more and more obvious that they were seeing something they didn't like. The salesman noticed and started to roll down his window to say something to them. I said be cool, man. They're just trying to figure out what a 'n****r' would be doing driving a Lexus. Happens all the time."

No matter who you are or how successful you may be, there is no advantage to being Black in America.

But back to Hawk. He cut two consecutive hundred million dollar grossers. From that time on, he was never without work and could mostly choose his jobs. He had two daughters with his European wife, all of whom lived a comfortable life in Tinseltown.

Our friendship grew during our time in Hollywood. When Hawk decided to take a swing at directing, while he was still cutting the Ed Wood features, he employed me in his second feature. His first had done well, in an independent release sort of way. The second didn't do so well. But more importantly, Hawk got too stressed in the director's chair. It would be cutting exclusively from then on.

When this job came up in New York, Hawk knew that I was going to be leaving for Australia.

"Hey, Wallace," he said on the phone one day.

"Yeah. How you doing, Hawk?"

"Good, brother, good. Listen I've got a proposition for you."

"Let's hear," I said.

"You know, I got a job cutting a film that's shooting in New York in a couple of weeks. And I'm taking Rita and the kids with me for a little TDY. They haven't been back there in years," he said.

"Yeah, so?"

"So, here's what I'm wondering. How would you like to house sit for us? It'll mean you have to live at our house for maybe three months. Can you put off your trip to Australia that long?"

"Probably," I answered.

"OK. Here's what I'll do to sweeten the deal for you. You'll live rent free, of course. But I'll give you some dough on top."

"Oh…"

"No, brother. Wait a minute before you go 'Oh-ing' on me. You can use some extra scratch, right?"

"Yeah, but…"

"Hey, man, 'yeah but' is just another 'Oh.' Tell you what I'll do. I'll buy your plane ticket to Australia."

"Hey, Hawk…"

"It's either that or I give you cash. You decide."

That's how my trip to Australia got financed.

Staying in Hawk's house was a luxury I hadn't enjoyed much in Hollywood. The best and worst thing about it was waking up and reaching to the bedside table for the remote. Hawk had ten million channels, half of which were playing movies dating from the twenties to the nineties. Not a morning went by when I jumped out of bed before grabbing the remote – unless, of course, I had a job or another appointment. I must have seen fifty million movies in those three months. And if I didn't, it wasn't for lack of trying.

It was also a novelty going from the bedroom to the kitchen to the dining room to the living room to the back yard to the bathroom. It was so civilized. It was like being back in Smalltown, in a real house where you didn't have to look at the same walls endlessly. I didn't realize what a claustrophobic life I had been leading until I spent those few months at Hawk's. How quickly we adjust and adapt to our surroundings, whether they are luxurious or limited.

CHAPTER FORTY SEVEN

Hawk, Rita and I went to dinner at a Vietnamese restaurant somewhere on La Cienega. It was brightly lit and open. Atmosphere was not the draw, the food was.

"Before we get into a pissing contest," Hawk announced, "I'm getting this. I know you're a rich Aussie and all that shit but we're taking you to dinner. Got that?"

"Cool," I said. "I was planning to fumble for money at the end anyway."

"So, how do you like Australia?" Rita asked politely.

"I'm there," I answered. "There are a lot of similarities between there and here." And I went into my standard pitch about the things that make Australia unique: the limited population, the egalitarian nature of the culture, its diversity, its social safety net, the optimism couched in humility, its cringe factor and the tall poppy syndrome.

"See, I always thought you would do good in Australia," Hawk said. "You remember I told you when you left that you'd be better off there where you could be a bigger fish in a smaller pond?"

"I do remember that," I said.

"I don't know if I told you but when we did that feature, the cinematographer took me aside when we did your scenes and said he wanted to get a tighter shot of your face. He thought you had magic."

"No, man, you never told me that."

"That's what the brother said," Hawk said. "I told the motherfucker he was full of shit. Wallace ain't got no magic. But he wouldn't listen and went in for a tighter close-up anyway."

"Yeah. Me and George Clooney. We got faces. All I know is that they haven't caught on yet in Australia."

"Do you plan to stay there?" Rita asked.

"I don't plan much," I said. "I just tend to drift along in my little stream and see where it takes me. But, having said that, I certainly don't have any plans to leave. Mostly because I don't know where I'd go."

"You don't ever miss America? Do you ever think about coming back?" she asked.

These were questions I wasn't prepared for. Did I miss America? Did I ever think about coming back? It took me a minute to consider them. "As far as missing America, I don't get much of a chance. Many of the television shows and most of the movies come from here. The media is filled with American stuff. The world's pop culture is American. So from that point of view, there's no opportunity to miss it. And I can keep in touch with friends thanks to the Internet and telephone. So, no. And about coming back, I don't think about that. It's more like I've been there, done that and got the tee shirt. If I were to leave Australia, it would be to go live somewhere else probably. But who knows?"

We talked about the girls and what they were doing. Both were growing into lovely, intelligent and accomplished women. They were moving in two entirely different circles. One had studied and was working in government planning. The other studied dance in Europe.

We went back to their new house for a cup of tea. Hawk and I sat up for a few hours reminiscing about the old days in New York and Hollywood and catching up on everyone's activities from then.

Hawk was also good for some up-to-date Hollywood gossip. Being in the position he was in, all of the good stuff passed through his editing suite. If you were in the inner industry – and probably even if you weren't – there were no secrets in Hollywood for very long. If someone was fucking up anywhere, it was known instantaneously industry wide. If someone was fucking someone else's wife, same deal. If someone had a new joke, bang, everyone knew it before lunch. It was as if everyone in town was wired to the same mainframe computer.

After midnight, Hawk insisted on driving me back to where I was staying. I would never have found a bus that late anyhow. And a taxi would have been prohibitive. I accepted his offer. When we got there, Hawk got out of the car. "Listen, brother, if you tell anyone about this, I'm coming after you". And with that, he gave me a big hug.

"It's always good to see old friends," I answered. But as I said the words, I realized that it was only old friends that I had here. I was a visiting fireman. I was the cowboy riding back into town after a long cattle drive. The same refrain kept playing in my head: I didn't belong here.

I had nothing planned for the next day. I woke up that morning with a sense of adventure. I would just go somewhere and see what happened. Plenty of time to wander.

Santa Monica always held an attraction for me. If I'd stayed in L.A. and could wangle it, I'd have lived in Santa Monica. Where else on the planet could you find such a rich mixture of affluence, funk, kitsch, sustainability and homelessness?

I loved the idea that Santa Monica was a haven for the homeless. It is so civilized and generous for a community to look after vagrants. Australia's safety net functions in a similar way, even though there are still some who slip through. But somehow in Santa Monica, the homeless didn't have to sacrifice their dignity. And what better place to be homeless? The beach is conveniently near for a snooze in the sunshine. There were places around where you could find a meal. There may have been an underworld that I wasn't aware of but on the surface, at least, it seemed pretty good.

When I lived in Hollywood, a friend decided she was going to buy food to distribute at Christmas time to some homeless people who were more or less living in little parks in the San Fernando Valley. She asked me if I'd help.

She had bought tons of stuff and separated it into twelve or so bags. We loaded them up and headed for the first park. There were perhaps eight people congregated around a picnic table, having a smoke if they had them and looking generally needy.

"I've got some food if you want it," she announced.

"What do you have?" a guy asked. He was not insolent, just curious.

"There's all kinds of stuff here. There's some lunchmeat, bread, mustard, chocolate, some fruit, cereal. Have a look and use what you want. Maybe someone else will like what you don't," she said.

They began rummaging through the bags we gave them. I went to one of the men who was standing away from the group. He looked to be in his forties. He was clean and, in a Salvation Army sort of way, well dressed.

"What are you doing here?" I asked. "You don't look like you really belong with homeless people."

"Well, I am," he answered. It was a direct answer but not abrupt.

"How come?"

"I'm not gonna tell you my whole story, but it's pretty much typical. I had a job, had a family. I was responsible and all that. But things don't always go the way you plan. You know?"

I nodded.

"So, I don't know. One day, I guess, I realized that I wasn't living my life anymore. I was trying to be something I wasn't, I guess. I don't know. All I know is there came a point when I just couldn't deal with it anymore and I left. I didn't take all the money or anything like that. I just took a little, enough to get me out of there."

"You left your family?" I asked.

"Yep."

"Just like that?"

"Yep. Just like that."

"And?"

"And I'm happy. It's not like I have any security or anything like that. And if I get sick or something, I'm probably screwed. But I move around as I want. I scramble for a place to sleep and something to eat. I don't do anything illegal. Just live my life. It don't hurt anybody."

His sincerity and humility left me with nothing to say and definitely nothing to judge. "Good luck to you," I said. "I'm not sure you're not onto something."

"Naw," he smiled. "Believe me, you're a whole lot better off. This ain't no life, really. Just the one I'm living."

We shook hands. My friend and I left that park and went on to the next.

Thinking about it now, I see another example of a person living their own movie. Each person's life unfolds as it will, whether it's in Africa or South America or the Arctic. Each of us logs our time, doing what we do, and moves on. The homeless are just other people with stories too. They're all the stars of their own movie. Life decides whether or not it's a comedy or tragedy. Usually, it's a little bit of both. Sometimes a lot.

CHAPTER FORTY EIGHT

I was prepared for the stares next day when I took a bus to Hollywood and Highland, then caught the train to Union Station. This train was a new feature, talked about during my time in L.A. but not yet begun. It always seemed a tragedy to me and many others that the powers-that-be had paved over the elaborate network of trolley tracks that connected the far reaches of Los Angeles back before the auto, petroleum and concrete industries got hold of it. You could jump on an electric trolley and get anywhere in greater Los Angeles efficiently and conveniently. But that wasn't good enough for those industrial giants. They had bigger plans. The movie, *Chinatown*, comes to mind. How they would love to have those electric trolleys back today! It'd be like Melbourne with glitz.

Union Station is a landmark. It looks virtually the same today as it did when it was built in 1939. That was when train travel was at its zenith and Union Station was its West Coast Mecca. Old newsreels show the likes of Clark Gable and Gloria Swanson and Mary Pickford and Bob Hope rocking up on the Twentieth Century Limited, waving and smiling to the press as they made their way up the long, vast corridor, heels clicking against the marble floor. It takes very little imagination to thrust oneself back into that time today. It doesn't seem to have changed a bit.

My destination was a small town near the Hearst Castle on the central coast of California, about halfway between Los Angeles and San Francisco. My friend, Shirley, lived there with her husband, Andy.

Shirley and I met when I got involved with the actors' union. She was on staff. It was love at first sight – but not that kind of love. We instinctively knew that we would be the best of friends as long as we kept our private parts to ourselves. It was never even talked about.

We were buddies from the start. And she became one of my lifelines in Hollywood.

Shirley saw me through all my romantic misadventures, was by my side in all my extraneous creative pursuits and was always good for a laugh when it was needed. She was also basically from the same part of the country as I, except she was a big city girl and I was a small town boy. Our friendship immediately found a balance that allowed us to talk about everything with one another without judgment. Not without opinion or advice. But definitely without judgment.

Shirley was doing it pretty hard in those early days of our friendship. Her first marriage left her with an ex-husband who had gone to the desert to find himself, like some Old Testament prophet, and two daughters that needed stuff. She worked the full-time job at the union, then moonlighted as a bartender at a strip club in the San Fernando Valley. She was always tired but never flagged. And never complained. At least not for long. The two jobs paid her well enough to eventually buy a condo way out in the Valley, toward Northridge, and a Pinto convertible.

I went to the strip club once to see it and say howdy. It was not exactly a Gentlemen's Gallery. There was a little stage with a few chairs around it and a pole in the middle. On the opposite side of the room was the bar where Shirley ran things. Near the entrance were two pool tables and the rest was scattered tables and a hallway that led to the girls' dressing room and toilets. Seedy would be far too extravagant a word to use in describing this dump. But Shirley logged three nights a week there and made good tips. She could keep the boys at the bar laughing and drinking and that, she reckoned, was her job.

One night, when she came over to my place for pasta, she told me of her plan.

"You know, all those guys want to see my tits," Shirley said, twirling her fork through the linguini.

"With all those strippers, they want to see your tits too?"

"Well, that's just it. They get to see all those other tits all the time. They never get to see mine."

"Makes sense," I said, "guys being what we are."

"Right. So, I'm going to show them my tits."

"What?" This was not the kind of thing that Shirley would be casual about. She had standards. And, of course, if the union knew that she was baring all, there might be repercussions.

"Don't worry," she assured. "I'm only going to do it once and I'm going to advertise. Those girls make stupid money in tips. I do all right at the bar but it doesn't compare to what they get. So, I'm going to do a onetime only strip and cash in."

She was so determined that I didn't even try to find an argument against it. She set her date and began teasing the boys at the bar about seeing her boobs. Walt Disney couldn't have done a better job of hyping this show. She let the momentum build and build. She teased and teased. It got so she was getting bigger tips at the bar just in anticipation of the coming event.

The night finally came. I wasn't there. I'd like to have been, but Shirley told me in no uncertain terms that if I showed up, she'd kill me and pour acid on my grave.

I could hardly wait to call her the day after her big night. She was at work.

"So?"

"So what?" she asked nonchalantly.

"Don't give me that shit. How much did you make last night? Was it fun? Did you get off on it? Come on. Let's have it."

"You're not going to believe it. First of all, the place was absolutely packed. There wasn't room for another person. The girls were pissed off from the start. They couldn't draw that many people if they did a lesbian act with a female donkey. By around 10:30 they guys were chanting, *SHIRLEY! SHIRLEY! SHIRLEY!* So I went into the dressing room and put on my outfit. I decided to go real conservative to begin with. So I put on a long dress over a black bustier and garter belt. When I walked out, you should have heard them. They were hooting! Shit. My boss just walked in. I gotta call you back."

She left me dangling. In the meantime, I had to go out and when I returned, there was a message from her on my machine. Her voice said, "I'm coming over for pasta tonight. I'll tell you the rest of the story then."

While I cooked, she talked. "OK, so where was I?"

"Your boss just walked in and you were going to call me back," I said, chopping garlic.

"Very funny. OK. So did I tell you what I was wearing?"

"Shirl, as much as I love your fashion sense, I don't really give a shit about the wardrobe. Tell me about stripping."

"You're such a dick," she said. "So. I was beside myself, I was so nervous. But I figured it was too late to back out then. So I climbed onto the stage and the guys went nuts. The girls were all crowded around in the hallway watching. Eventually, I took off the dress and flung it to the side. Now all I had on was, well, underwear. Black, of course. And stockings. I kicked off my shoes and started dancing like I saw the girls do a million times. And if I do say so myself, I threw in some pretty cool moves. The guys started throwing money onto the stage. No coins. Only big stuff. Fives, tens and twenties. Lots of them. I took off the stockings and they hooted even more. I don't know what got into me but I started to really enjoy it. I mean, they were all screaming for me to take it off and I decided to tease them a little more. I mean, the girls just get up there and rip their tops off, bingo, like that. I decided I'd try to milk it a little, throw in a little Gypsy Rose Lee. So I started reaching back like I was going to unfasten the bustier. Then I stopped and said, 'If you really want to see these babies, it's gonna cost you, boys.' And they threw *more* money on the stage. By now I was laughing and having a ball too. So

I unfastened the hooks and held it on in front of me and showed a little side, then a little more and finally tossed it aside and stood there with only black panties and the garter belt. There were so many bills on the stage that I nearly slipped on them. It was great. I bounced around a little while longer to give them their money's worth and then picked up the money and laughed all the way to the dressing room. It was great."

"How much?"

"Guess."

"I don't know. Six hundred?"

"Guess again."

"More?" She nodded with a big smile on her face. "A thousand?"

"Guess again."

"No fucking way. More than a grand?"

"Thirteen hundred and eighty dollars. It's the easiest money I ever made."

***

Shirley and Andy were at the station when my train arrived.

"So, how was your train ride?" Shirley asked after she gave me a big hug and kiss and we made our way to the car, arm in arm.

"It was good. It's so beautiful, California," I said.

"We love it here, don't we, honey?" Shirley said.

"Sure beats the smog," Andy said, without much interest.

Their house was a multi-level structure backed up against the top of a hill. It was situated so that it provided a 360 degree view, about 160 of which was the ocean. From this height, its rich, blue vastness seemed endless. On a clear day, you could probably see Australia.

Shirley showed me to my room on the lower level. Living here had provided her with the opportunity she needed to make her home into a luxury instead of a necessity. This room was beautifully furnished with an Asian motif. Even with a limited budget, through her creativity, she was able to make it sumptuous and inviting. I called it my opium den while I was there.

The next level up was where the kitchen and living area were. There was lots of glass to allow for magnificent views. A proper, working fireplace dominated the living room, making it easy to imagine a cold winter night in its glare with maybe a cup of hot soup and a good book. Exposed beams and rafters gave the entire place a very welcoming and rustic feel. The kitchen was modern and functional and the perfect environment for Shirley's newfound domesticity.

The next level up was where you found the master bedroom and Andy's office/den. Decks surrounded the house on all levels. At the very bottom, under the house, was a large room used for storage or workout equipment or an art studio, depending on who was using it.

Shirley had always been artistically inclined. She had loaned me two of her charcoal sketches for the walls of my Hollywood apartment. They were brilliant by any standards, but she had never trained and, therefore, thought they couldn't be all that good. But once she moved to the Central Coast, she started dabbling more and more with watercolors. There were a number of other artists in her little town who banded together and started having art festivals. Before long, she was submitting her watercolors, having them accepted and, to no one's surprise except maybe hers, was actually selling paintings.

I was remembering all this as she handed me a cup of coffee.

"This place is fantastic," I said, once we settled in front of the fireplace.

"We love it," Shirley said again.

"How'd you find it?" I asked.

"This was my dad's place," Andy said. "After my mom died, he lived here but pretty much let it go to pot. Then when he died, my brother and I worked out a way to split things up so I got this place.

We've had to put a lot of work into it to get it in this shape. But it's worth it."

Shirley had often told me in emails and on the phone how much she loved her home. She had been raised in modest surroundings back in the Midwest, always longing for a place like this. Now she had it and never for a moment took it for granted.

After dinner, we were sitting by the fireplace talking. Andy and I didn't really know one another. Our only connection was Shirley. She told me that she made it clear to her husband that our friendship was and had always been platonic and not to be interfered with. But if she was married to this guy, there must be something about him I'd like.

"Let me ask you something," he said. "You've just been traveling around the world to interesting places. What do they think of this idiot we've got as president?" Before I could answer, he continued. "Not that the son-of-a-bitch was elected to anything. Those fucking Republicans steal everything that isn't nailed down. But anyway, what are people saying?"

"Depends on where you are. The people I was with in Africa make Republicans look like socialists." I told him about my conversation with the guy who organized mercenaries. I told him how I was received in Europe until I disassociated myself from Bush. "I always tried to distance myself even more by saying that I'm Australian but the accent gives me away."

"Let me ask you something about Australia," Andy said. "You know I drove a limo for a while in L.A."

"Actually I didn't but go ahead."

"Well, something I noticed that I always was curious about. I used to drive all the big stars around. We used to call Robert DeNiro *"No dinero"* because he was such a cheap bastard. Never tipped anyone. But what I want to know is: what's the deal with the Aussies?"

"What do you mean?"

"OK. Like, whenever I picked up Russell Crowe, he would jump in the front seat with me and start shooting the shit just like a regular guy. All the Aussies I picked up were that way. No Hollywood bullshit. Jump in the front and start talking. I never once drove an Aussie anywhere that he sat in the back of the limo. Never."

"I know. The first time I got in a cab there, I got in back like you would anywhere else on the planet. The driver looked around at me like I was a snob. After I learned better, I always sit in front now."

"Is everybody like that?" Shirley asked.

"Pretty much. Women usually sit in back but it's rare that a guy does. It has something to do with what they call *mateship* I think."

"Right. They all called me *mate*, like we were buddies or something," Andy said. "Fucking amazing."

I took those thoughts with me to bed. As I lay in my opium den, I thought about where I lived. This journey had been such an exciting adventure that I had lost sight of its starting point. I had spent so much time realizing where I no longer lived that I rarely considered where I now actually lived.

As we said our goodbyes next day, I was satisfied that Shirley was living the happy life she deserved with a man who was worthy of her. Their relationship was full. Their house was warm and inviting and comfortable. They had a naturalness and good-natured respect and tolerance and love for each other that were visible and palpable. I left knowing I didn't have to worry about my friend.

I sat in the waiting room of the little Central Coast train station. All my gifts had now been distributed. All stops made. All friends visited. This last train ride would take me back to L.A. I'd spend two more days there, then return to Australia. The Palindrome Adventure would come to an end.

I began to reflect on the past two months. I had visited four of the seven continents on the planet and flown over a fifth. The trip had compressed much of my personal history, from Smalltown to

Hollywood. I had observed how the lives of people I had known well, in what seemed to be a previous incarnation, were now manifested: people who had been my family, literally and figuratively, from whom I was now estranged; people who had been my carefree mates who now had growing and grown children, people with whom I had once dreamed who now lived practical, happy lives. I had seen the seemingly impregnable and noble country of my birth diminished in the eyes of the world as it began a shameful descent. It was only two short months, nothing in the history of humanity, perhaps, but profound as seen through my personal, historical lens.

I had said all my final goodbyes and once again found myself at an international airport. This time they announced departures to Tahiti, Fiji, Hong Kong, New Zealand, Japan, Indonesia and… Melbourne. Boarding the Qantas jet and settling into my seat to the strains of *I Still Call Australia Home*, I began thinking about the day I was in a large room in the Melbourne Town Hall. We were told that migrants from well over 100 countries were gathered together on this day. Someone official spoke and welcomed us and swore us in. A woman led the singing of *Advance Australia Fair*, or I should say, sang *Advance Australia Fair* since no one else in the room knew the song. My parents had been naturalized American citizens and I couldn't help recognizing that I was now becoming a naturalized Australian citizen. As I thought these thoughts, the same woman who had sung *Advance Australia Fair* went back to the mic and asked us to join her in singing *Waltzing Matilda*. Everyone knew the chorus of that international hit. And as I joined the others, much to my surprise and without shame, I began tearing up. That iconic Banjo Patterson song told me where I now belonged. I had taken a trip around the world, it seemed, just to remember that. Suddenly, I felt like Dorothy clicking the ruby slippers together and saying, "There's no place like home. There's no place like home. There's no place like home."

Fair dinkum.

AFTERWARD

As I write these words, **The Palindrome Adventure** *is a few years in the past. America did invade Iraq just as everyone knew it would. The son of a Luo was elected President of the United States. The promise of the Euro zone slammed into the reality of politics. Looking back makes the two months between September and November of 2002 seem quaint and simple and manageable.*

On a personal note, several other things unfolded. That pinochle game was the last. Both my brother and brother-in-law passed away. Gudrun turned me into another one of her desperate love affairs and emailed me for more than a year after I returned to Oz. I have now been in Australia long enough that I have old friends here too. But no matter what follows, it is certain that it will be unpredictable. For as long as one lives, other waters will inevitably continue to flow.

February 2011